Chinese in WASHINGTON

The Legacy of the Chinese Exclusion Act

TRISH HACKETT NICOLA

Published by The History Press
An imprint of Arcadia Publishing
Charleston, SC
www.historypress.com

First published 2026

Manufactured in the United States

ISBN 9781467147729

Library of Congress Control Number: 2025945133

Notice: The information in this book is true and complete to the best of our knowledge. It is offered without guarantee on the part of the author or The History Press. The author and The History Press disclaim all liability in connection with the use of this book.

To Loretta Chin—a friend and mentor

CONTENTS

Acknowledgements 7
Introduction 9
History Leading Up to the Exclusion Acts 11
Washington Territory Before the Chinese Exclusion Act 13
The Page Act of 1875 13
Anti-Chinese Riots in Washington Territory 14

1. The Chinese Exclusion Act of 1882: Renewals, Amendments, Repeal, and the Aftermath 17
The Chinese Exclusion Act of 1882 17
The Scott Act of 1888 19
The Geary Act of 1892 and the McCreary Amendment of 1893 19
The Immigration Act of 1924 (Johnson-Reed Act) 20
The Magnuson Act of 1943: Repeal of the Chinese Exclusion Act 20
The War Brides Acts of 1945 and 1946 20
The Chinese Confession Program, 1956–1965 20
The Immigration Act of 1965 (Hart-Celler Act) 21

2. Chinese People Born in the United States 22

3. Exclusion of Laborers 37

4. Merchants Exempt from the Act 45
Merchants 45
Children and Spouses of Merchants 56

5. Other Exemptions to the Act 69
Students 69
Travelers 78
Diplomats 89
Teachers 91

6. Women: How They Were Affected 92

7. Chinese Communities in Washington State 98
Seattle 98
Olympia 108
Port Townsend 113
Spokane 119
Tacoma 130
Walla Walla 134
Yakima and Other Communities 136

8. The 1909 Alaska-Yukon-Pacific Exposition 152

9. Others 157
World War II Veterans 157
Paper Sons and Daughters 160

Notes 161
Bibliography 169
Index 179
About the Author 191

ACKNOWLEDGEMENTS

Over the years, many volunteers have worked on indexing the Chinese Exclusion Act case files. Loretta Chin, the first volunteer to work on this project, started around 1993 when the case files arrived at the National Archives at Seattle. Loretta processed the fifty thousand files: She put them in archival folders, wrote the name and file number on each folder, and then started indexing them. It was a delight to have the opportunity to work with Loretta. She was a great teacher and made the work fun. When I started in 2001, Loretta became my mentor and friend. She took me under her wing and was always ready to answer my questions about Chinese culture and history. We both got excited about the unique documents we occasionally found in the files. And we loved the photos in the files, especially the ones of babies and children. The Chinese community, researchers, family historians, the National Archives, and I owe so much to Loretta Chin. Without her foresight, we would not have such an all-encompassing index.

Thank you to the staff, past and present, at the National Archives at Seattle. They have been very supportive: Candace Lein-Hayes, Susan Karren, Patty McNamee, Kenneth House, Valerie Szwaya, Brita Merkel, Crystal Shurley, Courtney Elliot, Eric Flores, Wendy Standley, Michelle Criner, and Marie Brindo-Vas. And thank you to the team of volunteers who index the files with me: Rhonda Farrar, Lily Eng, Hao-Jan Chang, Joyce Liu, Tamia Duggan, Jackie Lum, and Stan Ching. They also alert me to interesting educational files to put on the blog at ChineseExclusionFiles.com. Extra kudos to Lily Eng, our index expert and the one in charge of entering the indexed files into the database.

Thank you to the members of the Asian community near and far who have encouraged and supported me along the way: the late Al Young, whose enthusiasm made it all fun; Art Chin, Cathy Lee, and the Chinese American Citizen Alliance; Betty Luke, Vivian Chan, and staff at the Wing Luke Museum; Chinese researcher and artist Cheryll Leo-Gwin; Andrew Sandfort-Marchese; Mark Johnson, author, for asking me to share the stage during his presentation; and Linda Yip, Jeanie Low, Amy Chin, Marian Smith, and my immigration buddies, especially Linda Harms Okazaki, Grant Din, Ruth Chan, and Marisa Louie. Thank you to Peter Sage for being supportive of my research and the blog, and thank you to Benny Yi-Bing Chu, Debbie Jiang, Stephen Artick, John Carvala, Jeffrey L. Staley, Kam Yee, Elana Eng Lim, John Gong, and Richard Lou for sharing their family stories on the blog. Thank you to Kevin Lee from Sydney, Australia; Sue Fawn Chung; Marie Sheallene Lim-Yeo; and Darby Li Po Price for contributing their family stories to the blog. Thank you to the *Seattle Times* reporters Jerry Large and Eric Lacitis for publishing articles and a video on the Chinese Exclusion Act files at National Archives at Seattle. Special thanks to Natasha Mozgovaya of *Voice of America* for interviewing the CEA volunteers and publishing an online article referring to a few compelling stories from the files.

Special appreciation to Annette Kassis, who gave me copies of the books she has written for The History Press—an inspiration; to Sue Donaldson and Jean Godden for featuring the CEA volunteers on the *Bridge Radio* program; and to Sue Donaldson, again, for being such supportive friend and fellow volunteer. Lorraine McConaghy and Jill Morelli gave me encouragement when I needed it.

Deepest gratitude to Laurie Krill at The History Press, who helped me through this process as a very patient editor—perfect for a green newbie—and to Zoe Ames, copyeditor, for all her help.

And the biggest thank-you to my husband, Bud Nicola, and my children and their families, who patiently and lovingly put up with me during this long process.

INTRODUCTION

This book is a collection of summaries of the Chinese Exclusion Act case files at the National Archives at Seattle. The files are not biographies, but through interviews conducted by immigration authorities, they reveal portions of Chinese immigrants' lives. The files were created as a result of the passage of the Chinese Exclusion Act of 1882 and its renewals and amendments. The act was in effect until 1943. It was passed to limit the number of Chinese immigrants entering the United States, specifically laborers, and prevent the Chinese already in the United States from becoming naturalized citizens. The files consist of a variety of forms required or created by the government, correspondence, interrogations, and usually at least one photograph. The early files were generally handwritten and sometimes contained habeas corpus documents or other court papers. The law became more complicated when it was renewed or amended; standard forms were introduced. Most files are eight to ten pages long, but a given file could be only one or two pages or as many as fifty or sixty pages.

The files tell only a small part of the story of each person's life, as related by the immigrant, and may not always reflect the full truth. Even so, the files exemplify how difficult it was for Chinese immigrants to enter or leave the United States and to assimilate to the American way of life. They describe some of the everyday challenges the Chinese immigrants had in U.S. society and sometimes give clues about their previous life in China and their extended family in China and the United States. Some of the information in the files may not be accurate. The Chinese said what they needed to say to be admitted to the United States. Most of the essays in this book are about ordinary people, and a few are about prominent Chinese immigrants who are well known. The fifty thousand case files housed at the Seattle facility are for those who entered, reentered, or departed from the ports of Seattle, Port Townsend, and Sumas, Washington; Portal, North Dakota; and Portland, Oregon. These immigrants may have settled in any part of the United States, from Mississippi to New York or Montana. This book pertains to only Chinese immigrants who settled in Washington State, spent significant time here, or traveled through Washington State. Occasionally, I did a little more research to tell more of a person's story.

Many of the early Washington State Chinese settlers do not have an exclusion file at the Seattle facility. They either came before the Chinese Exclusion Act was in effect (1882) or entered through a port whose records are not housed at the National Archives at Seattle. Many Chinese immigrants entered through the Port of San Francisco and made their way up to Washington Territory or State through Oregon for mining, building the railroads, or support jobs in laundries, merchandise stores, or restaurants. Some were smuggled in through various ports on the West Coast or across the Canadian border. If they did not call attention to themselves or did not travel outside the U.S. borders, they might not have a file. Chinese people, even those born in the United States, would need to go through a complicated investigative process whether they were applying to travel to China or just cross the Canadian border.

The fifty thousand files at the National Archives at Seattle are all indexed by name and file number, but about one-third are still being processed to include an enhanced version of the index. This enhanced version includes the person's name, file number, married name, school name, other names and aliases (where they apply), certificate of residence or identity number, years the files cover, date of last entry, port of entry, vessel name, case city, last residence or destination, exempt status and/or occupation, gender, age, marital status, date and place of birth, cross reference sheet (sometimes referring to other files), photograph, interrogation transcript, disposition of the file (admitted; rejected; court papers; deported; left (did not return or unknown); rejected/appealed; unknown; application withdrawn; deceased; applied to leave; disposition unknown; application to leave approved; departure not shown), Alien Registration Number, and second case file number. There is a comments section for notes about anything unusual in the file: for example, drawings or maps of the person's village, house, or school; birth, marriage, or death certificates; passport; family photos; photos from trips over many years, which show both aging and assimilation; discharge by court papers; military service records; or anything that might help a researcher find the person. Since there are so many common Chinese names with a variety of spellings and an individual may have used several variations of their name, this extra information helps researchers pinpoint the file they are searching for, but it makes the task of indexing the files a long, slow process.

HISTORY LEADING UP TO THE EXCLUSION ACTS

The nineteenth century was chaotic in China. Between 1802 and 1840, its population increased by three hundred million, bringing the total population to over four hundred million. China's Great Recession began in 1838 and destabilized its economy for one hundred years. Floods, earthquakes, fires, and drought brought further devastation to the country. There were several wars.[1] After losing the Opium Wars, China was forced to pay large indemnities to the Western imperialist powers. The 1896–1902 Boxer Rebellion failed to rid China of its foreign occupants. The Chinese left China because it was so hard to make a living and survive. The Chinese government imposed high taxes on the remaining peasant farmers, who, when unable to pay their taxes, lost their lands. Displaced from the land, they were unable to find employment in the already limited industrial sector. Between 1840 and 1900, two and a half million Chinese left China for other parts of the world. Most laborers came from the Pearl River Delta, the area known as Guangdong Province (Kwangtung). About 90 percent of those leaving China were males. They hoped earn money and return to their families in China.

There were few Chinese immigrants in the United States by the late 1840s. They were usually small business owners and educated.[2] After gold was discovered in California in 1849, Chinese came to the United States to work in the gold mines and build railroads in the West. Some worked in farming and fishing or held support jobs for all the laborers, such as cooks and laundry workers. In 1869, the United States entered a treaty with China to open the door to Chinese immigration. The United States needed cheap labor for the mining and the railroad industry, and the Chinese were willing to provide it. As the number of Chinese immigrants in this country increased, so did the anti-Chinese sentiment.[3]

Guangdong Province, China. *TUBS, CC BY-SA 3.0m, https://creativecommons.org/licenses/by-sa/3.0, via Wikimedia Commons.*

After the completion of the building of the Union Pacific Railroad in 1869, there was an economic depression. Anti-Chinese riots occurred in states where Chinese were living and working, including California, Oregon, Washington, Colorado, and Wyoming. Soon, anti-immigration laws were passed to limit the number of Chinese coming into the country. These laws were also fueled by racial and cultural fears. It was difficult for Chinese to assimilate into American culture. They would never look Anglo-Saxon. They were usually assigned to do dangerous jobs not wanted by Caucasian laborers, such as working with explosives during the building of the railroads.[4] An economic downturn gave employers an opportunity to pit the Chinese against white workers and keep wages low. A cry to exclude the Chinese went out. Many U.S. laborers, although recent immigrants themselves, resented the Chinese being in this country and taking jobs away from "white" workers. There were many conflicting opinions, but the consensus was that the Caucasian workers wanted to severely restrict the number of Chinese coming into the United States.[5]

The 1870 U.S. census recorded about forty-nine thousand Chinese in California; by 1880, there were over seventy-five thousand.[6] Although this was less than 1.5 percent of the total population of the United States, it was enough to make the white population fight to have Chinese immigration halted.[7]

WASHINGTON TERRITORY BEFORE THE CHINESE EXCLUSION ACT

Only one Chinese person was enumerated on the 1850 Washington territorial census, but in 1853 a law was passed to deny voting rights to the Chinese. In 1863, they were prohibited from testifying against whites. The next year, a poll tax was levied against every Chinese person living in the territory.[8]

In the mid-1860s, some Chinese left California for Oregon and Washington Territory. They worked building railroads or in the gold mines or served the mining community as cooks, laundry workers, and grocery and supply store merchants. They found jobs in the fishing and canning industry, at lumber mills, and in farming and construction. The first Chinese business in Washington Territory, manufacturing cigars, was started in Seattle in 1867.[9] In 1870, there were only 234 Chinese people living in Washington Territory, mostly in Seattle and Walla Walla.

THE PAGE ACT OF 1875

The Page Act was passed in 1875 to prohibit Chinese contract laborers, convicts, and prostitutes from entering the United States.[10] The Page Act used racist and sexist language and assumed most Chinese women immigrating were prostitutes. Before leaving China, women were put through a rigorous interrogation. They were asked if they had engaged in prostitution or if they had led a virtuous life. If they passed that interview, they were questioned again on the ship and again when they arrived at the U.S. port. If any of their answers varied from their original testimony, they were sent back to China. Few women wanted to go through the ordeal. This created a mostly all-male Chinese population.[11] About 2,000 Chinese people had come in 1871 to work on the Northern Pacific Railroad between Kalama and Tacoma, Washington.[12] By 1880, the number of Chinese people in Washington Territory had increased to 3,186.[13]

ANTI-CHINESE RIOTS IN WASHINGTON TERRITORY

By 1885–86, the anti-Chinese agitation on the West Coast was in a frenzied state. Washington Territory passed a law in 1886 prohibiting aliens ineligible for citizenship (that is, Chinese people) from owning property.[14]

Seattle

In February 1886, the 350 Chinese in Seattle were rounded up and taken down to the waterfront to be sent out on the next ship. The sheriff and a few other courageous citizens confronted the mob. The mob rioted. Several dissenters were shot, and one died from his wounds. U.S. President Grover Cleveland declared martial law. Most of the Chinese left for San Francisco. In a matter of days, there were only a few Chinese people left in Seattle.[15]

Tacoma

In November 1885, about two hundred Chinese people living in Tacoma were rounded up and forced out of town, where they caught trains to Portland, Oregon. The next day, their shops and homes were burned. This became known as the "Tacoma method"—the Chinese in Tacoma had been not murdered but driven out. The ringleaders were prosecuted but never convicted. The Chinese did not return until the 1920s.[16]

Newcastle, Black Diamond, and Renton

Fire destroyed the homes and belongings of Chinese workers in these towns, or the Chinese were simply run off. The people responsible were never found and prosecuted.[17]

THE HATCH MILL, PACIFIC AVENUE, AS IT USED TO BE
The few Chinese shacks in the foreground were burned in 1885

"The Hatch Mill, Pacific Avenue [before 1885]. The few Chinese shacks in the foreground were burned in 1885." *From Herbert Hunt,* Tacoma, Its History and Its Builders: A Half Century of Activity *(S.J. Clarke Publishing, 1916). Public domain.*

Squak Valley (Now Issaquah)

In 1885, the Chinese in Squak Valley were threatened, intimidated, and forced to leave. Three were murdered. Their tents and possessions were burned.[18]

Olympia

Between 1884 and 1885, the Chinese were prohibited from working on road construction, and a twenty-five-dollar quarterly tax was levied on washhouses, which were primarily run by Chinese. In 1886, a mob ordered the Chinese to leave. At the time, there were about two hundred Chinese people in Olympia, or about one-tenth of its population. Olympia Sheriff William Billings arrested mob leaders, who were fined and received a jail sentence. Business leaders wanted to both keep cheap laborers and prove that Olympia was a safe place and capable of being the seat of state government. The Chinese did not feel reassured, and many of them left.[19]

Bellingham

Bellingham is close to the Canadian border, and many of the Chinese living there had crossed into the United States illegally or were smuggled in. Petitions and boycotts were used, and a deadline was given for their removal. It worked: The Chinese left, and the white citizens celebrated.[20]

Wherever the Chinese lived, they were subjected to expulsion.

CHAPTER 1

THE CHINESE EXCLUSION ACT OF 1882

Renewals, Amendments, Repeal, and the Aftermath

The Chinese Exclusion Act of 1882

An Act to execute certain treaty stipulations relating to Chinese.

Whereas in the opinion of the Government of the United States the coming of Chinese laborers to this country endangers the good order of certain localities within the territory thereof: Therefore,

Be it enacted by the Senate and House of Representatives of the United States of America in Congress assembled, *That from and after the expiration of ninety days next after the passage of this act, and until the expiration of ten years next after the passage of this act, the coming of Chinese laborers to the United States be, and the same is hereby, suspended; and during such suspension it shall not be lawful for any Chinese laborer to come, or having so come after the expiration of said ninety days to remain within the United States.*[21]

The Chinese Exclusion Act was approved on May 6, 1882, and renewed every ten years until it was repealed in 1943. Every time it was renewed, there were more provisions and details to address. All these transactions needed to be documented, and the burden of proof was on the Chinese. This produced a tremendous amount of paperwork on Chinese individuals living in the United States. By the time the law was repealed, thousands and thousands of case files with valuable personal and historical information had been created.[22]

Forty-seventh

Congress of the United States, At the First Session,

Begun and held at the CITY OF WASHINGTON, in the DISTRICT OF COLUMBIA, on Monday, the fifth day of December, eighteen hundred and eighty-one

An Act

To execute certain treaty stipulations relating to Chinese.

Whereas, In the opinion of the Government of the United States the coming of Chinese laborers to this country endangers the good order of certain localities within the territory thereof: Therefore, Be it enacted by the Senate and House of Representatives of the United States of America in Congress assembled, That from and after the expiration of ninety days* next after the passage of this act, and until the expiration of ten years next after the passage of this act, the coming of Chinese laborers to the United States be, and the same is hereby, suspended; and during such suspension it shall not be lawful for any Chinese laborer to come, or, having so come after the expiration of said ninety days, to remain within the United States.

Sec. 2. That the master of any vessel who shall knowingly bring within the United States on such vessel, and land or permit to be landed, any Chinese laborer, from any foreign port or place, shall be deemed guilty of a misdemeanor, and on conviction thereof shall be punished by a fine of not more than five hundred dollars for each and every such Chinese laborer so brought, and may be also imprisoned for a term not exceeding one year

Sec. 3. That the two foregoing sections shall not apply to Chinese laborers who were in the United States on the seventeenth day of November, eighteen hundred and eighty, or who shall have come into the same before the expiration of ninety days next after the passage of this act, and who shall produce

First page of the Chinese Exclusion Act of 1882. *National Archives, Washington, D.C.*

The Chinese Exclusion Acts underwent numerous interpretations and amendments. Some of the most consequential of these are listed in the following pages.

The Scott Act of 1888

The Scott Act of 1888 made it unlawful for any Chinese laborer who left the United States before the act was passed to reenter the country. It abolished the returning laborer's right to return to the United States. About twenty thousand U.S. resident Chinese laborers who had traveled abroad before the act was passed were not allowed to return even though they had return certificates. They challenged the law in the Supreme Court, but the law was upheld.

Teachers, students, government officials, tourists, and merchants were exempt from this prohibition, but they needed to obtain permission from the Chinese government.[23]

The Geary Act of 1892 and the McCreary Amendment of 1893

The 1892 Geary Act renewed the 1882 Chinese Exclusion Act. It required Chinese people in the United States to carry a certificate of residence to prove that they had legally entered the country. Chinese people already living in the United States were required to register to receive their certificate. Those without a certificate were subject to detention and deportation. The McCreary Amendment of 1893 required a photograph of the certificate owner to be attached to the certificate. These certificates of identity contained the applicant's name, age, physical description, local residence, occupation, date and place admitted, and photograph. The act placed the burden of proof of their right to be in the United States on the Chinese themselves, denied bail to Chinese people in habeas corpus proceedings, and made it the duty of all Chinese laborers in the United States to apply for a certificate within one year. The act required two white witnesses to testify to a Chinese person's immigration status.[24]

THE IMMIGRATION ACT OF 1924 (JOHNSON-REED ACT)

Immigration quotas were based the total number of people of each nationality in the United States as of the 1890 U.S. census, when most immigrants came from northern Europe, with a limit of 150,000 immigrants in total per year from all foreign countries. The wives and unmarried children under age eighteen of U.S. citizens were given non-quota status. Transportation companies that landed aliens in violation of established immigration law would be fined. Chinese and Japanese, who were ineligible to naturalize, were prohibited from entering the United States as immigrants. (The act was also biased against southern and eastern European immigrants.) The wives of Chinese merchants were still permitted to enter the United States, but Chinese wives of U.S. citizens were denied entry, as they were considered aliens ineligible for citizenship. (Marriage does not confer citizenship.)[25]

THE MAGNUSON ACT OF 1943: REPEAL OF THE CHINESE EXCLUSION ACT

With the passage of the Magnuson Act of 1943, all Chinese Exclusion Acts were repealed. The number of annual entry visas for Chinese was limited to 105. Chinese people could now become naturalized U.S. citizens.[26]

THE WAR BRIDES ACTS OF 1945 AND 1946

Following the passage of the War Brides Act of 1945, the alien wives of U.S. servicemen were allowed to enter as immigrants but still limited by the Chinese quota of 105 per year.[27]

When the War Brides Act of 1946 was passed, the Chinese wives of U.S. servicemen were allowed entry as immigrants on a non-quota basis.[28]

THE CHINESE CONFESSION PROGRAM, 1956–1965

Between 1956 and 1965, the Immigration and Naturalization Service (INS) ran a program for Chinese immigrants who had fraudulently entered the United States before September 1957. If the immigrant confessed, immigration authorities would adjust or correct his status. The immigrant needed to identify his "paper family" in great detail, implicating other people who were involved or who entered the United States with false papers.[29] This had a domino effect and created many files with lengthy investigations of all their "paper" relatives. The program required the Chinese community to place their trust in the very agency they feared most—the INS, long associated with the threat of deportation. Because of privacy issues, none of these files are included in this publication.

The Immigration Act of 1965 (Hart-Celler Act)

The Hart-Celler Act law repealed the quota system based on national origin that had been U.S. immigration policy since the 1920s and had made it difficult for non-white individuals to immigrate to the United States.[30]

CHAPTER 2

CHINESE PEOPLE BORN IN THE UNITED STATES

Woo Bak Sue

Child Born in the United States

Woo Bak Sue was born on August 10, 1884, in Seattle, Washington Territory, just two years after the Chinese Exclusion Act was passed and five years before Washington Territory became a state.[31] His parents, Woo Tai Gap and Chew See, took Bak Sue to China when he was about five years old. Bak Sue came back to the United States ten years later through Port Townsend in the summer of 1899. When he arrived, he was arrested, put in detention, and given a hearing. A writ of habeas corpus was issued stating that he had been detained without authority of law and that he was entitled to be released on the grounds that he was a native-born citizen. The writ served as protection against unlawful imprisonment. An order of discharge was made by Judge C.H. Hanford of the U.S. District Court, Northern Division, District of Washington. Woo Bak Sue was released after payment for the costs of his detention was made; records do not show who paid the fees. He asked that his photograph be attached to his discharge papers and that the papers be certified and sent to him, probably to avoid going through this same type of ordeal when he traveled again.

Woo Bak Sue made three trips to China after 1899: 1904 to 1905, 1910 to 1911, and 1915 to May 1938. When he applied to leave for China in 1903, he had two Caucasian witnesses, as required. They both swore that they were residents and citizens of Seattle for the last twenty years and were

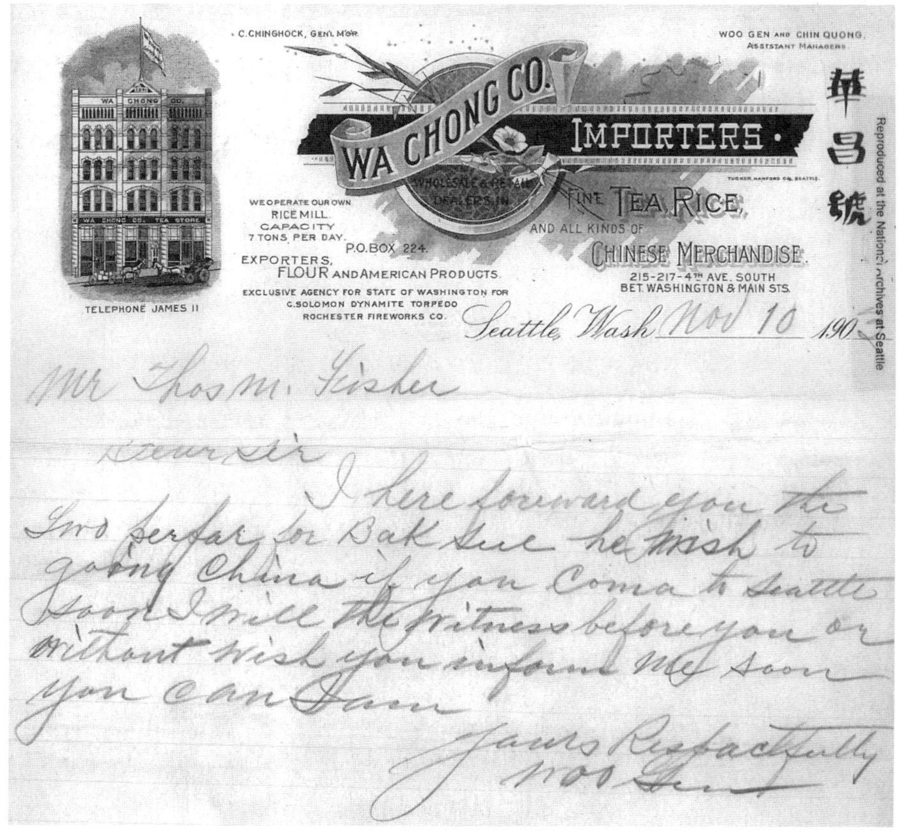

C. CHINGHOCK, GEN'L M'G'R.

WOO GEN AND CHIN QUONG, ASSISTANT MANAGERS.

WA CHONG CO.

IMPORTERS

WHOLESALE & RETAIL DEALERS IN

FINE TEA, RICE, AND ALL KINDS OF CHINESE MERCHANDISE.

華昌號

WE OPERATE OUR OWN RICE MILL. CAPACITY 7 TONS PER DAY.

P.O. BOX 224.

EXPORTERS, FLOUR AND AMERICAN PRODUCTS.

EXCLUSIVE AGENCY FOR STATE OF WASHINGTON FOR C. SOLOMON DYNAMITE TORPEDO ROCHESTER FIREWORKS CO.

215-217-4TH AVE. SOUTH BET. WASHINGTON & MAIN STS.

TELEPHONE JAMES 11

Seattle, Wash. Nov 10 1903

Mr Thos M. Fisher

Dear Sir

I here forward you the Two Serfar for Bak Sue he wish to going China if you Coma to Seattle soon I will the witness before you or without wish you inform me soon you can [illegible]

Yours Respectfully
Woo Gen

A piece of correspondence by Woo Gen on Wa Chong Company letterhead, 1903. *Woo Bak Sue, Chinese Exclusion Act (hereafter CEA) case file, file 7030/10966, record group (hereafter RG) 85, National Archives at Seattle, WA.*

well acquainted with Bak Sue and his parents. Woo Gen of the Wa Chong Company sent a letter on company stationery to Thomas M. Fisher, Chinese inspector, Office of the Collector of Customs in Port Townsend, saying he would be a witness for Bak Sue if requested.

When Bak Sue was returning in 1911, the immigration inspector asked him if he knew any of the Chinese people from his village at the detention house. He knew only Woo Bing Gee and his parents, but they were not from his village. No follow-up questions were asked, so it is not known why Bak Sue was asked this question.

Woo Bak Sue's son, Woo Sze Hong, arrived in Seattle in September 1938 and was admitted. In October 1938, Woo Bak Sue was in the process of applying to return to China because he wasn't feeling well. His application was approved. His son was settled in Seattle, and his wife and extended family were in his home village of Nom On in the Hoy San District. After being in his village from 1915 to 1938 and being sick, he may have simply wanted to go home.

The file contains photos of Woo Bak Sue from 1899, 1903, 1910, 1912, 1915, and 1938—from a young teenager to age fifty-four.

ROBERT QUAN

NEWSBOYS EXCURSION TO VICTORIA, BRITISH COLUMBIA, 1938

In late September 1938, Robert Quan (Quon/Quong), age fifteen, applied to go to Victoria, British Columbia, Canada, to attend a *Seattle Times* "newsboys excursion."[32] It was a one-day trip, departing on Sunday morning and returning to Seattle in the evening. Robert needed to get his Form 430, Native Return Certificate, approved before he could leave.

Robert's father, Eng Ah Quan (Harry Quong Eng), testified that he was forty-three years old and born in Dallas, Texas. He said he was an "American citizen, absolutely." He had never been to China. He married Jessie Quong, a Caucasian, in Omaha, Nebraska. They had four children, all born in Okmulgee, Oklahoma: two daughters and two sons, ages twenty-two to fifteen. Robert was their youngest. They were all living in Seattle. Erma and Dorothy attended Wilson's Business College, Harry Jr. went to Garfield High School, and Robert was enrolled at Washington Grade School. They lived at 436 Twenty-Third Street South. The spelling of Robert's surname varied from Quan to Quon and, sometimes, Quong. He was called Bob Quan at school. The children's birth certificates were registered at Okmulgee, Oklahoma, but they had only Harry's certificate. Robert's certificate was on order.

Mrs. Jessie Ethel N. Quong testified as a witness for her son, Robert Quong. Mrs. Quong was born in Omaha, Nebraska; she was white and had been married twice. Her second marriage was to Harry Quong (Eng) at Sapulpa, Oklahoma, in 1915.

Robert Quan testified that his father worked as a cook at the Moose Club. He thought his father went to China as a member of a crew once. Robert's father said he had never been to China, but the immigrant inspector ignored this discrepancy and recommended that Robert's application be approved.

Form 430 APPLICATION OF ALLEGED AMERICAN CITIZEN OF THE CHINESE RACE FOR PREINVESTIGATION OF STATUS TRIPLICATE

U. S. DEPARTMENT OF LABOR
IMMIGRATION AND NATURALIZATION SERVICE

Seattle, Wash.,
Sept. 30, 1938

To District Commissioner,
Officer in Charge, Immigration and Naturalization Service,
Seattle, Wash.

Age 15 Height 5 ft. 6½ in. (In shoes)

Marks Pin mole left side of face; faint pit in front of right ear; pin mole lobe of left ear.

SIR: It being my intention to leave the United States on a temporary visit abroad, departing and returning through the Chinese port of entry of Seattle, Wash., I hereby apply, under the provisions of Rule 16 of the Chinese Regulations, for preinvestigation of my claimed status as an American citizen, submitting herewith such documentary proofs (if any) as I possess, and agreeing to appear at such time and place as you may designate, and to produce then and there witnesses for oral examination regarding the claim made by me.

This application is submitted in triplicate with my photograph attached to each copy, as required by said rule.

Respectfully,

Signature in Chinese 簽唐字名
Signature in English 簽番字名 Robert Quong
Address 具稟人之住址 ROBERT QUONG 436 23rd So., Seattle.

管理外人入口委員知之我現欲暫離美國出遊外邦今由華人出入之港埠而去將來亦即由該埠而回茲依三十九款之例在美國出世所有之憑據呈上查驗亦親與證人到委員之公辦房詢問口供照例簽名稟上並附相三幅

Robert Quan's Application of Alleged American Citizen of the Chinese Race for Preinvestigation of Status, Form 430, 1938. *CEA case file, Quan Robert, file 7030/11495, RG 85, National Archives at Seattle, WA.*

Because Robert's father was Chinese, his file was reviewed and listed in Harry's file. Even a one-day round trip to Canada required interviews of Harry and his parents, forms completed, a photo taken, and verification of several documents.

Low Yow Edwin

U.S. Citizen Born in Alaska

In March 1939, Low Yow Edwin started the process of obtaining a citizen's return certificate at Immigration and Naturalization Service in Seattle.[33] Although Edwin's case file lists him as Low Yow Edwin, he testified that his full name was Edwin Low Yow and the American version was Edwin Low.

He was twenty-three years old, a cab driver, and was born on September 25, 1915, in Killisnoo, Alaska. He presented a certified copy of his birth certificate to the immigration inspector. His father, Low Yow, was born in China, and his mother, Martha James, was described as an Alaskan full-blood Eskimo native. Low Yow was a cannery contractor in Alaska and spent most of the summer months there for several years.

Edwin's mother, Martha James, died around 1916 when Edwin was about one year old and his sister, Amy Low Yow, was about two years old. Their father, Low Yow, lived in Seattle when he was not working in Alaska. His children were thought of as U.S. citizens. Anyone born in Alaska after 1905 (except Native Americans) was considered a natural-born citizen.[34]

Low Yow also had a second wife, Chin Suie Heung (American name Helen), in Seattle. Low Yow and Helen had four children together; two died in infancy. Helen did not find out that her husband had another wife, Martha James, in Alaska until after Martha James died. Low Yow brought the children to his home in Seattle when they were small and asked his second wife to take care of them. He did not admit that he was the children's father until he was on his deathbed. He died at age sixty-three at Seattle in March 1927.

Edwin's sister, Amy Low Yow, was a witness for her brother. She was married to Willard Jew (Jue), and they lived in Seattle. Willard Jue graduated from the University of Washington in 1929 with a degree in pharmacy but was unable to find work in his field because of prejudice against the Chinese. Eventually, he became director of the University of Washington herb garden. During his lifetime, he was president of the Chinese Historical Society of the Pacific Northwest, the Wing Luke Museum, and several other historical organizations.[35]

In 1939, Edwin was planning to leave for China through San Francisco, so he applied for a return certificate through the office there and his Seattle paperwork was transferred to a San Francisco file. Immigration requested his parents' death certificates. Amy obtained a certified copy of her father's Seattle, King County, Washington death certificate. She did not have enough information to get a copy of the death certificate for her mother, who died in Alaska.

Edwin and Amy's stepmother, Helen, testified that she was born in San Francisco around 1881 and that her childhood name was Chin Suie Heung before she married and became Mrs. Low Yow. She did not mention that Helen was part of her name. Her testimony about her daughters Daisy and Rose agreed with Edwin's and Amy's.

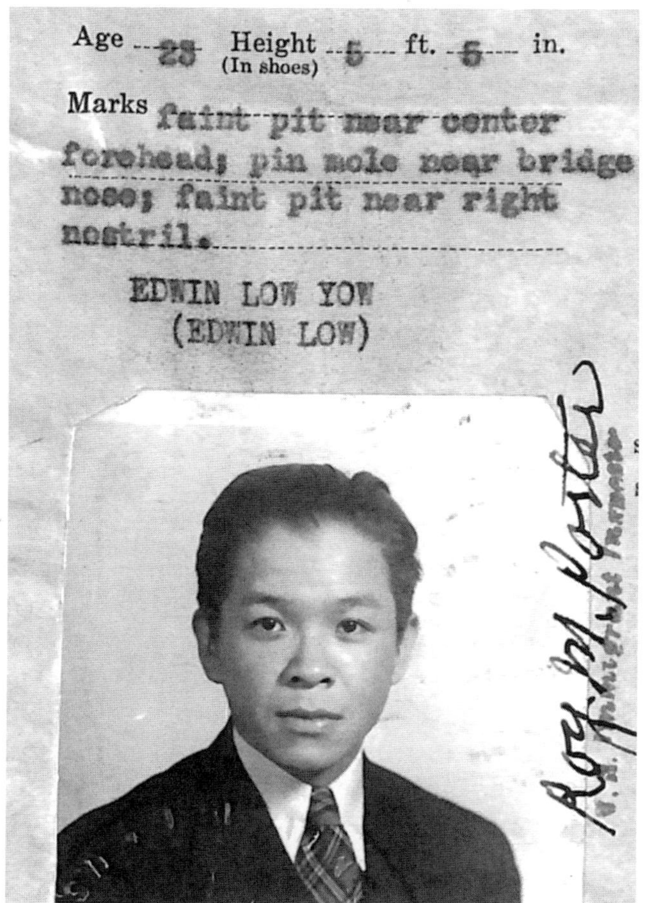
Age 23 Height (In shoes) 5 ft. 6 in.

Marks faint pit near center forehead; pin mole near bridge nose; faint pit near right nostril.

EDWIN LOW YOW
(EDWIN LOW)

Low Yow Edwin, Form 430 photo, 1939. *CEA case file, Low Yow Edwin, file 7030/11920, RG 85, National Archives at Seattle, WA.*

Edwin presented a copy of his birth certificate as proof of his citizenship. His application was approved. The reference sheet in Edwin's file contains the file numbers for his stepsister, Rose, and her husband, Harley.

This file shows you how complicated such files can be. It involved records in Alaska, Seattle, and San Francisco; a man with two wives and children from each wife; and names that are spelled differently on various documents. It took much research by several people to untangle the complete story.

Low Yow Edwin was the father of CEA volunteer Rhonda Farrar. Family stories spelled Edwin's surname Law, not Low. Rhonda discovered her father's file when she indexed the file as a volunteer at the National Archives at Seattle.

Rose Leong

Clerk at Boeing in Seattle, U.S.–Born Citizen

Rose Leong left Seattle by boat on Sunday morning, October 24, 1943, and returned a week later on the SS *Princess Alice*.[36] She was traveling with May Fun Kim (May Mar) and Kathleen Wong. They were visiting Vancouver, British Columbia, Canada, on vacation. Rose was twenty years old, born on May 12, 1923, in Seattle, the daughter of Leong Yip and Chin Shee. Rose was single, employed as a clerk at Boeing, and living with her family at 216 Seventeenth South, Seattle. She had never been out of the United States.

During Rose's application interview, she identified photos of her parents and her half brother, Leong Gim Lin, who went back to China around 1931 and did not return. She had two brothers and a sister in the United States. Her brother Robert Leong, age twenty, was serving in the U.S. Army at Camp Sheridan, Illinois. Her brother Jimmie Leong, age sixteen, and her sister Gene Leong, age eight, were both living at home. Rose attended Washington Grade School and graduated from Garfield High School in Seattle in June 1942. Her father, Leong Yip, who had been ill for the last three years, had recently died. Rose's mother testified that Leong Gim Lin was the son of her husband and his first wife.

The reference sheet in the file lists the names, case numbers, and relationships for Rose's parents; her brother in China; Leong Git Too, her nephew (son of her brother, Leong Gim Lin); and Jow Wah, her adopted brother. The immigrant inspector recommended approval of Rose's application, remarking that her documents were in order, she spoke English fluently, and she "has all the earmarks of being educated in this country. Her father had been well known to this office for more than twenty years."[37]

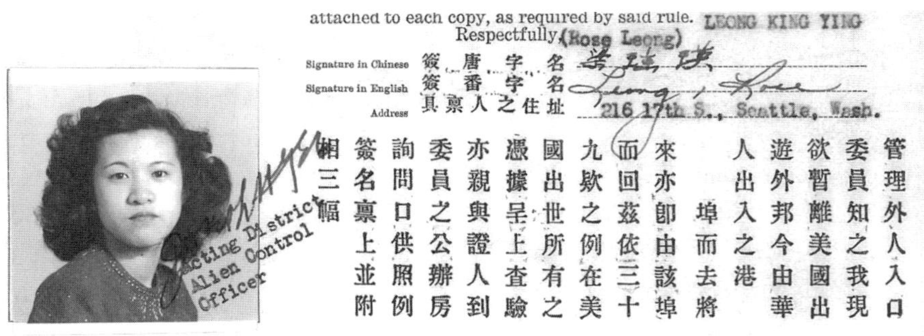

attached to each copy, as required by said rule. LEONG KING YING
Respectfully, (Rose Leong)

Signature in Chinese 簽唐字名
Signature in English 簽番字名 Leong, Rose
Address 具禀人之住址 216 17th S., Seattle, Wash.

管理外人入口委員知之我現欲暫離美國出遊外邦今由華人出入之港埠而去將來亦即由該埠而回茲依三十九款之例在美國出世所有之憑據呈上查驗亦親與證人到委員之公辦房詢問口供照例簽名稟上並附相三幅

Acting District Alien Control Officer

Rose Leong, Form 430, 1939. *CEA case file, Leong King Ying Rose, file 7030/13652, RG 85, National Archives at Seattle, WA.*

Lee Share Yung

San Francisco, Portland, Seattle

Lee Share Yung's file starts in 1888, just six years after the Chinese Exclusion Act was passed.[38] There were still many details of the law for ship captains and immigration inspectors to figure out. Lee Share Yung persevered through a long detention and court case, a good example of what the Chinese, even those born in the United States, had to go through to be admitted or readmitted to the United States after the act was passed. The long interrogations, though daunting for those who experienced them, give us a peek into the lives and villages of the Chinese in China.

On June 26, 1888, Captain W.A. Ward of the steamship *Gaelic* was ordered by the Circuit Court of the Northern District of California to release Lee Share Yung from imprisonment and detention. According to the "Habeas Corpus Judgment Roll" in his file, on November 27, 1888, after consideration by the court, he was finally discharged from custody. The judgment was certified and included his photo.

Lee Share Yung was born in San Francisco, California, in December 1871. He married Toy Shee, and they had two sons: Lee Gim, born in 1889, and Lee Ling Hung, born in 1901. Before Lee Share Yung left for a visit to China in 1900, he obtained an affidavit with his photo attached to ensure his reentry into the United States. He swore that he was a member of the Wau Yune Lung Kee Company, dealers in Chinese merchandise and provisions doing business in San Francisco. He had four Caucasian witnesses and returned on May 2, 1902.[39]

In 1920, he made another trip to China to bring his son Lee Ling Hung to the United States. By that time, he was a merchant for the Quong Sang Wo Kee Company in Portland, Oregon. He produced his 1888 discharge papers for the interrogator's inspection.

Lee Ling Hung first arrived in the United States at Seattle on January 21, 1921, and was admitted as a citizen, the son of a native.[40] He visited China in 1926 and returned in 1928. During his pre-investigation examination before leaving in 1926, he stated he had one son, Lee Gok Sui, born in 1921. On his return, he claimed a second son born while on that trip, Lee Gok Foo. In an application for another trip to China in 1930, he claimed that his second son's name was Lee Gok Gong and his third son was Lee Gok Foo. Because Lee Ling Hung's father Lee Share Yung's citizenship had been granted in 1888 through U.S. District Court discharge papers, immigrant inspector Roy M. Porter recommended that Lee Ling Hung's application for pre-

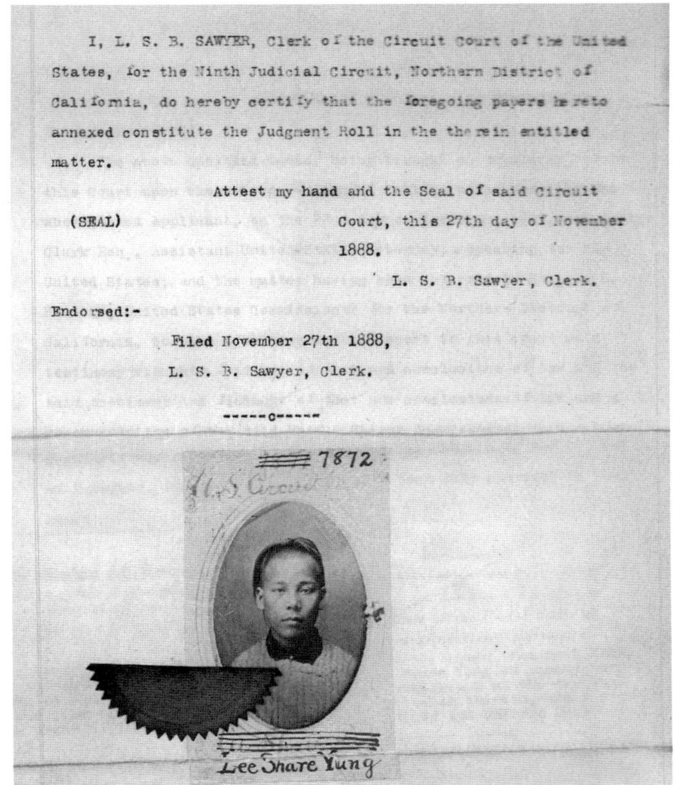

I, L. S. B. SAWYER, Clerk of the Circuit Court of the United States, for the Ninth Judicial Circuit, Northern District of California, do hereby certify that the foregoing papers hereto annexed constitute the Judgment Roll in the therein entitled matter.

Attest my hand and the Seal of said Circuit

(SEAL) Court, this 27th day of November 1888.

L. S. B. Sawyer, Clerk.

Endorsed:-

Filed November 27th 1888,

L. S. B. Sawyer, Clerk.

-----o-----

7872

Lee Share Yung

Left: Lee Share Yung, "Habeas Corpus Judgment Roll," 1888. *CEA case file, Lee Share Yung, file 1010/16-8, RG 85, National Archives at Seattle, WA.*

Opposite: Lee Share Yung, affidavit, 1900. *CEA case file, Lee Share Yung, Seattle Box 118, file 1010/16-8, RG 85, National Archives at Seattle, WA.*

investigation of status be approved. Confusion over the names of the second and third sons and their dates of birth caused the inspectors to distrust Lee Ling Hung's testimony, and this combined with other discrepancies made approval of Lee Gok Suey's 1937 arrival complicated.

Lee Ling Hung was a baker and lived in Portland, Oregon, for about six years before moving to Seattle. In August 1937, Lee Ling Hung swore in an affidavit that he was a citizen of the United States and the holder of a certificate of identity issued when he entered the Port of Seattle in 1921. He was applying to bring his son, Lee Gok Suey, to the United States.

Lee Gok Suey arrived in Seattle on December 20, 1937, on the *Princess Marguerite* and was admitted four months later after a difficult but successful appeal.[41] He was seventeen years old, a student and the son of Lee Ling Hung, a U.S. citizen, and Luey Shee. He was born on May 9, 1921, in the Hoy San District, China. Originally, Lee Gok Suey was denied admission by a board of special inquiry because he was not able to prove to the board's satisfaction his relationship to his father.

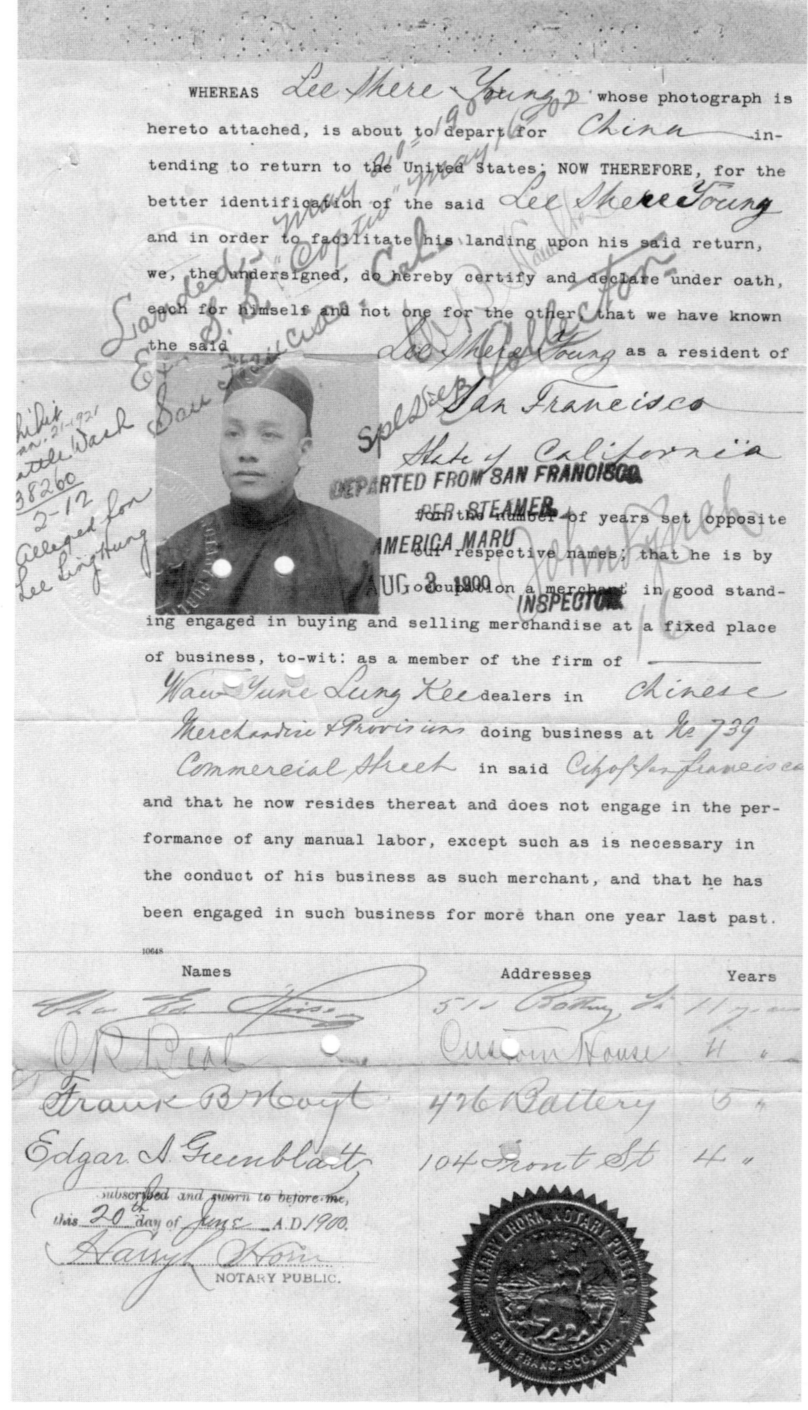

WHEREAS Lee Shere Young whose photograph is hereto attached, is about to depart for China intending to return to the United States; NOW THEREFORE, for the better identification of the said Lee Shere Young and in order to facilitate his landing upon his said return, we, the undersigned, do hereby certify and declare under oath, each for himself and not one for the other, that we have known the said Lee Shere Young as a resident of San Francisco State of California for the number of years set opposite our respective names; that he is by occupation a merchant in good standing engaged in buying and selling merchandise at a fixed place of business, to-wit: as a member of the firm of Waw Yune Lung Kee dealers in Chinese Merchandise & Provisions doing business at No 739 Commercial Street in said City of San Francisco and that he now resides thereat and does not engage in the performance of any manual labor, except such as is necessary in the conduct of his business as such merchant, and that he has been engaged in such business for more than one year last past.

Landed May 20 1902 S.S. "Coptic" May 16 02 San Francisco Cal. Collector

DEPARTED FROM SAN FRANCISCO PER STEAMER AMERICA MARU AUG 3 1900 INSPECTOR

John Lynch

Seattle Wash 38260 2-12 Alleged for Lee Ling Hung

10648

Names	Addresses	Years
Chas Ed Hiss	511 Battery St	11 years
O R Leal	Custom House	4 "
Frank B Hoyt	426 Battery	6 "
Edgar A. Greenblatt	104 Front St	4 "

Subscribed and sworn to before me, this 20th day of June A.D 1900.

Harry L Horn
NOTARY PUBLIC.

HARRY L. HORN, NOTARY PUBLIC SAN FRANCISCO, CAL.

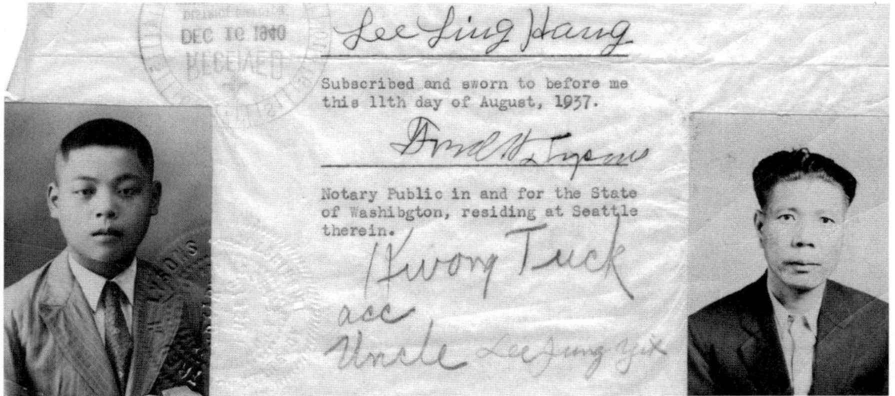

Affidavit photos of Lee Gok Suey and Lee Ling Hung, 1937. *CEA case file, Lee Gok Suey, file 7030/10684, RG 85, National Archives at Seattle, WA.*

Seattle's inspector in charge reopened Lee's case so additional evidence could be obtained. Affidavits from his father, uncle, and grandfather were submitted to the board for review. The applicant's attorney filed a letter and an affidavit of the applicant's alleged grandfather Lee Share Yung and included a photograph with a satisfactory resemblance to Lee Gok Suey. Because of several discrepancies in the witnesses' testimony, the board voted unanimously that Lee would not be admitted. His attorney argued that it had been fifteen years since the applicant's grandfather had been to China, so it was not unusual that his testimony might not completely agree with that of his two sons, who had been to China more recently. After Lee Gok Suey spent more than four months in detention, his arrival was approved.

In March 1938, Lee Share Yung testified that he was a bookkeeper at the Quong Tuck Company in Seattle. He was the father of Lee Gim Jeow and Lee Ling Hung and the grandfather of Lee Gok Suey. He was reexamined regarding some of the questions where there was some confusion. Were there twelve rows of houses in his village or thirteen? Lee Share Young said that there were thirteen rows, but the first row of houses was not a regular row because there was only a small house and some toilets there. It is easy to see how there could have been confusion over this trivial fact. Lee Hing Hung sent his father, Lee Share Yung, a photo of Lee Gok Suey in 1932. The interrogator asked how he could identify his grandson since he had not seen him since he was two years old. He replied, "I have to trust my son who sent me the picture." There were other discrepancies regarding the extended family and deceased ancestors, the location of neighbors' houses in their home village, and the applicant's school experience. Eventually, the board of special inquiry decided that there was enough information on which all the witnesses agreed, and they admitted Gok Suey Lee. In all, there were over fifty pages of interrogation. The witnesses were asked about the village; the location of roads, paths, hedges, ponds, shrines, the school, the cemetery, and stores; and many other minor details. They gave detailed descriptions of the houses, the buildings, and the people who lived in them. There were over one hundred houses in their village, so this could not have been easy. How many of us could describe our neighborhood in such detail?

Gok Suey Lee married Pansy Chin Lee. They had a son, Edwin Mah Lee, in May 1952 in Seattle. Edwin Mah Lee eventually moved to San Francisco and became the city's mayor from 2010 until his death in 2017. He died unexpectedly on December 12, 2017.[42]

Woo Quin Lock

Son of Citizen, Rejected/Appealed/Admitted

Twenty-year-old Woo Quin Lock, the son of a U.S. citizen, was finally admitted to the United States more than eight months after his arrival at the Port of Seattle on February 2, 1940.[43]

Woo Quin Lock was born in Kwong Tung, China. He was denied admittance to the United States on April 12, 1940. His case was appealed on May 10, and he was admitted on August 10. He received his certificate of identity two days later. The exhibits submitted in his case were an affidavit by his father, Woo Yen Tong; three letters written by the applicant to his father and their translations; a sample of the applicant's handwriting; four Woo family Seattle case files; and eight San Francisco files for various Woo family members.

Woo Yen Tong, the father of Woo Quin Lock, swore that he was a United States citizen and that he had proved his citizenship to the Immigration and Naturalization Service after his arrival at the Port of San Francisco in 1911. He attached a photo of Woo Quin Kwock, Woo Quin Lock, and a cousin, Woo Koon Sang, to his affidavit.

During his testimony, Woo Quin Lock stated that his father sent him 1,200 in Hong Kong currency (worth about 333 U.S. dollars in 1939) to cover his travel expenses.[44] His father owned two houses on the north and south side of the village and a social hall in Wan Jew village. Woo Quin Lock was

Affidavit photo of (*left to right*) Woo Quin Kwock, Woo Quin Lock, and Woo Koon Sang. *CEA case file, Woo Quin Lock, file 7030/12841, RG 85, National Archives at Seattle, WA.*

questioned about the location of the family's real estate holdings. Some of his testimony did not agree with his father's and brother's testimony.

The case file contains more than sixty pages of documents and testimony. Woo Quin Lock's father, Woo Yen Tong, who was always referred to as his "alleged father," was originally admitted at San Francisco in 1909 as the foreign-born son of a native, Woo Gap. He returned to China in 1919 and married Chen Shee, and their son, Woo Quin Lock, was born before he returned to the United States. He made several trips to China, and four sons were born. Woo Quin Lock's younger brother Woo Quin Kwock arrived from China in 1939 and was admitted. He was a witness for Woo Quin Lock.

There were many discrepancies between the testimony of the applicant and that of his brother about their method and date of departure for Hong Kong, where they stayed on the way, and when they got there. The brothers did not agree on when and where their alleged younger brother attended school.

The interrogation committee decided that the true relationship between Woo Quin Lock and his father and brother could not be established. They denied Lock admission to the United States, but he had the right to appeal. The case was reopened in April 1940 to reconsider the citizenship of his alleged father. Woo Quin Lock's uncle was called to testify. The uncle, Woo Fong Tong, presented his certificate of identity, which was issued to him in San Francisco in 1913. He testified that he was forty-four, born circa 1894 in Wan Jew village, Toy San district, China. He was a laborer living in the Chicago Hotel in Spokane. He had made two trips to China, in 1921 and 1929, and returned through the Port of San Francisco. He identified the photos that were attached to Fook Yen Tong's affidavit and a photo of Woo Gap, from Woo Gap's 1921 certificate of identity that was included in his San Francisco file. He correctly identified all the people in the Woo family photos from the Seattle and San Francisco files.

Woo Fong Tong described the burial ceremony for his father, Woo Gap. Woo Gap died in 1929, and Woo Fong Tong took his remains—his whole body, not just his bones—back to China in a regular wooden casket, which was placed in a wooden box lined with tin. After their arrival in Wan Jew village, the shipping box was removed, and the casket was placed outside the village for a day for visitation by the family. Then the casket was opened briefly to give everyone one last look at the body. There was a regular burial procession with the whole family accompanying the casket to the burial place at Fong Ngow hill, about two *lis* (less than a mile) north of Wan Jew village. After Woo Gap was buried, the family worshipped at his grave.

Woo Gap was married three times, and his father was married twice. There was much testimony in the case file about whether the Woo men were stepsons or half brothers.

In May 1940, P.J. Hansen wrote a reference letter for Woo Yen Tong, whom he called Raymond Woo. Hansen stated that Woo had worked for him for nine years as a cannery foreman and he considered him a conscientious and trustworthy employee. He offered his assistance in getting Woo's son admitted to the United States.

The legal brief for the appeal on behalf of Woo Quin Lock conceded that Woo Quin Lock was a foreign-born son of Woo Yen Tong but left open the question of his father's U.S. citizenship. Woo Yen Tong derived his citizenship through his father, Woo Gap. Woo Gap and his second wife, Lee Shee, were the parents of Woo Yen Tong. Woo Gap married Lee Shee before the death of his first wife, which was legal under Chinese law and custom. Woo Gap's first wife, Chow Shee, the mother of his four sons, was ill for many years and required constant care. Woo Gap's second wife moved into the household and cared for Chow Shee and the children. Woo Yen Ton was the son of Woo Gap and Woo's second wife, Lee Shee. He was born before Woo's first wife died.

Woo Quin Lock's attorney, Edward E. Merges, brought forward a May 1918 letter written by Philip B. Jones, immigration officer at San Francisco, to the commissioner of immigration at Angel Island stating the merits of Woo Gap's status as a merchant, one of the exemptions to the Chinese Exclusion Act. Woo Gap was born in the United States; a merchant in Santa Cruz, California; and well-known by the community and the immigration station. He resided with his wife and their son Woo Yen Tong. They provided a home and schooling for their son, which immigration authorities thought was sufficient proof of their relationship. They were also impressed that Woo Gap was honest about his dual marriage. Woo Yen Tong's case was submitted to the Central Immigration Office in Washington, D.C., and it was determined that Woo Gap was a citizen of the United States. His son, Woo Yen Tong, had been admitted as the son of a citizen. Finally, after an eight-month legal battle, Woo Quin Lock was admitted on August 20, 1940, as the son of a citizen. His new residence was at 725 King Street in Seattle.

CHAPTER 3
EXCLUSION OF LABORERS

Ah Soon
Laborer, Then Merchant, and Back to Laborer

Ah Soon's Chinese Exclusion Act case file starts in 1899, when he was a laborer in Montana.[45] Within a few years, he was working as a merchant for Ah King, one of the most substantial Chinese businessmen in Seattle and the Pacific Northwest. Ah Soon's Caucasian and Chinese witnesses on his immigration documents were well-known businessmen in the area. Ah Soon became a real estate broker and was involved in the 1909 Alaska Yukon Pacific Exposition in Seattle. He was a stockbroker for a local mining investment company. Not everything was as successful as it appeared. Immigration authorities thought he might be working as a laborer in Tacoma. He eventually changed his immigration status to laborer.

Ah Soon's affidavit, sworn on April 12, 1899, to the "Honorable Collector of Customs" in Port Townsend, Washington, states that he was a laborer applying for a certificate of departure. Ah Soon was a cook living in Helena, Montana, when he applied. His application was approved, and he left for China. He returned to the United States on March 14, 1900, with the status of laborer and was admitted.

By 1907, Ah Soon's life had changed. He was now living in Seattle and a merchant at the Ah King Company. In April 1907, he started the process of obtaining the necessary documents to make a trip to China. He swore in an affidavit that he was a bona fide merchant for the Ah King Company and that he had been a member of the firm for one year and did no labor except that which was necessary in the conducting of business. He was visiting China to bring his wife, Louie Shee, and his seven-year-old daughter, Ah Que, back with him. He would retain his interest in Ah King Company. His photo was attached to the affidavit.

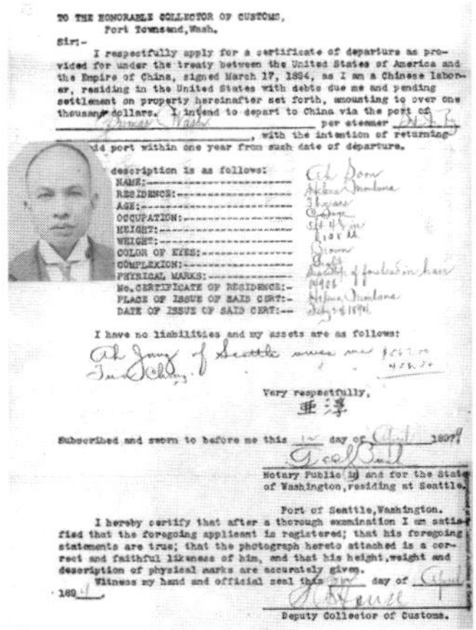

TO THE HONORABLE COLLECTOR OF CUSTOMS,
Port Townsend, Wash.

Sir:-

I respectfully apply for a certificate of departure as provided for under the treaty between the United States of America and the Empire of China, signed March 17, 1894, as I am a Chinese laborer, residing in the United States with debts due me and pending settlement on property hereinafter set forth, amounting to over one thousand dollars. I intend to depart to China via the port of ______ per steamer ______, with the intention of returning [to sa]id port within one year from such date of departure.

[My] description is as follows:
NAME:
RESIDENCE:
AGE:
OCCUPATION:
HEIGHT:
WEIGHT:
COLOR OF EYES:
COMPLEXION:
PHYSICAL MARKS:
No. CERTIFICATE OF RESIDENCE:
PLACE OF ISSUE OF SAID CERT:
DATE OF ISSUE OF SAID CERT:

I have no liabilities and my assets are as follows:

Very respectfully,

Subscribed and sworn to before me this ___ day of ___ 189_

Notary Public in and for the State of Washington, residing at Seattle.

Port of Seattle, Washington.

I hereby certify that after a thorough examination I am satisfied that the foregoing applicant is registered; that his foregoing statements are true; that the photograph hereto attached is a correct and faithful likeness of him, and that his height, weight and description of physical marks are accurately given.

Witness my hand and official seal this ___ day of ___ 189_.

Deputy Collector of Customs.

Affidavit of Ah Soon with photo, 1899. *CEA case file, Ah Soon, file RS 30384, RG 85, National Archives at Seattle, WA.*

On April 26, 1907, G.W. Upper testified concerning the application of Ah Soon for a certificate of departure and return. Upper's business was in the Colman Building at West and Wheeler. He had been living in Seattle for seventeen years. The Ah King Company was formerly called Wah Yuen Company, and Ah King had always been the head of it. Ah Soon managed the company while Ah King was in San Francisco on business. Ah Soon did no manual labor. Upper, formerly a teller at the National Bank of Commerce where Ah King Company did business, testified that Ah Soon had the authority to sign checks on the company account. Upper did not know the amount of capital stock of the company, but Ah King owned the building and paid more than $30,000 for it. They had a wholesale business and supplied Chinese logging camps throughout the West and Northwest.

The next day, witness Charles I. Lynch was interrogated. He had been living in Seattle for twenty-two years and had been employed at the post office for the last eight years. He recognized a photo of Ah Soon and identified him as a member of the Ah King Company. He had known him about nine months. Some of the members of the firm were Ah King, Charley Sing, Ah Foon, and Ah Soon. Besides selling Chinese merchandise, they took contracts for cannery help for five canneries. They also sold produce from a thirty-acre farm south of Seattle at Duwamish Junction.

Ah Soon was reinterviewed on May 2, 1907. He said he was forty-four years old and was born at Har Pong Village, San Ning, Canton, China. His other name was Hock Fong. He first came to the United States in KS 8, or 1882 (KS stands for Kuang-hsu or the reign of Guangxu, the Qing dynasty emperor who reigned from 1875 to 1908), arriving in California.[46] He was married and had one daughter. He was a laborer and had been working for his brother, Ah King, in Seattle for about two years. He was in Helena, Montana, before that for over ten years working as a cook at French Charlie's. He had a $1,000 interest at the Ah King Company, which sold Chinese groceries and general merchandise. He named ten of the members of the firm who each owned a $1,000 interest in the company.

Ah Soon said there were two other people in Seattle who were from his village, Har Pang. They were Hock Hung, who worked in Wah Yuan's store, and Ah King. He said they were cousins. In other interviews, Ah Soon said that Ah King was his brother. Ah Chung, a farmer, was another cousin from Har Pong living in Waitsburg, Washington.

G.W. Upper was recalled to testify on May 6, 1907. He swore that he had known Ah Soon at least four years and that he still believed that Ah Soon had been a member of Ah King Company for more than a year. Although he had known who Ah Soon was for four years, he'd known him more intimately on a business level for the last two years.

A few days later, Ah Soon was recalled to testify. He was asked how long he had known Charles I. Lynch (about two years) and G.W. Upper (about five years). The inspector pointed out that in his previous statement, Ah Soon said he had known Upper for only two years. Ah Soon agreed that two years was incorrect; it was actually about five years. People said what they thought they needed to say to get approved. Often, discrepancies were ignored.

Charles I. Lynch was also recalled on May 9. Lynch was asked about his earlier statement that he had known Ah Soon for about nine months. Lynch said that was incorrect; he had known Ah Soon for more than a year. To qualify as a reliable witness, one was required to have known the affiant for one year or more. Lynch was sure Ah Soon still had an interest in the Ah King Company.

On May 10, 1907, Ah Soon's Application for Preinvestigation of Mercantile Status for his trip to China was approved. Two days later, Ah Soon left on a train for Vancouver, British Columbia, to start his trip. Ah Soon applied to return in 1908. Ah King, manager of Ah King Company, testified on June 16, 1908, that Ah Soon was still a member of his company. Ah Soon's readmittance application was approved, but he did not return.

In March 1909, Ah Soon applied again for admission as a merchant. His application included the following information: Hok Fong (marriage name); age forty-six, height 5 feet, 3¾ inches, scar on back of left hand, wife and two children born in Har Ping, Sun Ning, China; residence at Ken Chung Lung Company, Seattle; member of company for one and a half years; $1,000 interest in company; twelve partners; position in firm: "traveling man." The testimony of Mar Hing, a merchant for the Ah King Company, agreed with Ah Soon's interview.

Ah Soon returned to the United States on March 13, 1909, and was admitted at Seattle as a returning domiciled Chinese merchant. There is no activity in Ah Soon's file from 1909 to February 1913.

On February 28, 1913, Ah Soon applied to travel abroad under the provisions of rule 15 of the Regulations of the Department of Commerce and Labor with the status of a domiciled broker. He had merchant status and claimed that he owned two thousand shares of the Canton Province Mining Company in Seattle.

On March 3, 1913, a Caucasian witness, George F. Ober, a thirty-nine-year-old mining engineer in Seattle, testified that he had lived in Seattle for over three years. He knew Ah Soon was a merchant and real estate broker who bought and sold restaurants and laundries. Soon worked with Wong Shin How at a curio exhibit for an Ah King concern at the Alaska-Yukon-Pacific Exposition in Seattle in 1909. Ah Soon was a stockholder in the Canton Province Mining Company and sold shares of the company on commission. The officers and trustees in the company were Ah King, president; Thomas W. Snaith, vice president; George F. Ober, secretary and treasurer; L.L. Thorp, trustee; Yee Onlai, manager; and Louie Kee, assistant secretary.[47]

Joseph H. Beaven, another white witness, stated that he was fifty-four years old and a superintendent of Baptist mission work. He had known Ah Soon for about twenty years. Ah Soon was employed and a stockholder at Ah King Company. About twenty years before, Ah Soon was a cook at a restaurant in Spokane, but he presently had an interest in his brother's store, the Ah King Company.

Later that day, Ah Soon testified that he had misplaced his certificate of residence but was classified as a merchant. He was a mining stockbroker, living at the Ken Chung Lung Store in Seattle. He owned two thousand shares in the Canton Province Mining Company. He paid $0.06 to acquire a share and got 15 percent commission on every dollar's worth of stock he sold. He had sold over $2,000 worth of stock in a little over two years. He also sold goods on commission from the Ken Chung Lung Company. He denied doing any manual labor in the past twelve months. He signed his statement in Chinese characters.

On March 12, 1913, a letter from Ellis DeBruler, immigration commissioner, stated that he was not satisfied that Ah Soon met the requirements to receive a return certificate as a domiciled exempt broker.

OFFICERS AND TRUSTEES

PRESIDENT AH KING

Ah King is a prosperous Chinese merchant in the city of Seattle. Was one of the men instrumental in securing for the Alaska-Yukon-Pacific Exposition the fine display from his native land. He is the owner of the well known Chinese farm near Seattle.

VICE-PRESIDENT THOMAS W. SNAITH

Thomas W. Snaith has made and lost a small fortune at mining more than once. He has followed the business for years and went through the Alaska boom.

SECRETARY AND TREASURER GEORGE F. OBER

Mr. Ober is the president of the Ober Engineering Co., Seattle, Wash. Is a Colorado man, where he was raised. He is a graduate and a mining and metallurgical engineer, and was U. S. mineral surveyor for Colorado and Wyoming ten years. He had the government contracts for surveying in the Ute reservation and has been the manager of a number of large mining enterprises.

TRUSTEE L. L. THORP

L. L. Thorp is a mining man residing at North Yakima, Wash. He was elected a trustee at the annual meeting this year.

MANAGER YEE ONLAI

Yee Onlai, the active manager, is an Americanized Chinese. He is a mining engineer and has been mining in Tucson, Arizona, where he had charge of copper mines. Was manager for the Dragon Mountain Mining Company and the Fook Hing Mining Company in China, where he now resides.

ASSISTANT SECRETARY LOUIE KEE

Louie Kee is the manager and part owner of the Peking restaurant in Seattle. Previous to coming to this country he was an office holder of the Chinese government.

List of mining investment officers and trustees in the Canton Province Mining Company, including assistant secretary Louie Kee, 1913. *CEA case files, Ah Soon, file RS 30384, RG 85, National Archives at Seattle.*

DeBruler thought Ah Soon's white witnesses also could not testify that he met the requirements. Ah Soon was sometimes referred to as Ng Ah Soon, and his name was sometimes written as (Ng) Ah Soon.

About a week later, J.V. Stewart, Chinese inspector, put a note dated March 20, 1913, into Ah Soon's file saying that he found Ng Ah Soon "acting" as a cashier in the Peking Restaurant in Tacoma. J.A. Wilkens, A.S. Fulton, and watchman Sylvester were witnesses also.[48]

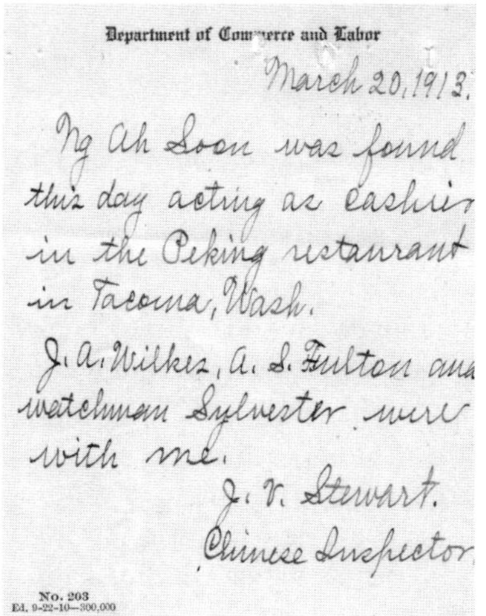

Department of Commerce and Labor

March 20, 1913.

Ng Ah Soon was found this day acting as cashier in the Peking restaurant in Tacoma, Wash.

J. A. Wilkes, A. S. Fulton and watchman Sylvester were with me.

J. V. Stewart.
Chinese Inspector.

No. 203
Ed. 9-22-10—300,000

Note from Chinese inspector regarding Ah Soon, 1913. *CEA case files, Ah Soon, file RS 30384, RG 85, National Archives at Seattle.*

The case files sometimes refer to a person's "baby name"—given to young people before they get married. Chinese men usually obtained a "marriage name" after they got married; this practice is no longer common in modern society. In July 1913, Ah Soon testified that his "baby name" was Gong Sen, Hock (Hok) Fong was his marriage name, and his American name was Ah Soon.[49] He was fifty years old, born in Har Ping village, Sun Ning District, China. He originally came to the United States through San Francisco. He had been back to China twice, in KS 24 or 25 (1898 or 1899), returning KS 26 (1900) through Port Townsend as a laborer. He went to China in KS 33 (1907) and returned in 1909 through Seattle as a merchant and a member of Ah King Company. In 1913, he was living in Tacoma and working as a laborer at the New York Laundry. He earned $40 per month. Charley Dan owned the laundry. Ah Soon based his claim for a return certificate on his loan to Charley Dan for $1,100 so Charley could buy an interest in the Peking Café and buy a laundry. Ah Soon got the money from his brother Ah King (sometimes he said Ah King was his cousin) when he sold his interest in the Ah King Company store in Seattle.

Ah Soon was married to Lou Shee (Louie Shee). They had two children, a boy and a girl. Their son, Gong Sen/Kwong Sin, born in 1908, was six years old, and their daughter, Ah Que, was about fourteen years old. Ah Soon was cautioned that he should not collect any part of his loan to Charley Dan while he was in China because it would change his status and he would not be able to return to the United States. Ah Soon signed his statement in Chinese and English. Charley Dan, baby name Men Dan, was his witness. Charley Dan, his wife, and his infant daughter were living at the laundry at 1508 South D Street in Tacoma. Dan was a native-born citizen. He went to China when he was six years old, returned when he was nineteen years old, and was admitted at Port Townsend.

A letter from the immigrant inspector in Tacoma to the commissioner of immigration in Seattle sent on July 9, 1913, confirmed that Ah Soon

No. 25/1915

CHINESE OVERTIME CERTIFICATE.

Hongkong, April 8, *1915*.

I, J. B. Sawyer American Vice ~~and Deputy~~ Consul ~~General~~ at Hongkong hereby certify that Ah Soon holder of Laborer's Return Certificate No. 30384 dated July 21, 1913 at Seattle, Wash. who departed from said port on August 5, 1913 was unable to return to said port within the period of one year allowed by the Return Certificate mentioned, by reason of a disability beyond his control, namely: illness:- Rheumatism.

and I further certify that his departure on the return passage from this port by the Steamship Talthybius on April 16, 1915. is a return by him at the earliest practicable date, within the additional period of one year, after the removal of the disability above mentioned.

He has offered in addition to his own statements the following proof of the disability: corroborative statements of Chin Gee Hee and Ng Kun.

J. B. Sawyer

American Vice ~~and Deputy~~ Consul ~~General~~

Ah Soon, Chinese overtime certificate, 1915. *CEA case files, Ah Soon, file RS 30384, RG 85, National Archives at Seattle.*

was issued a certificate of residence as a laborer in Helena, Montana, on February 24, 1894. Ah Soon's status was changed from merchant to laborer. On August 5, 1913, Ah Soon made another trip to China.

Ah Soon was unable to return by August 1914, within the allowed one-year period, because he was sick with rheumatism. He provided corroborative statements by Chin Gee Hee and Ng Kun. Ah Soon obtained a Chinese overtime certificate signed by the American vice consul in Hong Kong, which gave him permission to return at a later date—but as early as possible. He was able to return in May 1915 and testified that a son, Quong Ock, was born in July 1915 after Ah Soon left China. He now had two sons. His daughter died around 1912.

Ah Soon applied for a laborer's return certificate in July 1915 to return to China. He had recently made a loan of $1,000 to Mah Fook Hing, a merchant at Yik Fong Company at 705 King Street in Seattle. Hing was interviewed, and although he did not sign a promissory note, he substantiated Soon's testimony. Ah Soon planned to leave for Hong Kong within a few days and would be staying at the Sam Yik Company. This application is the last document in his file; he probably did not return to the United States.

CHAPTER 4
MERCHANTS EXEMPT FROM THE ACT

MERCHANTS

A merchant is a person engaged in buying and selling merchandise, at a fixed place of business, which business is conducted in his name, and who during the time he claims to be engaged as a merchant, does not engage in the performance of any manual labor, except such as is necessary in the conduct of his business as such merchant.

He shall establish by the testimony of two credible witnesses other than Chinese the fact that he conducted such business as herein before defined for at least one year before his departure from the United States, and that during such year he was not engaged in the performance of any manual labor, except such as was necessary in the conduct of his business as such merchant.[50]

Leong Yip

Pacific Northwest Pioneer

Leong Yip's Seattle Chinese Exclusion Act case file starts in February 1912.[51] His previous files were brought forward, and there are no documents in this file from before 1912, but his 1917 and 1919 interviews tell us about his earlier life. He spent many years in Astoria, Oregon, before relocating to Seattle around 1914.

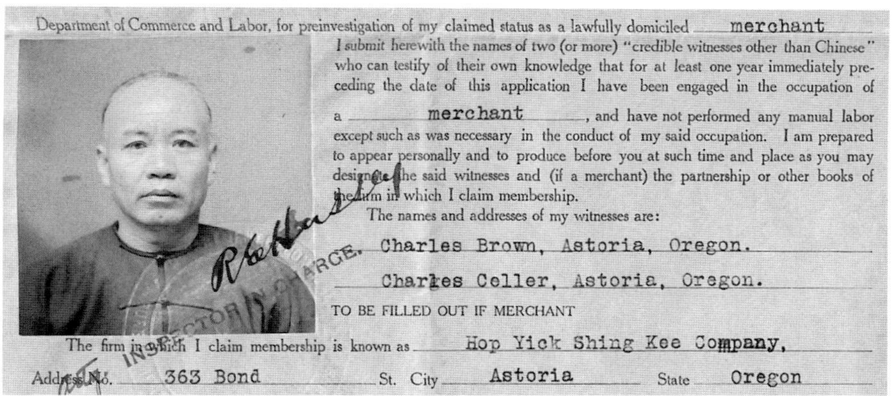
Department of Commerce and Labor, for preinvestigation of my claimed status as a lawfully domiciled merchant I submit herewith the names of two (or more) "credible witnesses other than Chinese" who can testify of their own knowledge that for at least one year immediately preceding the date of this application I have been engaged in the occupation of a merchant, and have not performed any manual labor except such as was necessary in the conduct of my said occupation. I am prepared to appear personally and to produce before you at such time and place as you may designate the said witnesses and (if a merchant) the partnership or other books of the firm in which I claim membership.

The names and addresses of my witnesses are:

Charles Brown, Astoria, Oregon.

Charles Celler, Astoria, Oregon.

TO BE FILLED OUT IF MERCHANT

The firm in which I claim membership is known as Hop Yick Shing Kee Company,

Address No. 363 Bond St. City Astoria State Oregon

Leong Yip, Form 431, 1912. *CEA case files, Leong Yip, file 34847/5-3, RG 85, National Archives at Seattle.*

In 1912, Leong Yip was fifty-five years old, a manager of Hop Yick Shing Kee Company in Astoria, Oregon, and he spoke some English. His first wife died in China in 1911, and he married Chin See of the Shee Chong village, Sunning district, China. Leong had recently spent four and a half months at Canoe Pass Packing Company in Alaska acting as overseer of the workers and as bookkeeper and treasurer. In 1910, he gave half of his $1,000 interest in the company to his son but retained all his duties.

J.D. Robb, a foreman at the Canoe Pass Packing Company cannery, was a witness for Leong. As a child in Astoria, Robb knew Leong, who contracted for Chinese labor and managed the Hop Yick Company. Robb testified that Leong did not engage in manual labor during the time he knew him.

W.L. Robb, father of J.D. Robb and president and manager of Canoe Pass Packing Company, testified that he had known Leong Yip for about twenty years. Robb was collector of customs at Astoria from 1902 to 1906 and frequently did business with Leong. He also testified that Leong was a merchant and did not do any manual labor. The Commission of Immigration in Seattle issued Leong Yip a merchant's return certificate. In July 1913, when Leong Yip returned to the United States, his certificate of identity was canceled, and he received a certificate of residence in its place.

Around 1914, Leong relocated to Seattle and became the manager of Ying Shing Lung Company, a Chinese grocery business with eighteen other members.

In his interview, Leong explained that he had been a laborer from 1881 to 1885 before becoming a merchant. He still owned his share of the Astoria firm. He paid $40 a month rent to his landlord, Goon Dip, the Chinese consul. He paid about $9 to $10 a year in taxes. His white witnesses were James Shea, an exchange teller at the National Bank of Commerce, and Peter Bremmeyr, a plumber. Leong's business made a little over $10,000 a year, and his inventory was worth about $2,000.

Shea testified that when Leong arrived in Seattle, he presented the Seattle bank with a letter of recommendation from the Astoria Savings Bank commending Leong very highly as a merchant who had conducted business with the bank for twenty-five years. Leong Yip made several trips back to China. Charles Brotchi, deputy sheriff, a witness for his 1919 trip, testified that Leong was one of the best-known merchants in Chinatown, president of the Chinese Masonic Lodge in 1918, and a man above reproach and clean and honest in every respect.

Leong Yip returned to Seattle in July 1920 with his wife and his son, Jow Wah, and was admitted. Leong Yip's June 30, 1943 *Seattle Times* obituary is included in his file. It called Leong Yip "a Chinese patriarch and one of the most colorful of Pacific Northwest pioneers." One of his sons was then serving in the army during World War II.[52]

Chin Hing Yee

The first document in Chin Hing Yee's file is his July 1900 Application for Readmission of Chinese Merchant form.[53] It includes an affidavit by two Caucasian men, John Thompson and Edward Maus. They swore that they were citizens of the United States and residents of the State of Washington and that they had been residing in King County more than ten years. They testified that they personally knew Chin Hing Yee, whose photograph was attached to the affidavit, and that Chin was thirty years old; he'd resided in Seattle for more than six years in the past; he was a merchant at Coaster Tea Company; he had a $500 interest in the company; prior to his departure for China, he was engaged in the business of buying and selling merchandise for the firm; and he did not perform manual labor in the twelve months before his departure. Chin Hing Yee fit the description of a merchant in every aspect.

When Chin Hing Yee returned to the United States in November 1901, John Thompson and Edward Maus again swore in an affidavit to the same information they had sworn to when Chin left for China in 1900. Thomas M. Fisher, Chinese inspector for the Customs District of Puget Sound, Washington, reported to Colonel F.D. Huestis, the customs collector in Port

Townsend, Washington, that he had examined the witnesses for Chin Hing Yee and believed the applicant was entitled to admission. Chin Hing Yee was readmitted in November 1901 at Port Townsend.

In 1909, Chin Hing Yee, sometimes known as Chin Hing, applied to go to China again. He swore in an affidavit that he was born around 1870 in Chin Bing village, Sun Ning district, China. He had been a resident of Seattle for many years, and he was a merchant doing business at Bow On Drug Company at 216 Washington Street. He was formerly a member of the Coaster Tea Company at 1305 Second Avenue. Fred R. Harvey and Edward Maus swore in an affidavit that they were white citizens who had resided in Seattle for several years; they knew Chin was a merchant at a fixed place of business; he was not a laborer; and for the last twelve months he had not performed any manual labor. Edward Maus was in the fire insurance business and had lived in Seattle since about 1888. He had known Chin Hing Yee for fifteen years. Fred R. Harvey, a resident of Seattle for ten years, was a contractor at the Collins block and had known Chin for about five years.

Chin Lai, a manager of Bow On Drug Company, was asked to draw up a partnership list for the company. He swore that Chin Hing Yee invested $500 in the company and became a partner. Other partners were Louie Hay, Chin Sang, Hong Sing, and Toy Sam. Sales were about $600 or $700 a month and rent on the store building was $120 a month. They rented out part of the building for a restaurant and received $60 a month in rent.

In 1911, Chin Hing Yee was working as a bookkeeper, was admitted as a returning merchant, and was asked to prepare a partnership list also.

Chin Hing Yee signed his name in English and Chinese on all his documents. When Chin went back to China in early 1915, he was a laundryman. Because he changed his status to laborer, it was necessary for him to show that he was owed $1,000. The Chinese Exclusion Act required that a laborer who wanted to leave be owed more than $1,000 that could be collected only when he returned. Chin Lai testified that he was owed the required amount by Chin. When he returned to Seattle in October 1915, Chin claimed he had two sons and one daughter and his wife was "in the family way."

In 1919, Chin Hing Yee testified that he was originally admitted to the United States in 1885 at the Port of San Francisco as the minor son of a merchant. He was fourteen or fifteen at that time. Henry A. Monroe, the examining inspector in Seattle, thought Chin must be mistaken "because that was before the court had decided that minor sons of exempts

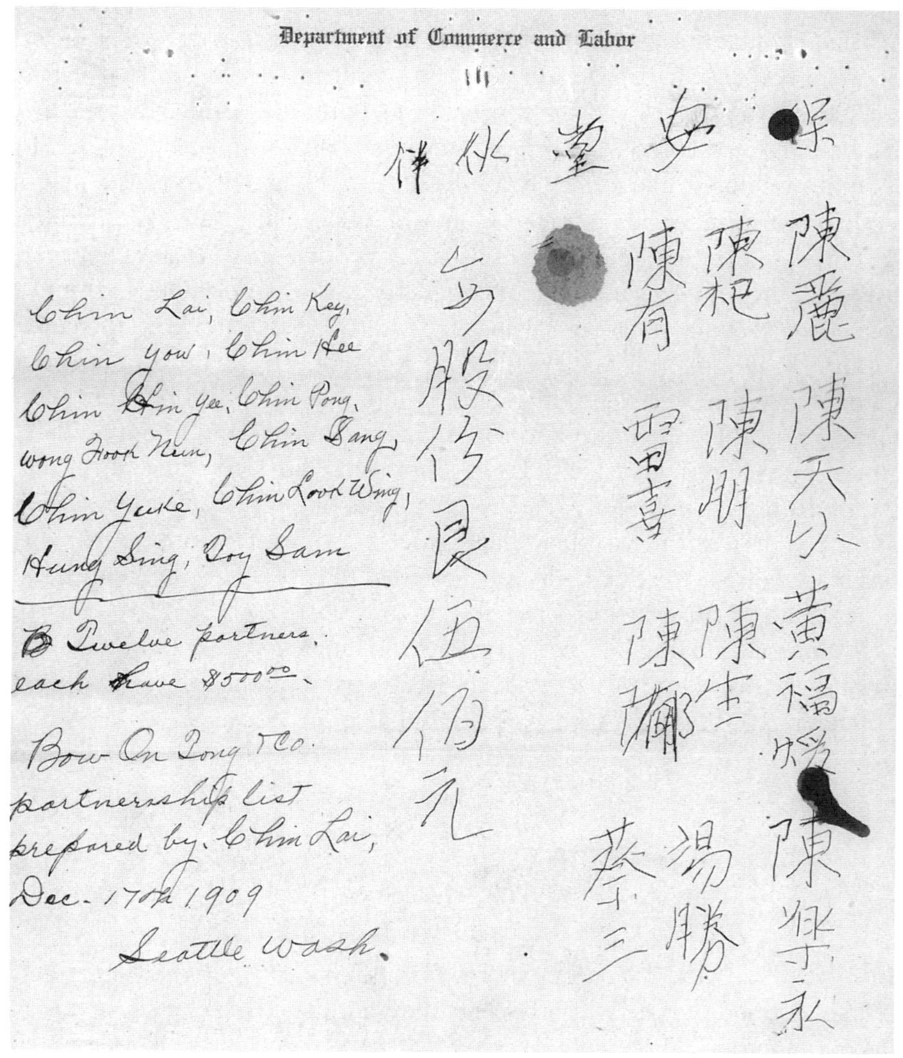

Department of Commerce and Labor

保安堂伙伴

陳麗 陳[illegible] 黄福[illegible] 陳樂永
陳杞 陳明 陳生 湯勝
陳有 雷喜 陳[illegible] 蔡三

每股[illegible]伍佰元

Chin Lai, Chin Key,
Chin You, Chin Hee
Chin Hin Yee, Chin Pong,
Wong Foork Num, Chin Sang,
Chin Yuke, Chin Look Wing,
Hung Sing, Toy Sam

Twelve partners.
each have $500.00.

Bow On Tong Co.
partnership list
prepared by. Chin Lai,
Dec. 17th 1909
Seattle Wash.

Chin Hing Yee, merchant partnership list, 1911. *CEA case files, Gin Mon Louie, file 7032/521, RG 85, National Archives at Seattle.*

(merchants) could be admitted without being in possession of the certificate required by Section 6 of the Act of 1884." Monroe thought Chin was first admitted in 1901 as a member of the Coaster Tea Company. Monroe suspected that Chin was still a laborer, but since Chin had previously been admitted as the son of a merchant, a laborer, and then again as a merchant, Monroe—wanting to be consistent—could only recommend that his application be approved.

When Chin Hing Yee applied to leave in 1919, he was issued a certificate of identity. He was applying for a return certificate as a laborer. He had $1,000 on deposit in the University State Bank of Seattle and showed his bank book as proof. Chin was reminded that he would be entitled to readmission only if the money was still on deposit when he returned.

Before making another trip to China in 1923, Chin Hing Yee testified that he was fifty-three years old, his wife's name was Lim Shee, and they had five children, four sons and a daughter, ranging in age from four to twenty-four. Two of their sons were living in Canada. He was unable to return within the allotted year because his wife was seriously ill, so he obtained a Chinese overtime certificate that allowed him to stay up to one more year. Chan Yee and Chan Go gave corroborating statements, and Maurice Walk, American vice consul at Hong Kong, approved Chin's overtime certificate. (Hong Kong was frequently rendered "Hongkong" in early case files.) Chin Hing Yee returned to Seattle in September 1924, just two months after his original one-year deadline. He was admitted. There is no mention of the health status of his wife in his file.

Because Chin Hing Yee made five trips to China, there are photos of him from each trip, from 1901 to 1923. He wore his traditional Chinese clothes and hat in 1901 and an American suit and tie in 1923.

Gin Mon Louie

Chinese Herbalist in Seattle

In 1912, Gin Mon Louie applied to visit China. His witness, Willard A. Norse, testified that he was fifty years old and owned two hotels, at 114½ Second South and 122 Second South in Seattle.[54] For the past five years, M. Hee Woo (He Wo), a Chinese doctor, rented five rooms at the hotel on 122 Second South. Dr. Woo was Gin Mon Louie's employer, and when Woo visited China in early 1912, Gin Mon Louie took over the business for him until his return. Then it was Gin Mon Louie's turn to visit China.

F.T. Carlton, a druggist living in Seattle, also testified for Gin Mon Louie. They worked in the same building and saw each other four or five times a day. Carlton knew that Gin Mon Louie was going to China to get married. Gin Mon Louie's application was approved. He visited China, married, returned in September 1913, and received his certificate of identity.

When Gin Mon Louie applied to visit China in 1921, his witnesses were Dr. J.E. Godfrey, a physician and surgeon, and Axel Hedberg. Godfrey had lived in Seattle since 1914 and knew about a couple dozen Chinese people. He knew that Gin Mon Louie was a Chinese herb doctor, not a regular licensed physician but a "sanipractor" (drugless healer/naturopathic doctor). Dr. Lamb was his partner. Godfrey and Gin Mon Louie were friends and saw each other about once a month.

Gin Mon Louie's other witness was Axel Hedberg, publisher of the *Swedish Tribune*. Hedberg did not know many Chinese but was acquainted with Gin Mon Louie because Louie advertised in his newspaper. Hedberg went to Louie's office monthly to collect the five dollars owed him for the ads.

I yesterday visited the M. Hee Wo Company, at the address given by applicant, and he there exhibited to me what he claimed was a copy of his income tax report to the Government, which was made out on the blank form furnished by the Internal Revenue Department. This income report showed the income of the M. Hee Wo Company for the year 1920 to be as follows,

Salary of Gin Mon Louie	$900.00
" Gin Wing Fun	40.00
" John (porter)	96.00
" Office help.	460.00
Gas and light	78.91
Telephone	81.00
Advertising	2,126.25
Heat	32.00
Stationery and wrapping paper, and miscellaneous expenses -	384.80
Rent -	$840.00

The total shown was $5,038.96, and the income tax paid $100.76.

I think there is no doubt as to applicant's exempt status. In addition, he seems to be known to other inspectors in this office, and from the evidence submitted I recommend that the certificate be granted applicant.

C. E. Keagy
Immigrant Inspector

Income report for M. Hee Wo Company, 1920. *CEA case files, Leong Yip, file 34847/5-3, RG 85, National Archives at Seattle.*

Immigrant inspector Keagy visited Dr. Louie at his office and obtained a copy of M. Hee Wo (Hee Woo or Dr. Woo) Company's income tax report for 1920. He recommended that Gin Mon Louie's application to visit China and return as a merchant be approved.

In 1924, Gin Mon Louie made another trip to China. Godfrey and Hedberg were his witnesses again.

Gin Mon Louie visited China again in 1934 and returned in 1937. The interrogators asked him about his interactions in China with Chinese residents of the United States. Did he visit with anyone in his village who was from the United States? Did he attend the wedding of anyone from the United States? Did he arrange to appear as a witness for a prospective applicant for admission to the United States? Louie answered no to all these questions, and there were no follow-up questions.

The examining inspector, Roy C. Matterson, reviewed information from when Gin Mon Louie originally came into the United States. He was first admitted at San Francisco as a student in 1904 and was sometimes known as Jin Mon Yuey. Immigration listed him as Chan Man Yai, but Gin Mon Louie thought his name had been either misspelled or mispronounced. Matterson updated Gin Mon Louie's family information. His marriage name was Jin Lip Moon. He was married to Yee Shee, and they had two sons, Jin Ok Jung and Jin Hing Lok, both living in China. The immigration inspectors were satisfied with the results of their interrogation, and Gin Mon Louie was admitted to the United States.

Lew King, Merchant and Laborer

Canadian and U.S. File

It is unusual that a copy of Lew King's (or Loey King's) twenty-two-page Canadian file was included in his Seattle file.[55] Lew King's Canadian record was made in accordance with the laws of the Dominion of Canada—specifically the Chinese Immigration Act of 1906, as amended by acts assented to July 20, 1908, and July 25, 1917. A copy of the 1906 act as amended is included in the file.

On August 23, 1920, Wong Wam Fong, the manager of the Man Sing Lung Company at 92 Pender Street East, Vancouver, swore that the partnership was started in March 1919. It dealt with groceries, general merchandise, and drugs. Lew King was a member of the partnership, a

Lew King, Form 432 photo, 1921. *CEA case files, Lew King, file 7032/521, RG 85, National Archives at Seattle.*

merchant, and was interested in coming to Vancouver from Hong Kong to become an active partner.

Louis Gar On, the managing partner of the Man Sing Lung Company in Victoria, British Columbia, claimed that Lew King had been a partner of the company for several years in Victoria and was also registered as a partner of Man Sing Lung Company in Vancouver. He believed that Lew King should be entitled to enter Canada exempt from the Canadian $500 capitulation tax. The tax was levied as part of the Canadian Chinese Immigration Act of 1923 to discourage immigration of Chinese people into Canada, and the tax was gradually increased to $500.[56]

During Lew King's interrogation, he testified that he was a merchant for Man Sing Lung Company in Vancouver, British Columbia. He arrived in Vancouver on November 23, 1920. He had a Canadian Chinese Exclusion Act file. His exemption as a merchant was rejected, and he was admitted after paying the $500 head tax. In his statement and declaration for registration, he said that he was a salesman. He was born in Ing Gar Hong, Sin Ning district, China, around 1892.

Lew King left Vancouver and was admitted at the Port of Seattle in August 1921 as a section 6 merchant. The 1888 Scott Act, an amendment to the Chinese Exclusion Act, exempted merchants, teachers, students, travelers, and diplomats from the act.[57] Lew King continued working as a merchant, and over the next few years, he made two trips to China. When he applied for a laborer's return certificate in 1935, the Seattle immigration office chose to verify his original admission in Vancouver in 1921. The Vancouver office initially recommended that Lew King not be approved. Seattle immigration asked Vancouver immigration to reexamine its file. Roy M. Porter, immigrant inspector in Seattle, reviewed the Vancouver office's report. Porter did not think there was sufficient evidence to prove that Lew King's admission to the Canada or to the United States in 1921 was fraudulent. He reasoned that if the admittance was not approved, Lew King's appeal would probably be sustained, so he recommended that his laborer's return certificate be approved. Porter probably did not want to call attention to the fact that King's admittance in 1921 and his two succeeding admittances were approved, even though there was a slight chance that there may have been something fraudulent in the initial admittance.

At the time of his interview to leave the United States on April 5, 1935, Lew King presented a treasury bond for $1,000 as proof of his statutory right for a laborer's return certificate. He left the bond with the Goon Dip Company in Seattle. He was reminded by immigration authorities that the bond must be intact in the United States at the time of his return for him to be entitled to legal readmission. Lew King (married name Doon Hen) was forty-two years old and living at 214 Washington Street in Seattle. He left Seattle on April 13, 1935, on the SS *President McKinley*.

According to section 7 of the Chinese Exclusion Act of 1888, as amended, Chinese laborers were required to return to the United States within one year.[58] As of September 1937, Lew King had not returned, so Marie A. Proctor, district commissioner of the Seattle District Immigration Office, canceled his certificate of identity. This would have made it difficult for him to be admitted to the United States if he returned. There is no indication in his file that he tried to return.

Leung Man Hoi

Merchant Certificate from Swatow

Leung Man Hoi arrived in the Port of Seattle on May 15, 1915.[59] He passed his medical exam. He did not have hookworm or trachoma. If he'd had either, he would have been sent to the hospital until he recovered or was deported.

Leung was interviewed by immigration inspector Henry A. Monroe. He testified that his marriage name was Leung Yum Gong, he was thirty years old, and he was born on March 10, 1886, in Kai Gock village, Moy Yuen district, China. He was married to Chin She, and they had two young sons, Sik Chee and Sik Yuen. Leung was in the rice and wine business at Bo San Wo Company, Chung Sar Market, China. Leung Man Hoi was admitted to Seattle on his day of arrival as a section 6 merchant and received his certificate of identity. His destination was the King Chong Lung Company, 217 Washington Street, Seattle.

When questioned by inspector Henry A. Monroe, Leung Man Hoi said that he was examined in China by a consular representative in Swatow, a city

NIPPON YUSEN KAISHA.

S. S. YOKOHAMA MARU Voy. 14 out. Sailing H. K. 5/4/15

Name Mr. Leung Man Hoi Sex Male Age 30 years

Destination SEATTLE, Wash., U. S. A.

I hereby certify that I have microscopically examined the faeces of the above named and have not found any Ova of Hookworm *present.* 9 APR 1915

APR 7 1915

Signed PASSED F. LINDSAY-WOODS. M.B.

I hereby certify that I have examined the above named passenger and {him/her} to be free from Trachoma.

Signed

Surgeon.

Eye examination fee $1
Payable by passenger.

Results of Leung Man Hoi's medical examination, 1915. *CEA case files, Leung Man Hoi (Yum Gong), file RS 29097, RG 85, National Archives at Seattle.*

in eastern Guangdong, China. Leung did not know the interviewer's name, but he said he answered his many questions truthfully. Leung did not have any relatives in the United States, only a friend whom he had not seen in ten years, Wong Shu Tong, who was living at the King Chong Lung Company in Seattle. Leung had only $10 in cash with him and what he claimed was a bank draft for $1,000 in gold drawn on Wah Young Company issued in Hong Kong. Inspector Monroe concluded that it was not a bank draft but only an order for the Wah Young Company to extend credit to Leung.

Inspector Monroe asked Leung if he knew Chin Tan in China. Chin solicited men of means to secure section 6 certificates so they could enter the United States illegally. Leung denied knowing Chin Tan. At the conclusion of the interrogation, Monroe reminded Leung that under no circumstances could he work as a laborer or he would be subject to arrest and deportation.

Leung Man Hoi applied to leave the United States in May 1920 from San Francisco. He filed his application for a return certificate as a merchant, and it was approved on June 12, 1920, by the commissioner at Angel Island Station in San Francisco, California, but with some reservations. This is an excerpt from a letter to immigration in San Francisco from the Seattle immigration office on May 28, 1920:

> *Please note that Leung Man Hoi is a so-called Swatow Section 6 merchant. A couple of years ago this office established to the satisfaction of the*

Department of Washington and the U.S. Court here, on Writ of Habeas Corpus, that all Swatow cases were fraudulent, and the last twenty-two from that place holding papers were returned to China, after Judge Neterer of the District Court here had discharged a Writ of Habeas Corpus obtained in their behalf. Since that time no Chinese holding Swatow certificates have applied at this port for admission. Testimony of the applicant given May 15, 1915, is interesting reading, in view of the subsequent developments in Swatow cases.[60]

In spite of the letter from the Seattle office about its doubts concerning the validity of section 6 merchant certificates issued in Swatow, Leung Man Hoi's papers were approved.

Children and Spouses of Merchants

Ng Back Ging

Child of Seattle Merchant

Ng Buck Look wanted to bring his son, Ng Back Ging, to the United States.[61] Ng Buck Look (sometimes referred to as Ng Buck Look or Bok Look) was born in China and came to the United States in 1923. Ng Buck Look, his son, and their witnesses were interviewed several times. Although these interrogations were tedious and repetitive, they did produce a tremendous amount of genealogical (not always completely truthful) and cultural information about the family, including documents and photographs.

In August 1925, Ng Buck Look testified that since his arrival in the United States, he had been a buyer and partner for the Quong Chong Company on King Street in Seattle. He and his wife, Wong Shee, had three sons; one died when he was two years old. He completed his affidavit and attached photos of himself and his son. Ng Back Ging was classified as the minor son of a merchant.

Ng Back Ging, age fifteen, arrived in the Port of Seattle in March 1926. He was born in Mun Low village, Sun Woy district, China, and had not seen his father in five or six years. His father had lived in China and Canada before coming to Seattle. His grandfather was a farmer in their village, and his great-grandfather was dead. He was asked about his mother's and father's extended families. He described the village where he grew up, the houses, and the neighbors. His family had a red marriage paper with his great-grandparents' and grandparents' names listed. The marriage paper was not included in the file. This paper likely would have contained the same information about his mother's side of the family. Ng Back Ging was asked about the tiles or stones in the house and the courtyard; if they had a sewing machine or ancestral tablets; what the floors were made of; where the large and small doors, the windows, and the bedrooms were located; if they had a rice mill or pounder; and if there were any pictures on the walls. Then he was asked for details about his neighbors, their families, their houses, and the village. Where was the shrine? Was there a wall around the village? What was it made of? Was there a pond or stream near the village? Any land for growing rice? Any stores? A watchtower? Who were the watchmen? Who was the head of the village? Ng Back Ging also described his school experience. His testimony was over six pages long.

A. Brattstom, a white witness for Ng Buck Look, was interviewed. As a salesman for the Mutual Paper Corporation, he sold paper, twine, bags, and other paper goods to Buck Look at the Quong Chong Company. He knew Buck Look was a partner with Sam Choi. Brattstom was in the store at least once or twice a week.

Ng Dok Foon, the manager of Quong Chong Company, also testified. There were eleven partners in the firm, and six of them were active. Its annual total sales were between $24,000 and $25,000. There was no gambling on the premises. The interpreter examined the company's books and found that the figures agreed with the testimony. Ng Dok Foon lived in the same village as Buck Look and could verify all the information that had been given in the interviews.

Ng Buck Look was interviewed at length. He described his father, Ng Dok Baw, who was about fifty-seven and worked in their home village in the rice fields. Buck Look's mother had died, and his father remarried. Ng Buck Look had five brothers and one sister. One of his brothers, Bok Fook, came to the United States and lived somewhere in Oklahoma. Ng Buck Look described his other siblings, their spouses and children, and the other details that his son described.

John A. Thompson, a meat cutter at Fair Market on King Street, was also a witness. He verified Ng Buck Look's photo, and their testimony agreed. They were in each other's stores frequently, sometimes once or twice a day. He considered Ng Buck Look a "pretty good merchant."

Ng Buck Look was recalled, and five more pages of testimony were taken. He was asked about his father, the neighbors and their houses and families, slave families, ancestral halls, fishponds, walls around the city, watchtowers, bridges and streams, markets, his son's school experience, and details about Ng Dok Foon to make sure their testimonies agreed. Ng Buck Look originally entered North America through Vancouver, British Columbia, Canada. He paid a $500 head tax when he arrived. He took one trip back to China while he lived in Canada. He planned on staying in Vancouver but decided to make a short visit to the United States, found a business opportunity in Seattle, and decided to stay. Ng Buck Look did not have his Canadian documents with him, so he was allowed to go retrieve them. He presented a receipt for the $500 head tax he paid and a card showing his admittance to Vancouver on March 12, 1923, under Certificate of Identity 9, No. 45482.

On March 9, 1926, the Department of Immigration and Colonization in Canada sent the Seattle immigration office certified documents showing Ng Buck Look's original entry to Canada. It added a reminder that Ng Buck Look had forfeited his right to be readmitted to Canada by remaining away longer than the statutory period of two years.

Finally, the Board of Special Inquiry (BSI) agreed that Ng Back Ging should be admitted. His father's merchant status was confirmed, the books of his company were examined and cleared, and two statutory witnesses who were not Chinese had been examined. His father was a member of one of the oldest Chinese stores in Seattle. There were no discrepancies in all the testimony. The father and son resembled each other and had similar mannerisms. The father had been in China at the right time to conceive a son with Ng Back Ging's date of birth. The decision to admit Ng Back Ging was unanimous. He was admitted on March 13, 1926.

In 1929, Ng Back Ging wanted to make a trip to China. The Immigration Act of 1924 made it complicated for him to get approval for his trip. The act prevented immigration from Asia except under certain circumstances. It capped total immigration at 165,000 and set the nationality quotas to 2 percent based on the 1890 census.[62] The total U.S. Chinese population in 1890 was 107,488, so only a little over 2,100 of those exempt from the Chinese Exclusion Act would be able to immigrate to the United States.[63]

The First Supplement to Chinese General Order No. 13 addressed this problem. If a husband or father who was admitted before July 1, 1924, had maintained his status as a merchant, his wife and minor children admitted after June 30, 1924, would be lawfully admitted to the United States.[64]

According to the file, Ng Buck Look, a merchant and the father of Ng Back Ging, was lawfully admitted to the United States prior to July 1, 1924;

THE DEPARTMENT OF IMMIGRATION AND COLONIZATION

CHINESE IMMIGRATION BRANCH

C. I. 9

No. 45482

March 12, 1923. 19

To the Controller of Chinese Immigration,
Port of Vancouver

I hereby give notice that I desire to leave Canada with the intention of returning thereto.

I propose to sail or depart from Vancouver for ~~xxxxxxxxxx~~ SEATTLE

on the C.P.R.Coast boat day of March 12th, 1923 19

I intend to return to Canada at the port of (1) Vancouver

I request registration and I attach my photograph hereto and give the following information for the purpose of my identification on my return.

My proper name is Ng Buck Look

I am sometimes known as

I first came to Canada in the year 1914 Emp. of Asia, May Vancouver.

My place of residence in Canada is Vancouver

Where I have resided since the year 4 years.

Certificate of Registration Form C. I. 5 No 87352

My present occupation is that of Clerk

My place of birth was Mon Low

My present age is 31

Height 5 feet 7 inches.

Facial marks or other peculiarities:—
Large brown mark front of R. ear.
Two moles right neck.
Pit outer corner right eye.

I am personally known to Lim Kee and

both of Vancouver to whom I would refer you for correctness of statements herein made.

吳壮祿
(Signature of Chinese Person)

Particulars and photograph hereon shown compared with applicant and approved by me this day. H. W. Wilson (Controller) for

Dated at Vancouver March 12th, 1923.

I have personally examined the person of Chinese origin who claims to be the person above described and whose photograph is affixed hereon, (2) who returned to Canada on the day of 19 , and declare him to be the same person.

Certified a true copy.
(Controller)

Dated at 19

(1) If the person of Chinese origin desires to return to Canada by any other port, other than the port of departure, this form must be taken in duplicate and the duplicate forwarded to the intended port of entry by mail.
(2) The initials of the Controller should be affixed in ink so that a portion thereof overlaps the photograph.

[OVER]

Ng Back Ging, Canadian certificate of identity, 1923. *CEA case files, Ng Back Ging, file 7031/120, RG 85, National Archives at Seattle.*

he maintained his merchant status, and Ng Back Ging was lawfully admitted after June 30, 1924.

In late December 1929, Ng Back Ging applied for a predetermination of status under General Order No. 13 to make a trip to China. He swore that his American name was Harold Ng and he was not married. He was born on January 11, 1913, in Mun Low village, Sun Woy district. He wanted to get treatment for his leg, which had been broken in August 1928 and was not healing. Since his arrival in 1926, he had attended Pacific College in Seattle. He was asked some of the same questions he was asked during his 1926 interview, and his answers were consistent with his earlier testimony.

Ng Back Ging's father was interviewed again. He testified that he worked at Lin Shing Jewelry Store in Vancouver, British Columbia, for about two years before he came to Seattle. He showed the interviewer his papers from his admittance in 1926. William Francis Roark and Ralph E. Olsen were interviewed and swore in an affidavit that they had been residents of Seattle for several years and were not Chinese. They had known Ng Buck Look for more than one year and believed that he was a member of the Quong Chong Company in Seattle and he had not performed any manual labor during that time. Olsen was in the wholesale meat business, and Roark was a passenger agent for the Milwaukee Railway. They both stated that the Quong Chong Company was not associated with a restaurant, laundry, or gambling house.

Purely G. Hall, examining inspector, visited the company, reviewed the partnership books for three current years, and noted that the gross sales for 1929 were over $40,000. He recommended that Ng Back Ging receive his certificate. Ng Back Ging returned from his trip to China on November 3, 1930, and was admitted.

Dorothy S. Luke Lee

Child of Merchant

Dorothy S. Luke Lee, born on March 15, 1910, in Seattle, was the daughter of Luke Lee and Down Cook.[65] When her family decided to go to China for a year, they needed to complete the paperwork for baby Dorothy and her siblings.

Dr. Cora Smith (Eaton) King, the family's physician for the previous five years, was a witness for the family. She testified that Dorothy's father, Luke Lee, was a merchant in Seattle. She knew that at least three of their children were born in the United States. She was present at the birth of the two youngest, Dorothy and Edwin S. Luke Lee, and she assisted in obtaining a certified copy of the birth certificate of Eugene Luke Lee, who was also born in the United States.

Dorothy's mother, Down Cook (Mrs. Luke Lee), testified that she was thirty years old in 1912 and was born in Quong Chaw village, Sunning district, China. She came to the United States in July 1907 through Sumas, Washington. At that time her husband was a merchant and member of Sing Fork and Company in New Haven, Connecticut. Their son, Luke Thick Kaye (Dorothy's older brother), born in Yen On village, Sunning district, China, came with them. Luke Thick Kaye testified that he was seven years

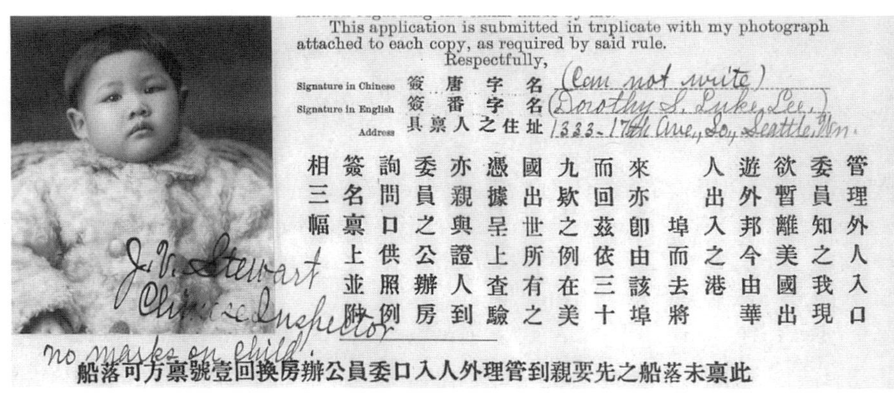
This application is submitted in triplicate with my photograph attached to each copy, as required by said rule.

Respectfully,

Signature in Chinese 簽唐字名 (Can not write)

Signature in English 簽番字名 (Dorothy S. Luke Lee.)

Address 具稟人之住址 1333-17th Ave, So. Seattle, Wn.

管理外人入口委員知之我現欲暫離美國出遊外邦今由華人出入之港埠而去將來亦即由該埠而回茲依三十九欵之例在美國出世所有之憑據呈上查驗亦親與證人到委員之公辦房詢問口供照例簽名稟上並附相三幅

J. V. Stewart
Chinese Inspector

no marks on child.

此稟未落船之先要親到管理外人入口委員公辦房換回壹號稟方可落船

Dorothy S. Luke Lee's Form 430, 1912. *CEA case files, Dorothy S. Luke Dee (Mrs. Kaye Hong), file #7030/11435, RG 85, National Archives at Seattle.*

old. He had been going to school for three years. His teacher at the Main Street School in Seattle was Miss Sadie E. Smith, and his present teacher at Colman School was Miss Rock.

Although Dorothy's brothers and parents have their own individual files, in many cases, some or all of a child's information is included in their parents' or siblings' files. Dorothy's file includes a reference sheet listing the file numbers of other family members.

Dorothy's file continues to September 13, 1938, when she applied to leave the United States from the Port of Seattle. She was now Mrs. Kaye Hong, age twenty-eight. She listed her address as 725 Pine Street, San Francisco, California, and was married to Kaye Hong (Hong Won Kee Kaye) on September 7, 1936. Dorothy, her husband, and some of his family were making a short trip to Canada. They returned the next day through Blaine, Washington, and were admitted.

Dorothy's brother, Keye Luke, attended the University of Washington in Seattle, majoring in architecture. After his father died, he designed sheet music covers for Harold Weeks's Melody Shop. He was an artist/illustrator before becoming an actor for films and television. He got his movie start by playing Charlie Chan's "Number One Son," Lee Chan.[66]

Dorothy and Keye's younger brother, Edwin Luke, was also an actor. He majored in journalism at the University of Washington and played in the Northwest Chinese Basketball Tournament.[67]

Ah Yen

Child of Merchant

Ah Yen, the minor son of She Get, a Chinese merchant from Port Townsend, arrived in Port Townsend on April 25, 1904, on the SS *Tremont.*[68] He was fifteen years old, weighed 108 pounds, and had a large scar above the center of his forehead near his hairline.

In his arrival interview at Port Townsend, Ah Yen stated that he lived in Cha Chung village in the district of San Ning, China, with his older brother and his wife and his younger brother. Their mother died in 1901. His village had about thirty houses, and their house was a few blocks from a large stream. When his father, She Get, visited him in their village in China around 1898, he stayed for one year. After She Get returned to the United States, they received letters from him. Ah Yen described his father as a tall, fat man who was a member of the Get Kee Company. She Get's witnesses described him as short and heavily built. Ah Yen was only about eight or nine when his father visited, so maybe his father seemed tall to him.

Inspector Fisher interviewed witness James W. Stockand, who had lived in Port Townsend for forty years and was a clerk in a store. Stockand said She Get had a legitimate store with a small stock of goods and he never saw any gambling there. He thought She Get was likely to provide for his son financially.

Another witness, Max Gerson, was a merchant in Port Townsend. He had lived there since 1882 and had known She Get for over two years. Gerson stated that She Get had a Chinese general merchandise store on Adams Street between Washington and Water. Gerson felt confident that if She Get's son was admitted, he would not become a public charge. He thought She Get was a man of some means, a gentleman who would support his son. Stockand and Gerson gave the same information in an affidavit and described She Get. They said he was forty-seven years old and about five feet, four inches with a heavy build, weighed about 180 pounds, spoke English very well, and seemed to be a very good businessman and that the photo of She Get attached to the affidavit was a good likeness of him.

She Get testified that he had lived in Port Townsend for a little over two years. Previously he lived in Spokane for fifteen years and Colfax, Washington, before that. He had been in the United States for twenty-five years. She Get sold Chinese merchandise at Yee Yuen Company in Spokane at 513 Front Avenue and had about $1,000 in stock. He sold his Spokane store and started a new store in Spokane and a business in Port Townsend in March 1902 with nine partners. His share was about $500 of the business's total stock on hand of $3,900 and he had about a $500 share in the new Spokane store. He registered as a merchant and had been back to China twice. He brought his son Ah Yen to the United States so he could attend school and help in the store. He was married to Sin Lim for twenty-seven years until she died in 1901.

In 1904, Ah Gee swore that he was a resident of Port Townsend and a member and bookkeeper of the Zee Tai Company. He was originally from Dow Dung, Sin Ning, Canton, China. On a 1901–03 trip to China, he visited Sha Chung (Cha Chung) to see She Get's son and give him and his brothers money from their father.

Another witness, Eng Gay, testified that She Get had three sons. The village of Cha Chung was a one-day, eighty-cent steamboat trip from Hong Kong. Witnesses were questioned each time an applicant arrived or departed. Frequently, their testimonies also appeared in affidavits at some point during the application process.

In September 1908, Ah Yen planned a trip to China. Max Garson and Milton Dobbs, citizens of the United States and residents of Port Townsend, swore that they were acquainted with She Get; he was a merchant, not a laborer, and a member and manager of Get Kee Company at 109½ Adams Street, Port Townsend; he performed no manual labor; no laundry, gambling

merchant,and none other than that specifically set forth herein to-wit,as manager of said firm for the year last past; that no laundry,gambling establishment or restaurant is connected with said firm; that he knows Ah Yen, the son of She Get,whose photograpg is attached hereto,who was admktted to the United States,at Port Townsend,April 30th,1904; that he has read She Get's affidavit,knows the contents thereof, and believes the same to be true.

And,he further states,that he has no interest whatsoever,in either She Get or Ah Yen.

Photo of Ah Yen, Gerson-Dobbs affidavit, 1908. *CEA case files, Ah Yen, file RS 2168, RG 85, National Archives at Seattle.*

establishment, or restaurant was connected with the firm; and they knew Ah Yen, son of She Get, who was admitted on April 30, 1904. Ah Yen's photograph was attached so he could be identified when he returned.

She Get swore in an affidavit that his son, Ah Yen, was about to depart for China. The purpose of the affidavit was to secure Ah Yen's readmittance into the United States. Ah Yen returned on May 31, 1909, arriving on the SS *Princess Victoria* in Seattle, and was admitted without a problem.

Lee Wing Hing (Lee Wong Hing)

Wife of Mar Hing, Seattle Merchant

In March 1908, James Shea and Frank Jobson, both residents of Seattle for more than five years, swore in an affidavit that they had known Mar Hing for more than two years. He was a merchant, partner, and cashier for the Ah King Company, and they thought he performed no manual labor. Mar Hing was about to go to Victoria, British Columbia, Canada, to get married. A photo of Mar Hing was attached to his affidavit and signed by the affiants.

Mar Hing had been a resident of the State of Washington for more than twenty years and was currently living in Seattle. He had a $500 interest in the Ah King Company, where he bought and sold general merchandise and was a cashier. He was going to Victoria to marry Lee Wong Hing.[69] They would be returning to Seattle in a few days. He attached a current photo of her to his affidavit.

Lee Wong Hing (Lee Wing Hing) was interviewed when the couple arrived in Seattle. She had been living in Victoria for nine years with her parents. Her father, Lee Hong Gue, was a Chinese interpreter and merchant. Lee Wong Hing and Mar Hing were married according to Chinse custom and English law. Their certificate was inspected by the inspector and approved. It is not included in the file. Lee Wong Hing was admitted to the United States as a member of an exempt class, the wife of a domiciled Chinese merchant.

The following July, Lee Wong Hing and her infant son, Gim Wing, visited Victoria for a few weeks, returned, and were admitted on August 21, 1909. Daniel Landon, Frank L. Mitten, and her husband were witnesses for her.

In the summer of 1917, Lee Wong Hing, now twenty-nine years old and the mother of five children, ages one to nine years old, applied to visit her family in Victoria. The children, Harry (Mar Wing), Clarence (Mar Lun), Howard (Mar Shew), James (Mar Gum Shu), and Myra (Mar Saung Gew),

I am about to go to Victoria, British Columbia, for the purposes of being married to Lee Wong Hing, a Chinese lady, and I expect to return within a few days after my departure from Seattle bringing my wife with me, and I make this affidavit to insure our reentry to the United States. My absence will be temporary only and for the purposes aforesaid.

The photograph attached to the affidavits of the white witnesses hereto annexed, are good likenesses of myself. The photograph attached to the this affidavit is that of said Lee Wong Hing.

Mar Hing

Subscribed and sworn to before me this 25th day of March, 1908.

Notary Public in and for the State of Washington, residing at Seattle.

Above: Affidavit of Mar Hing with photo of Lee Wing Hing, 1908. *CEA case files, Lee Wing Hing (Mrs. Mar Hing) file 7032/3680, RG 85, National Archives at Seattle.*

Right: Lee Wong Hing family photo (with a number above each person's head and their corresponding name listed below the photo), 1917. *CEA case files, Lee Wing Hing (Mrs. Mar Hing), file 7032/3680, RG 85, National Archives at Seattle.*

were all born in Seattle. Their family physician, Dr. U.C. Bates, identified the family from their photo. Miss Won Mee Menie, age eleven, accompanied them on the trip to help with the children. At about this time, Lee Wong Hing started appearing on documents as Lee Wing Hing.[70]

Lee Wing Hing made a few brief trips to Victoria and Vancouver from 1943 to 1944. She was the mother of eight children: five were living in Seattle, and three were in the U.S. Army. Harry was working in a mine in Oregon, Clarence was working in a shipyard in Seattle, James and Howard were both in the army, and Howard was stationed in Alaska. In February 1944, Lee Wong Hing and three friends applied to go to Victoria for a weekend to attend a wedding. She registered under the Alien Registration Act of 1940 and renewed her registration when it was about to expire. When asked why she was getting her card revalidated, she said she "may want to visit Canada again." Her file lists another trip to Canada in May 1944.

Lee Wing Hing's reference sheet in her file lists the file numbers for her four sons, one daughter, and her children's helper in 1917, Won Mee Menie. One son and one daughter were born after the 1917 trip and are not included on the list. The file numbers would be helpful for anyone researching the family.

Additional information not included in the file: Lee Shee Mar Hing died on January 18, 1946, age fifty-six, in Seattle.[71]

Look See

Wife of Merchant Chin Quong

When Look See traveled to China, her official status was spouse of a merchant.[72] She was married to Chin Quong, a manager of the Wa Chong Company, located at 719 King Street in Seattle. According to her file, she made two trips in China, one in 1904 and another in 1917.

Before she left for China in 1904, Look See was interviewed by the immigration inspector at Seattle. Her husband's status as a merchant was investigated and verified. She was readmitted to the United States at Port Townsend on June 22, 1905, one day after she arrived. She testified that she was thirty-six years old and first came to the United States with her sister, Mrs. Chin Gee Hee, in about 1882 or 1883 when she was around thirteen years old. When asked if she knew any white men in Seattle, she said that she knew Mr. Whitlock, a lawyer, and three white ladies: Mrs. Hambeck, a Christian teacher; Mrs. Thomas, an old lady, also a teacher; and a Mrs.

State of Washington)
) SS.
County of King.)

Chin Quong, being first duly sworn, on oath, says: That he is now and has been a bona fide resident of Seattle, King County, State of Washington, United States of America, for the last thirty years; that he is now, and for many years last past, has been a merchant, and a member and one of the managers of the firm of Wa Chong Company, doing business at No. 406 Main Street in the City of Seattle; that his interest in said firm of Wa Chong Company amounts to several thousand dollars; that at Seattle, Washington, on the ____ day of October, 1886, he was married to Look See, and she has resided with him as his wife ever since said time; that she desires to make a visit to the Empire of China, to be absent a year or two, and to return to the United States when said visit is over; that to aid her identification he attaches hereto her photograph, which is a good and correct likeness of his said wife, Look See, at the present time.

Chin Quong

Subscribed and sworn to before me, this 12th day of November, 1904.

A. S. Turner

Notary Public for Washington residing at Seattle.

Affidavit of Chin Quong with photo of Look See (Mrs. Chin Quong), 1904. *CEA case files, Look See, file 35205/1-4, RG 85, National Archives at Seattle.*

Greene. Chin Kee was her Chinese witness. He testified that Look See and Chin Quong had been married according to the Chinese custom for at least twenty years and that they had six children, three sons and three daughters, all born in Seattle. Her maiden name was Ah Quan. Chin Gee Hee, a merchant, labor contractor, and well-known early settler in Seattle, performed their wedding ceremony at Chin Ching Hock's place in October 1886. They had a red marriage paper that probably listed their parents, grandparents, and possibly more generations. The interviewer noted the paper but did not ask to see it or comment on it.

Look See's husband Chin Quong testified that he had been a member of the Wah Chung Company (Wa Chong) since about 1890. There were seven other partners whose capital stock equaled $60,000 (worth over $2 million in today's dollars). Besides himself, the partners were Chin Quok Jon, Woo Jen, Chin Wing, Chin Wing Mow, Chin Wing Yon, Chin Yen Gee, and Chin Ching Hock. Chin Quong was also a manager at the Wah Chung Tai Company in Butte, Montana.

Witness John C. Whitlock testified that he was forty-eight years old and had lived in Seattle more than sixteen years, having arrived in the spring of 1898. Since he collected the rent from the Chinese tenants of the Wah Chung building, he was well acquainted with Chin Quong. Whitlock usually had to go to the building night after night to find all the tenants. He was aware that Look See was in the detention house in Port Townsend when his testimony was taken. Whitlock, Justice of the Peace Samuel F. Coombs, and Chin Quong all testified in affidavits in Look See's favor in 1904 before she left for China. Look See was admitted when she returned.

Look See left Seattle again in September 1916 with her sons Chin Dan and Ah Wing and her daughter Ah Lan. She returned in June 1917 with her son Chin Dan and her daughter, her son-in-law Pang Chung Cheong, and their infant son. They were admitted.

Included in the reference sheet are the file numbers for Look See; Archie Pang, her son-in-law; Annie M. Chin, her daughter; Victor Ernest Pang, her grandson; Chin Dan, her son; Chin May Goon, the daughter of her husband by his secondary wife; Anna Pang (Annie M. Chin or Chin May Young), her daughter; and Chin Quong, her husband. This information would be helpful for anyone researching the extended family.

CHAPTER 5

OTHER EXEMPTIONS TO THE ACT

The Chinese Exclusion Act (22 Stat.58) of 1882 suspended immigration of Chinese laborers for ten years; permitted those Chinese in the United States as of November 17, 1880, to stay, travel abroad, and return; prohibited the naturalization of Chinese. The 1888 amendments (25 Stat.476) created a "Section 6" exempt status for teachers, students, merchants, and travelers.[73]

STUDENTS

Mah Sun Inng

1922 Graduate of Wilson's Modern Business College

Mah Sun Inng is listed in the eight-page program for the twenty-seventh annual graduation exercise for Wilson's Modern Business College, which contains information about the class officers, class honors, the graduation program (invocation, presentation of diplomas, class song, prophecy, poem, history, and so on), and the graduates of the 1921 courses for shorthand, "full commercial course," bookkeeping, and "scientific salesmanship."[74]

Mah Sun Inng was born in Bak Sar village, Sunning district, China, around 1901. He was the son of Mah Sin Dung, a merchant in Vancouver, British Columbia, Canada. His mother lived in China. Mah landed in Seattle in 1919 and was admitted as a section 6 student. After graduating

PROGRAM
Twenty-Seventh Annual
Graduation Exercises

Wilson's
Modern Business College
Seattle

The Emblem
of the
Efficient School

Masonic Temple, Feb. 2, 1922

Wilson's Modern Business College graduation exercises program, 1922. *CEA case files, Mah Sun Inng, file 35100/4978, RG 85, National Archives at Seattle.*

from Wilson's Modern Business College in February 1922 from the bookkeeping course and the scientific salesmanship course, he became a merchant for Quon On Company on 660 King Street in Seattle. He had worked there part time as a salesman while he was going to school.

In 1922, Mah Sun Inng applied for a one-week visit to his father in Vancouver, British Columbia. Earl H. Senn, an electrician in Seattle, was a witness for Mah. Senn testified that he had done a lot of work on Mah's car. H.E. McGoldrick, an automobile electrician, also testified that he had worked on Mah's car. Neither one mentioned what type of car Mah owned, and the interrogators did not ask about it.

Fok Cheu

Student, Arrived in Walla Walla in 1908

See Kin, Fok Cheu's father, was a merchant and member of the Hong Chong Wo Company in Walla Walla, Washington. He wanted to bring his son over from China to go to school in Walla Walla. He was interviewed by an immigration inspector to make sure he qualified for the status of a merchant; to be considered a bona fide merchant, he would have to have done no manual labor in the last year, and he needed to have two credible witnesses (who were Caucasian).

See Kin testified that he was forty years old and had been living in the United States for about twenty-seven or twenty-eight years. He arrived in San Francisco around 1881 or 1882 and then lived in Portland before settling in Walla Walla in 1886. He had a $1,000 interest in the Hong Chong Wo Company at Sixth Street between Main and Rose. His partners were Wong Sui, See Yick, Get Tuck, Yee Hep, Eng Hong (See Fat), Sing Kuan, and Yee Sing. He had visited China three times since his arrival in the United States.

Affidavit photo of Fok Cheu (Fook Chew) taken when he was sixteen years old, in 1908. *CEA case files, Fok Cheu, file RS 2063, RG 85, National Archives at Seattle.*

The immigration inspector of Seattle asked T.M. Fisher, the Chinese inspector at Walla Walla, to obtain Fok Cheu's "Canadian Pacific head tax guarantee." He described the guarantee as "printed on a piece of paper about 2-½ by 5 inches, the face of which is green and the back yellow." The head tax guarantee was required from Chinese arriving in the United States from British Columbia ports en route from China.

Fok Cheu, a student, was sixteen years old, five feet tall, and weighed eighty-two pounds.[75] He had a small mole on the bridge of his nose and a scar over his left temple. He was born at Si Ben Hong, a village with two hundred to three hundred houses in the Sun Ning district, Kwong Tung province, China. He had last seen his father in 1905, three years earlier. His older brother Fook Yung was already living with his father in Walla Walla. He had two younger brothers living in China with his mother, Lee Shee.

Lee Poo (married name Gee Woon), a gardener in Walla Walla, was a witness for Fok Cheu. In 1903, on a trip to China, he visited the Fook family. Poo's village was about three miles from Fook's village.

Fritz Lehn, a clerk and member of the Walla Walla city council, and Theodore Rondema both swore in an affidavit that they had known See Kin as a merchant for more than eight years; that See Kin had done no manual labor for the past year; and that the photo attached to the affidavit was a true likeness of See Kin. Eng Fang (married name Jam Mon), a gardener, age forty-five, testified for Fok Cheu and recognized a photo of him taken when Fok Cheu was nine or ten years old. Fred M. Pauly, a cigar and tobacco business owner in Walla Walla, also testified for See Kin. Pauly had lived in Walla Walla for about twenty years and did business with the Hong Chong Wo Company. He thought the company carried about $2,000 or more of Chinese merchandise and groceries. Fok Cheu's file contains no more information after he was admitted in 1909.

Ng Shue Tong (Eng Se Tong)

Student at Whitman College

In 1921, Ng Shue Tong, son of the late Ng Joon Sam, applied to the U.S. Consulate General at Canton, China, to come to the United States with a section 6 student exemption.[76] He was twenty years old and wanted to finish his education at Whitman College in Walla Walla. His father had died recently, and he had a scholarship to Whitman. He could speak a little English and eventually planned on returning to China as a missionary. His brother Soon En was living in Chicago.

Stephen B.L. Penrose, president of Whitman College from 1894 to 1934, wrote a letter of recommendation for Ng Shue Tong (Eng Se Tong) to the immigration officer in Seattle and attached a current photo of Ng. Penrose personally knew Ng's brother and uncle. He arranged for Arn Allen of the

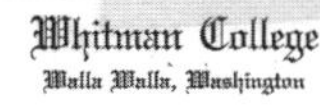

Whitman College
Walla Walla, Washington

January 17, 1922

States Immigration Officer
Seattle, Washington

Dear Sir

A Chinese boy, Tong Se Eng, has been admitted to Whitman College upon credentials from the Union Middle School of Canton, China. He is coming to this country as a student to prepare himself for later missionary work in China. He sailed from Hong-kong on the Empress of Asia due to arrive in Vancouver, B.C., on the 23rd of January. He is travelling second class and his room number on board the Empress of Asia is 376-A. He is due to arrive in Seattle on the 24th or 25th of January. He is eighteen years old, 5'4" in height, and his brother and uncle are personally known to me. I enclose his photograph. I hope that his papers will be in satisfactory shape and that he will have no trouble in regard to his admission to this country. I have asked Mr. Arn S. Allen, of the Y.M.C.A., to have a representative of that organization meet him and assist him in getting to the train for Walla Walla. The boy is of excellent family, has high ambitions, and is said to be an excellent student.

With high regards, I am

Very truly yours

Stephen B.L. Penrose

SBLP:JM

Left: Letter from Stephen B.L. Penrose to immigration, 1922. *CEA case files, Ng Shue Tong (Eng/Ng Se Tong), file 39540/3-1, RG 85, National Archives at Seattle.*

Opposite: "The Success of Whitman College" brochure, 1922. *CEA case files, Ng Shue Tong (Eng/Ng Se Tong), file 39540/3-1, RG 85, National Archives at Seattle.*

16 The Success of Whitman College

of the Faculty have made notable record for public service. In Red Cross work during the war, in public health movements, and in useful service generally the Faculty have illustrated the spirit of the founders and have cheerfully labored, despite the pressure of poverty, for the common good.

No Radicalism

This spirit of service on the part of Faculty and students is combined with a spirit of sanity. Enthusiasm is united with common sense. The College has felt that its mission was in large degree to contribute to political and moral sanity. The influence of the graduates of the College has been described by Judge Burke of Seattle, President of The Board of Overseers:

"The number of graduates which Whitman College has sent out is not large, but it has had in remarkable degree the qualities of mental poise combined with moral purpose. This well-known fact is not a matter of accident but is the result of forces deliberately set at work upon the campus in the lives of the undergraduate students."

The Success of Whitman College

WHITMAN COLLEGE QUARTERLY
Volume XXIV No. 3

YMCA to have someone meet Ng when he arrived at the Port of Seattle to make sure he got on the train for Walla Walla. Penrose ended his letter by saying, "The boy is of excellent family, has high ambitions, and is said to be an excellent student." When the Seattle immigration inspector interviewed Ng Shue Tong, he gave him this advice:

> *You should not become a laborer as you are to be admitted as a member of the exempt class and under your admission as a section six student you are not to become a common laborer, and if you do you are subject to arrest and deportation to China.*

Ng Shue Tong had hookworm when he arrived, so he was temporarily denied entry at the Port of Seattle. He applied for hospital treatment, was cured, and admitted at Seattle; from there, went to Walla Walla.

A sixteen-page brochure, "The Success of Whitman College," is included in the file.[77] A December 1933 letter from immigration services in Los

Angeles, California, to the San Pedro office with a copy to the Seattle office said immigration services had approved Ng Shue Tong's laborer's return certificate for his trip to China in the next few days. It is not known when or if he returned.

Lam Mai

Lam Mai (Mai Euon Lam) arrived from China with his mother, his brother, and the rest of his family He was admitted as a student at the Port of Seattle in December 1922.[78] He was nine years old. Since he was so young, his brother, Lam Yuk Tsun, filled out the paperwork for him. His brother was a college student, and his sister-in-law was a practicing physician. They lived in Tacoma, Washington, and Lam Mai went to school at Central Public School until he moved to Portland, Oregon. He graduated from Lincoln High School in June 1931 and attended North Pacific College, majoring in pharmacy. In February 1932, Lam Mai applied for a return permit as a student. One of his teachers was a witness for him. Charles W. Abbott testified that Lam Mai was a very good student and he did not know why Lam Mai left school.

Lam Mai, return permit photo, 1933. *CEA case files, Lam Mai (Mai Euon Lam), file 7032/2234, RG 85, National Archives at Seattle.*

Lam Mai's reason for leaving his pharmacy studies is not mentioned in his file, but he left to attend pilot training school at Swan Island Airport in Portland. The Adcox School of Aviation in Portland trained thirty-six pilots over two terms. Most of them went to China and flew for the Chinese Air Force after Japan's attack on Manchuria in 1931. By 1937, Lam Mai was a chief test pilot for the Chinese Air Force. Sadly, Lam Mai was shot down over Nanchong, China, in December 1937 and died from his injuries.[79]

Ng Fung Yuen

Student, Son of Merchant

In 1915, She Chew, a merchant at Tsue Chong Company, 412 Eighth Avenue South, Seattle, applied to have his son, Ng Fung Yuen, a student, join him in Seattle.[80] Two white witnesses swore in an affidavit that they knew She Chew was a merchant, not a laborer, and that he had a fixed place of business. She Chew swore to the same information in his affidavit and said he had a more than $500 interest in his firm, Tsue Chong Company. He attached photos of his son and himself to the affidavit.

In E.C. Mullin's witness statement, he said he sold eggs and poultry to the Tsue Chong Company, which manufactured noodles. Mullin visited the business twice a week. When asked, he said there was no restaurant, laundry, or gambling room connected with the business. Louie Lavinthal, the other white witness, was born in Russia and had been in Seattle for about six years. He was a drayman with a one-horse wagon and delivered goods to and from Tsue Chong Company, which shipped noodles and rice to Port Gamble and Port Townsend.

She Chew testified that the company sold the noodles in ten-, fifty-, or one-hundred-pound cases. The heaviest cases would sell for $8.50 to $9.00 per case. He was asked about his family. His wife in China was fifty-five years old and had bound feet. His older son was in Port Townsend. His second-oldest son died in Seattle in 1914. He was applying to bring his son Ng Fung Yuen to Seattle. He had a daughter who died shortly after birth.

J.V. Stewart, Chinese inspector, visited the business, examined the books and the list of partners, confirmed the business's bank transactions, and reviewed all the testimony from the admission records of all parties involved. He was satisfied with his findings.

Unfortunately, the Chinese and immigration inspector, John F. Dunton, was not happy with his analysis of over thirty pages of testimony and six files of family members and witnesses. The application was rejected because Ng Fung Yuen did not answer many of the questions accurately. The applicant did not know the family name of his aunt's husband, if they had any children, or where they lived. He did not know if his mother's parents were living. He did not know how many houses were on his side of the street. He did not know how many children his neighbor had or if his other neighbor had any sons—and on and on. Dunton listed three pages of unknowns or discrepancies. Inspector Dunton was not impressed with Ng Fung Yuen's

No. 2039

DEPARTMENT OF LABOR

IMMIGRATION SERVICE.

In The Matter of the Application of SHE CHEW, a domiciled Chinese, merchant, for the admission of his minor son FUNG YUEN.

State of Washington)
: ss.
County of King)

I, SHE CHEW being first duly sworn upon my oath depose and say: That I am a lawful resident of the United States and for many years last past have been and now am a merchant, having a fixed place of business at to-wit: No. 412-8thAvenue South, Seattle, Washington, where I am conducting business under the firm name of Tsue Chong Company, my interest in said firm amounting to more than Five Hundred ($500.00) Dollars; that for more

than twelve months last past, I have conducted business at such place and been engaged therein by buying and selling Chinese merchandise and during said time have performed no

3

Above: Affidavit of She Chew with photos of She Chew and "two poses of Ng Fung Yuen," 1915. *CEA case files, Ng Fung Yuen, file 7032/469, RG 85, National Archives at Seattle.*

Opposite: Ng Fung Yuen (exhibit G1 and G2), undated photos. *CEA case files, Ng Fung Yuen, file 7032/469, RG 85, National Archives at Seattle.*

demeanor during his interview. He thought what little knowledge Ng Fung Yuen had about the family was probably obtained from coaching. Since Tsue Chong Company's principal function was manufacturing and selling noodles, Dunton thought Ng Fung Yuen was performing the work of a laborer rather than a merchant. To be considered a merchant, She Chew could not perform any manual labor. Dunton recommended that Ng Fung Yuen's status as son of a merchant be denied.

Mr. Frye, the lawyer She Chew hired, believed that She Chew was sincere and that his son, Ng Fung Yuen, was probably overcoached to say the correct answers and was too nervous or afraid to answer the questions honestly. She Chew wrote to his son and told him not to be afraid and to simply answer the questions truthfully. Photos of Ng Fung Yuen at home in China were introduced.[81]

An appeal was filed, and Ng Fung Yuen was reexamined. The testimony of additional witnesses—Ah Gow, Ng Yee Loon, and Ng Soon Aim—agreed with that of the applicant. Over eighty pages of testimony was given. The previous decision rejecting the applicant was reversed, and Ng Fung Yuen was admitted.

The Tsue Chong Company still exists. Its manufacturing plant is in Kent, Washington, and its retail store is at 508 Eighth Street in Seattle. According to Loretta Chin, Seattle resident and expert on the Chinese Exclusion Act files, during the 1950s, the owner and his daughters would throw packets of fortune cookies to the crowds at the early Seafair parades.

TRAVELERS

Unfortunately, files for travelers such as actors, actresses, acrobats, magicians, and vaudeville members usually do not contain much information. Most do not include a photograph, but these files speak to the cultural and social events that were popular at different time periods.

Long Tack Sam

Internationally Renowned Magician and Acrobat

The files for Long Tack Sam and his troupe are unusual: they contain photos.[82] Their travels took place over several years.

On May 7, 1923, while in Minneapolis, Minnesota, Long Tack Sam wrote a letter on his company stationery to Seattle immigration services asking them to see that Chang Chang Ching, one of the young men in the troupe, get on board the SS *President Jefferson* for his return trip to Shanghai. Long Tack Sam attached a photo of Chang to the letter.

The cover sheet of the file shows that it contains information on all the actors who were members of the Long Tack Sam Company in one file. They were admitted at Blaine, Washington, arriving on a Great Northern Railway train on June 17, 1923. The members of the company were listed as Long Tack Sam, Long Lieu (Lan Ludovika), Fang Ching Hai, Sih Qua Ling, Sang Chi Hwa, Wang Kuh Yong, and Li Koy Dohien.[83]

On June 23, a letter from Pantages Theatre Company in Tacoma, Washington, to the U.S. immigration office in Seattle notified them that the Long Tack Sam Company of Chinese magicians would be returning to the port of Seattle on Sunday, June 27, 1923.

The initial correspondence in the files was for the troupe's 1929 tour. On that tour, they left the United States in March for vaudeville engagements at Winnipeg, Calgary, and Vancouver, Canada, and reentered at Seattle in April

38772
1-6

Long Tack Sam Company
LONG TACK SAM
SOLE OWNER

Minneapolis minn
May 7th 1923

U.S, Department of LABOR
Immigration Service
SEATTLE, Washington

Dear Sir
I have One Chinese Boy will Leaving you port in Seattle for Shanghai Chna May the 26th S,S, Presdent Jefferson Kindly see that he get on Board his name is Chang Chang Ching please let me now soon as he leaving also Kindly Notiffy at Washington Office

Respectfully Yours
Long Tack Sam

Long Tack Sam
c/o Paul Tausig
104 East 14th St
New York City

RECEIVED MAY 11 1923 U.S. IMMIGRATION SERVICE SEATTLE

Chang Chang Ching

Correspondence of Long Tack Sam with photos of Chang Chang Ching, 1923. *CEA case files, Long Tack Sam Company, file 38772/1-6, RG 85, National Archives at Seattle.*

1929 to continue their tour in the United States. The troupe was bonded by the National Surety Company, which was granted by the Department of Labor. They were allowed to stay in the United States for six months. A bond of $1,000 was paid for each member of the troupe. The substantial amount of the bond was to ensure that all the members of the troupe would depart the United States at the end of the six-month period.

On November 23, 1932, Long Tack Sam's daughters, Long Mi-Na, age twenty-three, and Long Nee-Sa, age twenty-one, joined the troupe.[84] They were actresses and members of the Long Tack Sam Troupe and made several tours in the United States and Canada. On this trip to Vancouver, British Columbia, they left Seattle by boat and returned via the Great Northern Railway. They were admitted at Blaine one week later.

1

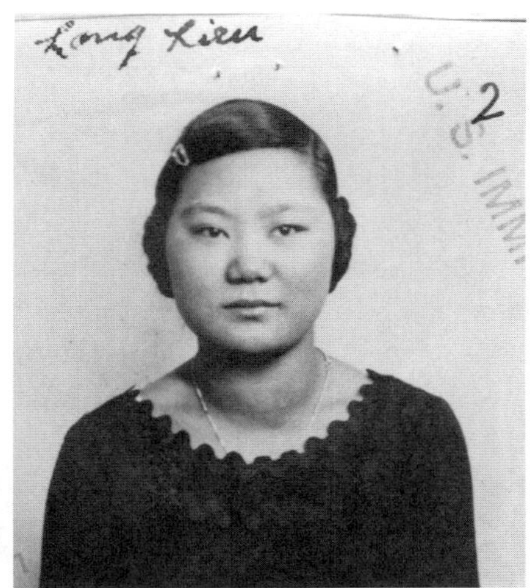
2

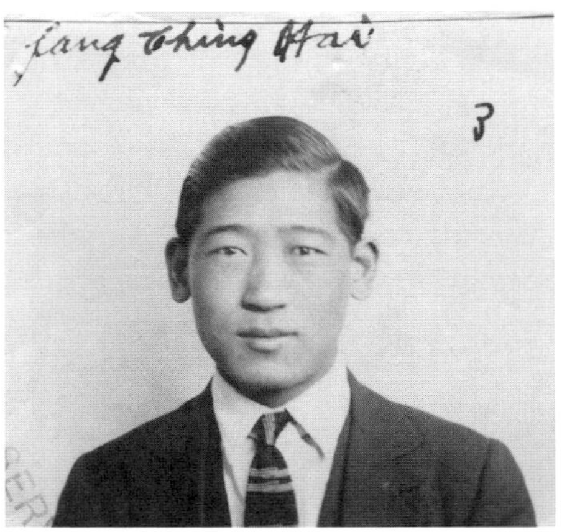
3

4

5

6

Opposite, clockwise from top left: Long Tack Sam, 1923; Long Lieu (Lan Ludovika), 1923; Sih Qua Ling, 1923; Wang Kuh Yong, 1923; Sang Chi Hwa, 1923; Fang Ching Hai, 1923. *Right*: Li Koy Dohien, 1923. *CEA case files, Long Tack Sam Troupe, files 38772/1-1 to 1-9, RG 85, National Archives at Seattle.*

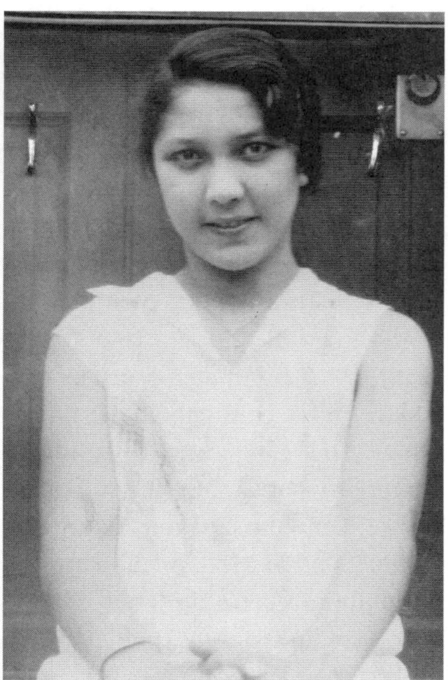

Left: Photo included with letter from Long Mi-Na to the commissioner of immigration in Seattle verifying that she would be traveling to Canada, 1929. *CEA case files, Long Mi-Na, file 7022/18-3, RG 85, National Archives at Seattle.*

Right: Photo included with letter from Long Nee Sa to the commissioner of immigration in Seattle verifying that she would be traveling to Canada, 1929. *CEA case files, Long Nee Sa, file 7022/18-4, RG 85, National Archives at Seattle.*

Most Chinese Exclusion Act case files capture small, fragmented moments in a person's life, but the files can give clues about their lives over a long period of time. For more information about Long Tack Sam, see the book and the documentary *The Magical Life of Long Tack Sam*, both by Ann Marie Fleming, Long Tack Sam's great-granddaughter.

Soong May Ling

The Future Madame Chiang Kai-shek

Soong May Ling (sometimes spelled Soong Mai-ling), age nine, and her sister, Soong Ching Ling, age fourteen, arrived in Port Townsend on the SS *Minnesota* from their home in Shanghai, China, as section 6 students and were admitted.[85]

The 1907 section 6 certificate for Soong May Ling is the only document in the file. The file contains correspondence from 1943 between Earl G. Harrison, commissioner of immigration and naturalization in Philadelphia, Pennsylvania, and Raphael P. Bonham, district director of immigration and naturalization in Seattle. Harrison asked Bonham to confirm that Soong May Ling was admitted into Seattle as a student in 1907. Bonham replied that a "charming little Chinese maid" had arrived with her sister, "now also a lady of renown." Bonham asked a local Chinese consul to examine the document and verify its authenticity. It passed his scrutiny. Bonham concluded that Soong May Ling "was the now world-famous and accomplished Madame Chiang Kai Shek." Bonham had the photo from the 1907 certificate copied and sent three prints and the negatives to Harrison, hoping that he would forward one to Madame Chiang Kai-shek.

Bonham received a letter dated May 5, 1943, from Harrison saying he had passed the photos on to Mrs. Eleanor Roosevelt, who sent a note saying she appreciated Bonham's kindness and planned to send one of the photos to Madame Chiang.[86] President Franklin D. Roosevelt repealed the Chinese Exclusion Act on December 13, 1943.

Information not in the file: Soong May Ling and her sister graduated from Wesleyan College. Soong Ching Ling became the second wife of Sun Yat-sen, one of the leaders of the 1911 revolution that established the Republic of China.[87]

In 1943, Madame Chiang Kai-shek "became the first Chinese person, and only the second woman, to address a joint session of the United

Photo of Soong May Ling from Chinese Certificate for Section 6 Student Exemption, 1907. *CEA case files, Soong May Ling (Madame Chiang Kai-shek), file RS 1483, RG 85, National Archives at Seattle.*

States Congress as she sought to have the United States repeal the Chinese Exclusion Act, which had been in effect since 1882 and prohibited new Chinese immigration."[88]

Shao Chang Lee, Diplomat

Charge for Alien Passenger Manifest

Shao Chang Lee, age twenty-nine, made a short trip to Vancouver and Victoria, British Columbia, Canada, in March 1919.[89] He was living in San Francisco and was secretary of the Chinese branch of the YMCA. He was also a student. On his return trip, he booked passage on the *Princess Charlotte* with a stop in Seattle. Shao Chang Lee's file is only five pages long and gives us very little personal information about him. It tells us more about the

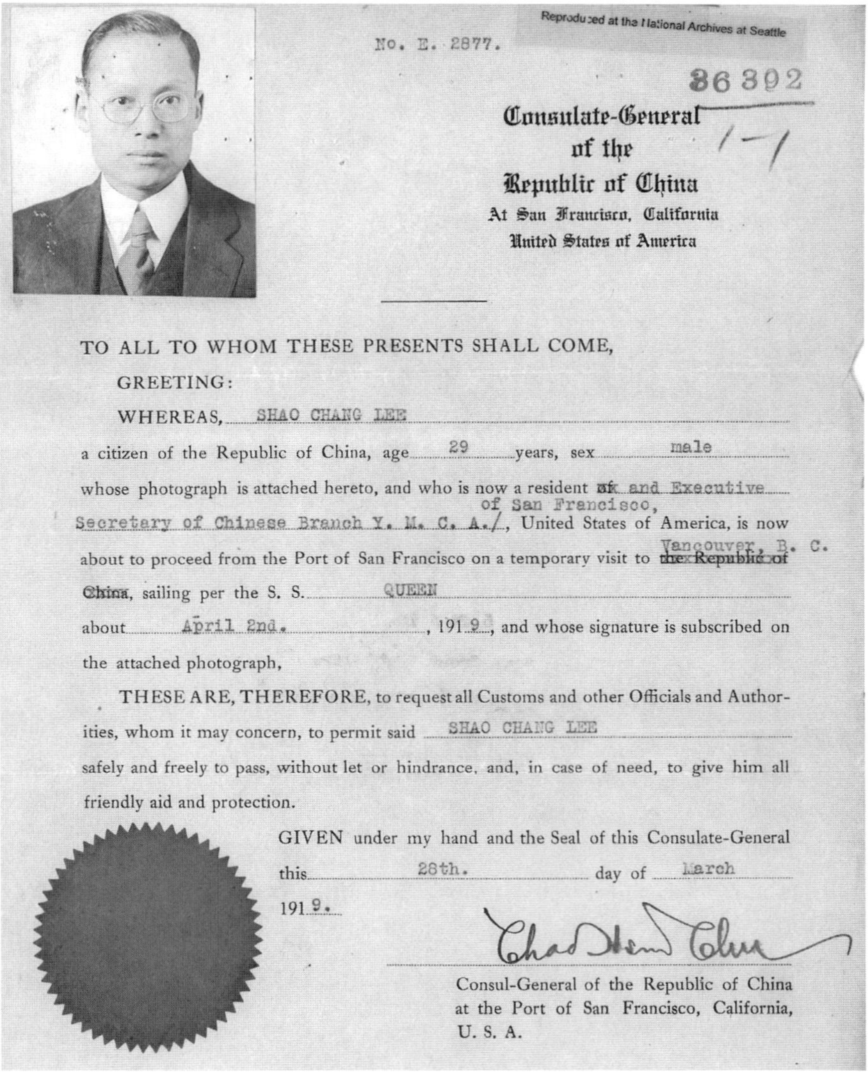

No. E. 2877.

36392

1-1

Consulate-General
of the
Republic of China
At San Francisco, California
United States of America

TO ALL TO WHOM THESE PRESENTS SHALL COME,

GREETING:

WHEREAS, SHAO CHANG LEE
a citizen of the Republic of China, age 29 years, sex male
whose photograph is attached hereto, and who is now a resident ~~of~~ and Executive Secretary of Chinese Branch Y. M. C. A./ of San Francisco, United States of America, is now about to proceed from the Port of San Francisco on a temporary visit to ~~the Republic of China~~ Vancouver, B. C., sailing per the S. S. QUEEN
about April 2nd., 1919, and whose signature is subscribed on the attached photograph,

THESE ARE, THEREFORE, to request all Customs and other Officials and Authorities, whom it may concern, to permit said SHAO CHANG LEE safely and freely to pass, without let or hindrance, and, in case of need, to give him all friendly aid and protection.

GIVEN under my hand and the Seal of this Consulate-General this 28th. day of March 1919.

Chao Hsin Chu

Consul-General of the Republic of China
at the Port of San Francisco, California,
U. S. A.

Shao Chang Lee, Form No. E. 2877, 1919. *CEA case files, Shao Chang Lee, file 36392/1-1, RG 85, National Archives at Seattle.*

tension between the international immigration offices and their rules and personnel than about Lee.

Form No. E. 2877 from the Consulate-General of the Republic of China at San Francisco, California, is included with an attached photo of Shao Chang Lee, requesting that all customs and other officials and authorities permit Shao Chang Lee to safely pass.

When Lee arrived in Seattle after his brief trip to British Columbia, Canada, he complained to Henry M. White, immigration commissioner in Seattle, about being charged one dollar to have his name entered on the alien passenger manifest in typewriting and said he was instructed to go to a certain typewriter to fill in the information. White sent a letter to the inspector in charge of immigration services in Victoria, British Columbia asking about the charge.

White received a reply from S.J. Burford at immigration services in Victoria:

> *I beg to inform you that the above gentleman has either deliberately made a misstatement of the facts or was under the impression that he was in the U.S. Immigration Office when going to the Dominion Immigration office to see about being checked out on his return to Seattle.*
>
> *Under your rulings, it is necessary for a Chinese residing in the United States who comes here for a few days visit, to be manifested on Forms 500 and 418 on his returning to Seattle, the former form under the present law being typewritten....*
>
> *The local agents of the C.P.R. (Canadian Pacific Railroad)...have no wide-carriage typewriters....Necessary for them to have the manifest prepared themselves.*[90]

The file also contained a business card for John E. Rieke, who was associated with the YMCA in Seattle but not mentioned in the file. And an undated, unidentified newspaper article titled "Pays Honor to Visiting Chinese: China Club Meeting Is Marked by Program of Lectures—Judge Thomas Burke Presides" was included in the file. The article mentions Judge Thomas Burke, president of the China Club of Seattle, and other prominent citizens of Seattle: Chin W. Kee and Shao Chang Lee, Charles M. Schwab, Mrs. J.J. Connell, and Paul Fung. The article notes, "Mr. Lee is an extremely progressive and forceful character and possesses a marked degree of wit and simple humor."[91]

Chinese Basketball Team Touring the United States in 1929

Twelve basketball players from China were admitted at the Port of Seattle on January 31, 1929, as temporary visitors for five months, each with a $1,000 bond. Two of them had section 6 student status certificates and could remain for one year. The governor general of Manila, Philippines, recommended that his office grant temporary visas to twelve members of the basketball team of Chinese students from Manila. The captain of the team, Domingo Rufino Choa, was a full-blood Chinese man from the Philippines. In a letter to the U.S. Department of Labor Immigration Service, Luther Weedin, commissioner of immigration in Seattle, said,

> *All members of this party are of a superior type of Northern Chinese, and most of them speak English fluently. A Souvenir booklet describing the basket ball* [sic] *team is enclosed.*[92]

According to their files, the players were not from northern China. Most of them were from southeastern China and were studying in the Philippines, where several of them were born. The souvenir booklet was not in the file.

Chen Ping-Huang

Chen Ping-Huang, Section 6 Precis, application for temporary visa (with photo), 1929. CEA case files, Chen Ping-Huang, file 10360/1-1 RG 85, *National Archives at Seattle.*

The American Consular Service (as it was called in 1929; it is now known as the U.S. Consulate General Shanghai) in Shanghai, China, stated that Chen Ping-Huang attended St. John's University and Kwang Hu University in Shanghai.[93] His father was a well-to-do export merchant at Changehow near Amoy, Fukien, China, a sub-provincial city in southeastern Fujian, China, with property valued at $150,000 Mexican silver dollars. Mexican currency was frequently used for business transactions in Asia for over three hundred years, until about the 1930s.[94] Chen's travel plans were to be with the basketball team as team secretary for five months and complete his year in the United States by finishing his studies at the University of Pennsylvania at Philadelphia. He had a recommendation from Tang (Tseng) Chin-Yun of the University of Washington in Seattle. Chen Ping Huang also has a New York file, no. 151/82.

Choa Domingo Rufino

Choa Domingo Rufino, 1929. *CEA case files, Choa Domingo Rufino, file 10360/1-2, RG 85, National Archives at Seattle.*

Choa Domingo Rufino (Itsan Choa), born in the Philippines, presented a passport issued by the governor-general of the islands.[95] He was captain of the basketball team. There was some confusion over Choa's name. Inspector Harris consulted with the China Club and David Young, secretary to the Chinese consul, both in Seattle, and it was decided that Itsan Choa and Choa Domingo Rufino were the same person. Itsan Choa was his Chinese name, and Choa Domingo Rufino was his Filipino name.

Choa's file also mentions a souvenir booklet titled *Souvenirs China & Japan Tour, Chinese Basket Ball Team*, published by C.C. Lim of Manila. Unfortunately, the booklet was not included in any of the basketball players' files. The booklet was printed in English with photos of the trophies the team won during their tour of Japan and China.[96]

Some biographical information on the other players is mentioned in Chen Ping-Hauang's file. Their individual files have only a visa application and a photo.

Lim Chu Cong

Lim Chu Cong (C.C. Lim) was born in 1902 in Amoy, China. He spent two years in Manila as a merchant before joining the Chinese basketball team of Manila.[97]

Lim Chu Cong, Declaration of Non-Immigrant Alien photo, 1929, CEA case files, Lim Chu Cong (C. C. Lim), file 10360/1-2, *RG* 85, *National Archives at Seattle.*

Left: A. Chua Ciong, Declaration of Non-Immigrant Alien photo, 1929. *CEA case files, A. Chua Clong, file 10360/2-3, RG 85, National Archives at Seattle.*

Middle: Co Yong, Declaration of Non-Immigrant Alien photo, 1929. *CEA case files, Co Yong, file 10360/2-3, RG 85, National Archives at Seattle.*

Right: Wee C.G. (Wee Guan Chuan), Declaration of Non-Immigrant Alien photo, 1929. *CEA case files, Wee C.G., file 10360/2-10, RG 85, National Archives at Seattle.*

Chua Ciong

Chua Ciong was born on April 1, 1894, in Manila, and for the past two years, he had been a student there.[98]

Co Yong

Co Yong was born on June 8, 1907, at Amoy, China, and for the past two years, he had been a student in Manila.[99]

Wee C.G. (Wee Guan Chuan)

Wee C.G. (Wee Guan Chuan) was born on March 3, 1906, in Amoy, China.[100] He was a student in Manila before arriving in Seattle with the basketball team. He stayed on as a student and graduated from the University of Louisville, Kentucky. He married Mary Virginia Payne, a Caucasian woman of Irish, German, and English descent from Evansville, Indiana. Their son George

Richard Wee (Wee Guan Wee) was born in 1931 in Louisville, Kentucky. They left the United States via Seattle on July 15, 1932, destined for the Philippine islands, where Wee planned to practice medicine.

According to an article in the *Seattle Daily Times*, it was thought that the University of Washington Huskies basketball team might play the Chinese team. C.L. Tseng of the University of Washington Chinese Student Club was trying to arrange a playoff, but plans did not materialize. The team was scheduled to play games in Vancouver, Denver, Charleston, Buffalo, St. Paul, San Francisco, Kansas City, New York, Chicago, Portland, Los Angeles, Louisville, Montreal, and Milwaukee.[101]

Diplomats

> *SEC.13. That this act shall not apply to diplomatic and other officers of the Chinese Government traveling upon the business of that government, whose credentials shall be taken as equivalent to the certificate in this act mentioned and shall exempt them and their body and house-hold servants from the provisions of this act as to other Chinese persons.*[102]

Sullivan T. Mar

Sullivan T. Mar (Teh-Chien Mar) was the chancellor of the Chinese consulate in Vancouver, British Columbia, Canada.[103] On January 11, 1927, he traveled from Vancouver by train, stopping in Blaine, Washington, before arriving in Seattle. He was thirty-one years old and was born in Foochow, China. He had a diplomatic passport issued by the Chinese consulate in Vancouver and a U.S. passport issued by the U.S. Consulate General. According to the Bureau of Immigration in Washington, D.C., since Mar was admitted as an official, he was not required to comply with the rules governing alien students even though he had originally been admitted as a student at the University of Washington.

Mar made a short visit to Vancouver on July 17, 1928. The immigration services office in Seattle gave him a one-page certificate for identification. It contained his photo and signature and was valid for only one week for his readmission through the Port of Seattle. It could not be used as a certificate of residence or certificate of landing. He returned the next day and was admitted with his diplomatic passport.

U. S. DEPARTMENT OF LABOR
IMMIGRATION SERVICE
DISTRICT No. 28

IN REPLYING REFER TO
No. 38/543

DISTRICT HEADQUARTERS
U. S. COMMISSIONER OF IMMIGRATION
SEATTLE, WASH.

July 17,1928.

TO WHOM IT MAY CONCERN:

This is to certify that Mr. SULLIVAN T.MAR, the bearer of this certificate, whose photograph and signature appear below for identification purposes, is en route to Vancouver, Canada, on a pleasure trip for a period not to exceed one week.

This certificate is given to Mr.Mar for the purpose of identification only on his return to the United States, and is not to be used as a certificate of residence or a certificate of landing, but to be used simply for identification purposes, to be surrendered by him to the Immigration Service at Seattle on return.

This certificate is issued under the authority of the Third Supplement to General Order No. 30, and Bureau file No. 54214/4, and valid for readmission only through the Port of Seattle.

Luther Weedin
Commissioner.

Immigration Service correspondence regarding Sullivan T. Mar, 1928. *CEA case files, Sullivan T. Mar, file 7031/120, RG 85, National Archives at Seattle.*

Although there is no more official immigration activity in Sullivan T. Mar's file, an undated newspaper clipping was inserted into his file. Mar wrote to the editor of the *Seattle Daily Times* regarding the Imperial Japanese Army's September 1931 invasion of Manchuria, China.

Japan had suffered heavy financial losses from the 1929 Great Depression, and Manchuria was rich in natural resources, forests, and fertile farmland. Japan had already invested in Manchurian railroads and wanted to expand its holdings in China. These activities led to the Second Sino-Japanese War, which began in 1937 when China began full-scale resistance to the expansion of Japanese influence in its territory.[104]

Mar wrote a letter to the editor because he disagreed with a speech Dr. Herbert H. Gowan had given on December 18, 1931, at the Lions Club concluding that Japan's military activities were not an act of aggression. Mar was a former student of Dr. Gowan at the University of Washington. He respected Gowan's knowledge of "Orient history" but thought Gowan was ill-informed about the current conditions. Mar listed six points of disagreement with Dr. Gowan's stance: the large number of troops entering Manchuria, Japan's 1915 Twenty-One Demands, President Wilson's response to the demands, Japan's demand that China recognize the demands, Japan setting up a puppet government in Mukden, and Dr. Gowan's presumption that he had more knowledge of the situation than the U.S. government and League of Nations. Mar suggested American business interests should consult with the reports on file at the State Department and the Department of Commerce for a history of Japan's efforts to control trade in Manchuria.

He signed his letter S.T. Mar (Sullivan T. Mar). A handwritten note beside the newspaper clipping written on Department of Labor stationery says, "One S.J. Mar has an oriental shop in Shafer Building—across from F & N [Frederick & Nelson]. Also Telephone Book shows S.J. Mar 700—8th Ave."

Teachers

Although there are several files for Chinese people with the status of teacher, those connected to Washington State were in fact students or laborers or did not spend much time in the state. There may be some files of those with a teacher's status that have not been indexed by occupation yet.

CHAPTER 6
WOMEN

How They Were Affected

Loss of Citizenship

According to the 1907 Expatriation Act, U.S. women citizens who married noncitizens took on the citizenship of their husband, therefore losing their U.S. citizenship.[105] The Cable Act of 1922 stipulated that women could keep their U.S. citizenship if they married a man who could become a citizen.[106] Chinese men were not eligible to become U.S. citizens.

Fannie Seto More

Born in Olympia, Lost U.S. Citizenship

Fannie Seto More (Lew Tue or Lew York Lue) was born on July 9, 1890, in Olympia, Washington.[107] In 1913, she married Seto More, a Canadian Pacific Railways passenger agent and Canadian citizen whose parents were born in China. Because Fannie married a non–U.S. citizen, a Canadian citizen, she lost her U.S. citizenship. When she traveled to the United States from her home in Vancouver, British Columbia, her classification under the Chinese exclusion laws was "traveler." Her two children, Wilfred and Maysien, were both born in Vancouver. Wilfred Bientang Seto was born on August 21, 1915, and Maysien Geraldine Seto was born on April 30, 1918. The three traveled from Vancouver, British Columbia, to Blaine,

Washington, via train many times, had Canadian certificates of identity, and became well known to immigration officials.

Fannie's file starts in 1909 and covers her many trips between Vancouver, British Columbia, and Seattle, Washington, until 1940. Fannie's parents were Lew King and Lee Shee. She had three brothers and one sister. Her father, Lew King, a merchant, was a member of Jong King Company and Wah Hing Company in Seattle. He died in August 1908. Her mother, Lee Shee, was born in Kin Ham village, Sunning district, China. She was admitted to the United States in 1873 as the wife of a merchant about seven months after she married Lew King. She died in Seattle in 1914.

In 1909, Fannie traveled from Seattle with student status. Her mother, Lee Shee, and brother, Lew York Lon, were witnesses for her. Lee Shee testified that she and her husband moved to Seattle in 1883. Seven months after they arrived, someone set fire to their store on old Third Avenue South. They moved nearby to the apartment above the Hong Yee Chung Company store and stayed there until the Great Fire of Seattle in 1889. After the fire, they lived in Olympia for a few years until they returned to Seattle.

S.L. Crawford was a Caucasian witness for Fannie Seto More in 1909. He testified that he had been living in Seattle for thirty-four years, since 1875. Crawford was a reporter for the *Post Intelligencer* during the Chinese riots in 1886 and city editor for many years. He had frequent dealings with Lew King and knew him intimately. Lew King had been a Chinese interpreter for the court when Judge Lind was on the bench. Judge Lind was a Thurston County judge in the early 1900s and appears in several files. Crawford identified photos of Lew King's children, including the applicant.

Witness Louie Kay, also known as Yin Lim and Hong Po, testified that he was a member of the Lew family but not related to Lew King. He came to Seattle in 1879, was away during the riots, and came back about two months after the 1889 fire. He was questioned about many things concerning the extended Lew family, but most of the information did not pertain to Fannie.

Fannie's mother underwent a serious operation in Seattle in 1913, but because Fannie had lost her U.S. citizenship, she was unable to secure a section 6 traveler certificate to cross the border to visit her. The consul at Victoria refused to approve her certificate on the grounds that she was not a Canadian citizen even though her husband was a member of the exempt class in Canada. One of her brothers, Lew Geate Kay of the Chinese consulate in Seattle, made an appeal to the immigration authorities, and Fannie was allowed to land without a section 6 certificate. Commissioner White informed the commissioner-general of immigration in Washington,

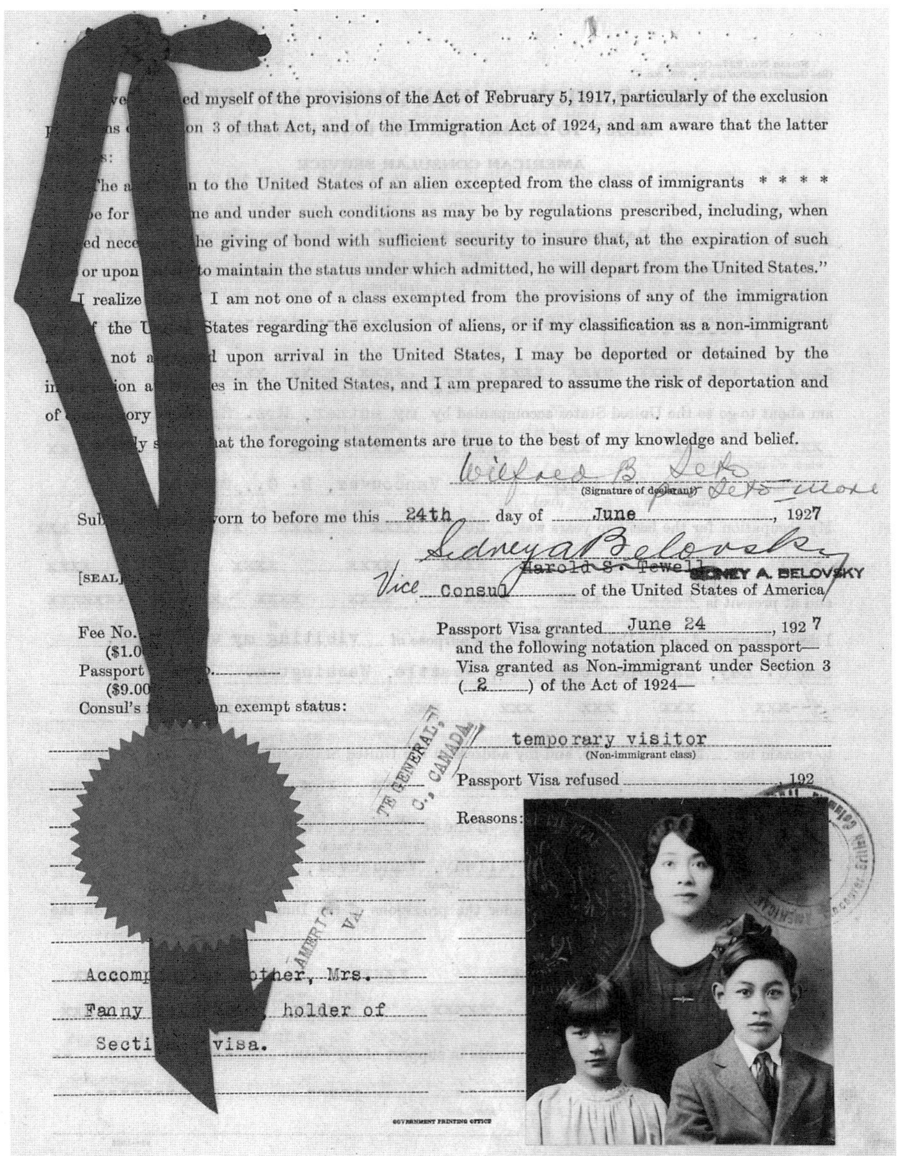

ed myself of the provisions of the Act of February 5, 1917, particularly of the exclusion
on 3 of that Act, and of the Immigration Act of 1924, and am aware that the latter

n to the United States of an alien excepted from the class of immigrants * * * *
e for ne and under such conditions as may be by regulations prescribed, including, when
ed nece he giving of bond with sufficient security to insure that, at the expiration of such
or upon o maintain the status under which admitted, he will depart from the United States."
I realize I am not one of a class exempted from the provisions of any of the immigration
f the U States regarding the exclusion of aliens, or if my classification as a non-immigrant
not a l upon arrival in the United States, I may be deported or detained by the
in ion a es in the United States, and I am prepared to assume the risk of deportation and
of ory
y at the foregoing statements are true to the best of my knowledge and belief.

Wilfred B. Seto
(Signature of declarant) p. Seto More

Su orn to before me this 24th day of June, 1927

[SEAL]

Sidney A Belovsky
Harold S. Tewell SIDNEY A. BELOVSKY
Vice Consul of the United States of America

Fee No.
($1.0
Passport
($9.00
Consul's n exempt status:

Passport Visa granted June 24, 1927
and the following notation placed on passport—
Visa granted as Non-immigrant under Section 3
(2) of the Act of 1924—

temporary visitor
(Non-immigrant class)

Passport Visa refused 192

Reasons:

Accomp other, Mrs.
Fanny holder of
Secti visa.

Seto More Fannie with her children, passport visa photo, 1927. *CEA case files, Seto More Fannie (Lew Tue Fannie), file 7030/12060, RG 85, National Archives at Seattle.*

D.C., about what had happened. His letter of explanation is in Fannie's file. Fannie knew influential people who helped her through trying times.

A 1921 letter from Frederick M. Ryan of the American Consular Service in Vancouver, British Columbia, confirmed that Mrs. Fannie Seto More acquired British citizenship through the naturalization of her husband. In 1921, Fannie and her children were issued section 6 certificates by the controller of Chinese immigration in Vancouver, British Columbia. John J. Forester, of Vancouver, swore in a 1927 affidavit that he knew Fannie Seto More and her children and could identify them.

By 1933, Mr. Seto More was manager of the Chinese Department of the Canadian Pacific Railways in Vancouver.

In 1938, Fannie traveled to visit her brother, Lew G. Kay, a staff member at the Chinese consulate in Seattle, with a stopover in Oakland, California, to see her sister. The file ends with Fannie's and her daughter's visit to Seattle in February 1939. Her file contains photos of her from 1908, 1914, and 1938 and photos of Fannie and her children from 1921, 1924, 1927, and 1933, in addition to the passport photo from 1927.

Rose Chin

Lost U.S. Citizenship After Marrying a Chinese Native in 1927

Rose Chin had never been out of the United States, and in 1927, she and her husband wanted to make a trip to Canada.[108] Rose applied with immigration services to make a temporary visit abroad.

In her application, Rose Chin Kee testified that she was born on April 15, 1911, to Mr. and Mrs. Chin Kee of 219 Washington Street in Seattle. Rose's father, Chin Kee, was a merchant and interpreter at immigration services in Seattle. He died in China around 1920. Her mother was born in San Francisco and had been to China sometime before Rose was born in 1911. Rose's birth certificate says her mother was born in China, but the interviewer did not ask her about this discrepancy. Rose was comfortable with the English language and approved of her interview being conducted in English. She had five brothers and four sisters, who were all born in Seattle, and one adopted sister. Her oldest brother, Tom Chin Kee, was the only one of her siblings to visit China. He left and returned when Rose was a small child.

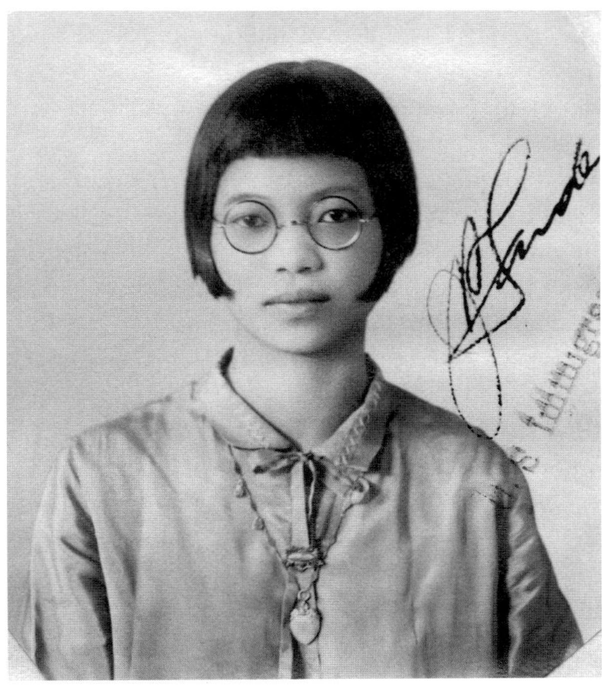

Left: Rose Chin's Form 430 photo, 1927. *CEA case files, Rose Chin, file 30-3706, RG 85, National Archives at Seattle.*

Below: Rose Chin's birth certificate, proof that she was born in Seattle. *CEA case files, Rose Chin, file 30-3706, RG 85, National Archives at Seattle.*

30/3706

V. S.—No. 8.

MARGIN RESERVED FOR BINDING

WRITE PLAINLY, WITH UNFADING INK—THIS IS A PERMANENT RECORD.

N. B. *In case of more than one child at a birth, a SEPARATE RETURN must be made for each, and the number of each in order of birth, stated.*

PLACE OF BIRTH

WASHINGTON STATE BOARD OF HEALTH

BUREAU OF VITAL STATISTICS

CERTIFICATE OF BIRTH

County of King

City of Seattle or Town of Wash (No. St.; Ward)

Record No.

File No.

Registered No.

FULL NAME OF CHILD Rose Chin Kee

{If child is not yet named, make supplemental report, as directed.

Sex of Child girl | Twin, Triplet or other? | and Number in order of birth | Legitimate? Yes | Date of Birth April (Month) 15 (Day) 1911 (Year)

FATHER

Full Name Chin Kee

Residence 219 Washington St

Color Yellow — Age at last Birthday 55 (Years)

Birthplace (State or Country) China

Occupation Merchant

MOTHER

Full Maiden Name Mrs Chin Kee

Residence 219 Wash. St.

Color Yellow — Age at last Birthday 38 (Years)

Birthplace (State or Country) China

Occupation —

Number of child of this mother 5 — Number of children, this mother, now living 5

CERTIFICATE OF ATTENDING PHYSICIAN OR MIDWIFE*

I hereby certify that I attended the birth of this child, and that it occurred on April 15, 1911 *at* M.

{* *When there was no attending physician or midwife, then the father, householder, etc., should make this return.*}

(Signature) Mrs T. Jakshitz

Midwife

(Physician or Midwife)

Give name added from a supplemental report April 20, 1911

Address 420 - 27 Ave N.

Registrar.

Filed , 1911

Registrar.

Rose married Pong Mon on May 15, 1927, at home in Seattle. They obtained their license from the county clerk, and a white man performed the ceremony. Rose Chin lived in Seattle all her life and knew inspector Mangels, interpreter Quan Foy, and Mr. Monroe from immigration services. She attended Main Street and Pacific public schools. She provided her birth certificate for inspection.[109]

Although the inspectors verified Rose's birth certificate, knew her family, and had known her since she was a small girl, they could not approve her application. Her husband, a Chinese native, could not prove that he was a U.S. citizen. According to the 1922 Cable Act, Rose Chin lost her U.S. citizenship when she married a Chinese native.

Rose was born in the United States, as were her parents and all her siblings. The immigration officials knew Rose and her family. Her father had been an interpreter. Rose had never been out of the country, but because she married a Chinese national and lost her U.S. citizenship, her application was not approved.

CHAPTER 7
CHINESE COMMUNITIES IN WASHINGTON STATE

SEATTLE

Chu Yong

Reprimand to the Seattle Office from the Bureau of Immigration, Washington, D.C.

On April 27, 1923, the U.S. Department of Labor Immigration Service District No. 16 sent a letter to several shipping companies in Seattle and Tacoma—Blue Funnel Line, Admiral Oriental Line, Osaka Shosen Kaisha, and the Canadian Pacific Railway Company—reminding them that the last paragraph of section 7 of the 1888 Chinese Exclusion Act stated that a "Chinese laborer shall be admitted to the United States only at the port from which he departed."

For some time, the Bureau of Immigration—as it was known until it became the Immigration and Naturalization Service (INS) in 1933 and then U.S. Citizenship and Immigration Services (USCIS) in 2003—had been having a problem with laborers not returning to the East Coast port they departed from. This came to a head when two returning East Coast laborers were deported because they did not return to the correct port. Leo B. Russell, special immigrant inspector, ended a 1923 letter to the commissioner of immigration in Seattle with this sentence:

> *Each case of this kind should be brought to the Bureau's attention, and if it appears that the warning given to the steamship companies is not being heeded, the Department will be asked to direct exclusion.*

Form 538

U. S. DEPARTMENT OF LABOR
IMMIGRATION SERVICE

BOND FOR CHINESE IN TRANSIT

Know all Men by these Presents:

That we, C H U Y O N G, *a citizen and subject of China, as principal, and* Wong On *residing at* Seattle, Wash. *and* ______ *residing at* ______ *as sureties, are held and firmly bound unto the United States of America in the full and just sum of Five Hundred Dollars ($500), to be paid to the United States, for which payment well and truly to be made, we, and each of us, do bind ourselves, our heirs, executors, and administrators, jointly and severally, firmly by these presents.*

Sealed with our seals and dated this 23d *day of* February, 1923 *, 191*

Whereas, Chu Yong *a Chinese alien, aged* 48 *years, claiming to have been born in* China*, whose height is* 5 *feet and* 6 *inches, whose complexion is* dark*, the color of whose eyes is* brown*, whose physical peculiarities consist of* pock-marked face; scar in hair back of left ear; several brown spots left neck

who arrived at the port of Seattle, Wash. *on the* 22d *day of* February, 1923 *, 191 , by* s. s. "President McKinley"*, claims to be bound for* Boston , Mass.
and requests the privilege of a continuous transit through such part of the United States territory as it may be necessary to pass through in order to continue the journey to the destination above mentioned via the port of Boston, Mass.*;*

14—570

Chu Yong, Bond for Chinese in Transit, 1923. *CEA case files, Chu Yong, Seattle, file 41010/3/4, RG 85, National Archives at Seattle.*

This was the fourth letter immigration services sent to the immigration office in Seattle in April 1923 regarding Chu Yong.[110] Each letter sounded more cautionary.

Chu Yong, a forty-seven-year-old Chinese laborer, departed for China in 1921 via the port of Boston and returned on February 22, 1923, at the port of Seattle. He had an authorized overtime certificate showing that he had been unable to return within the required one-year period because of illness. Because he did not return to his port of departure, he landed under a $500 transit bond with the understanding that he would proceed directly to Boston and present himself for admission. Luther Weedin, immigration commissioner at Seattle, sent an update on Chu Yong's status to the Boston office the next day.

When Chu Yong finally arrived at the Boston immigration office, almost a month later, on March 20, he said that although he knew he was supposed to proceed across the country immediately, he'd gotten permission from Wong On, the surety on Chu Yong's $500 "Bond for Chinese in Transit." Wong On, Chu Yong said, had telephoned the inspector, who said Chu Yong could stay in Seattle a "little while." There was no follow-up with the Seattle office to see if Chu Yong had actually spoken to Wong On.

Chu Yong spent more than a month visiting friends in Seattle, Chicago, and New York before proceeding to Boston. After Chu Yong was interrogated on March 29, 1923, the Boston Chinese inspector, W.P. Callahan, recommended that he be admitted. He was fortunate to be admitted. The Seattle immigration office received the brunt of the anger and frustration from the U.S. Department of Labor Immigration Service.

Look Gom Hong

Son of Deceased American-Born Chinese Citizen

Look Ah Pong, an American-born Chinese citizen, died on January 7, 1921, and was buried at Mount Pleasant Cemetery in Seattle on January 10.[111] His original certificate of identity and the invoice for his burial gave his son, Look Gom Hong, the necessary proof he needed to get his immigration documents approved.

Look Gom Hong was born in Sing Shu Village, Fook Chung, Sun Ning, China, and originally entered the United States through the Port of Seattle in 1923. He received his certificate of identity on arrival. After his entry was approved, he joined his older brother Look Gim Yook (York) in New York City.

PHONE EAST 199

Seattle, Wash., Jany 10 192[illegible]

M Hip Sing Co
513 – 8th Ave. So

Account of Ah. Pong. Deceased

To COLLINS BROS. UNDERTAKING CO., Dr.
PROFESSIONAL FUNERAL DIRECTORS
911-13 EAST PINE STREET

Casket and Trimmings (Complete)	75
Outside box and trimmings	
Burial suit or dress	8 50
Underwear, Hose, Shirt, Collar, Tie, Cuffs	
Hearse service	10
Pall bearers conveyance	
Family and friends conveyance	
Burial place	
Sexton, opening and closing grave, box and decorations	13 50
Gloves, Candles, Paper notices	6
Filing death certificate, Permits, Etc.	
Preparing remains	
Washing, Dressing, Shaving, Embalming	
Music Minister	
Professional service, Attention at funeral, Etc.	12 5
Auto for Minister to cemetery and return	
Cremation	125 50
Telephone and Telegrams	
~~Vault~~	

Died January 7 – 1921.
Buried January 10 – 1921.

EXTRAS

Paid – Jany 24. 1921
Collins Bros.
[illegible]

Collins Bros. Undertaking statement, 1923. *CEA case files, Chu Yong, file 41010/3/4, RG 85, National Archives at Seattle, RG 85, National Archives at Seattle.*

In 1935, Look Gom Hong filled out his Form 430, Application for Pre-investigation of Status, for his upcoming trip to China. He was twenty-five years old and a waiter at Li Chee Gardens Restaurant in New York City. In over five pages' worth of interrogation, Look Gom Hong described his father's and mother's siblings, his grandparents on both sides of the family, their extended families, and many details about their village.

Look Gim Yook (York) testified on behalf of his brother. He swore that he was with their father when he died at Hai Ping Fong, a house in Seattle where Chinese who were ill were taken. He did not have his father's death certificate, but he gave the interrogator a bill addressed to the Hip Sing Company from Collins Brothers Undertaking Company for $125 for the burial of his father. He surrendered his father's certificate of identity, which was issued in 1911. His father's certificate of identity was valuable proof of the family connection. Immigration wanted certificates returned to it when someone died so that the certificate could not be sold or given to a Chinese person who was trying to enter the United States illegally. For the same reason, immigration services also held the certificates of Chinese people leaving the United States until they returned. After obtaining Look Ah Pong's certificate, the interrogators asked Look Gim Yook (York) the same questions about the family and their village as his brother.

Look Kim Fun, who was admitted to the United States in 1922, was from the same village and testified for Look Gom Hong. He was asked the same questions about the family and their village and stated that the village had thirteen houses and a watchhouse. Since it was such a small village, everyone knew each other's families, making Look Kim Fun a credible witness.

The inspectors reviewed the interrogations and decided that the testimony of the three witnesses agreed. Look Gom Hong made a favorable impression, the brothers resembled each other, and they were prompt and frank in their testimony. Look Gom Hong's application was approved. The reference sheet in the file includes the names, relationships, and file numbers for Look Gom Hong's father, brother, two nephews, two uncles, two cousins, and a "distant relative."

Chin Fook Hing

Generation Book

Chin Hing, circa 1910. *CEA case files, Chin Hing (Chin Fook Hing), file 39666/1-1, RG 85, National Archives at Seattle.*

Chin Hing was a merchant whose family history was recorded for eighteen generations.[112] His marriage name was Chin Fook Hing, but he also went by Hing Henry. He was born in Canton, China, on September 1, 1875, at one o'clock in the morning. It is very unusual to see the time of birth listed in a file. His father, Chin Suey, was born in San Francisco and his mother, Woo Shee, was born in China. Family information was included in a Bible and a "generation book" of the Chin family. The interpreter explained to the interviewer that the generation book was a history of eighteen generations of Chin Fook Hing's family for dating back over three hundred years. Chin Hing's grandfather Chin Yick was one of the first Chinese immigrants to come to San Francisco. He was married to an Indian (Native American) woman and worked in the gold mines and then a fruit orchard. After the Chin Yick's wife died in 1874, he and his son Chin Suey went to China. Chin Suey married Woo Shee soon after he arrived, and they had a son, Chin Hing. The family moved back to San Francisco around 1881. Years later, they moved to Seattle, and Chin Hing became a merchant at Kwong Wa Chong Company.

In 1910, Chin Hing visited China and married Tah Soo Len, who was born in Los Angeles. Their two children, Chin Hing Henry and Chin Josephine, were born in Seattle. At the time of his interview in 1922, Chin Hing was a merchant and member of Chong Hing and Company at 676 King Street in Seattle. His business card is included in his file.

Witnesses for Chin Hing were Julius Schweigart, who was in the art and picture business and had been a resident of Seattle since 1906; Otto Guthman, a salesman at National Grocery Company in Seattle and a resident of Seattle since 1905; and Woo Gen, merchant and member of Kwong Wa Chong Company, Wa Chong Company, and Washington Rice Mill Company and a resident of Seattle for thirty-six years. Chin Hing (Chin Fook Hing) died in Seattle on November 16, 1941. A copy of his

Telephone Main 2391
CHIN HING, Manager
昌興號
Chong Hing & Co
舍路埠
IMPORTERS & MANUFACTURERS
WHOLESALE AND RETAIL
MAKERS OF SWEATERS IN ANY STYLE
CHINESE FANCY GOODS, STATIONARY,
CLOTHING & TOILET PREPARATIONS.
676 KING STREET,
SEATTLE, WASH., U. S. A.

Chin Hing's business card, circa 1910. *CEA case files, Chin Hing (Chin Fook Hing), file 39666/1-1, RG 85, National Archives at Seattle.*

obituary and photo from the November 22, 1941 edition of the *Seattle Times* is included in the file.

Excerpts from the obituary:

> *A German knitter befriended Mr. Chin and taught him the knitting business and in 1911, with no capital, Mr. Chin established the Chong Hing Knitting Company, 504 12th Ave. S. of which he was general manager until his death....*
>
> *Mr. Chin was the first Chinese to serve as a juror in King County Superior Courts. He was past treasurer of the Seattle Chinese Patriotic League and the Seattle Chinese Nationalist Association.*[113]

Chin Wing You

Seattle History in Interrogations

Chin Wing You was the youngest of three sons born in Seattle to Chin Gem (Jim) Wah and Me Wing Wah.[114] He was born in 1887. The family traveled to their family village, Hing Lung Lay, in Sun Ning district, China, in 1888.

The father made several trips between China and Seattle between 1888 and 1907. His son Chin Ah Wing joined him at the Wa Chong Company in Seattle in 1900. His son Chin Wing Moy died in China in 1907. Chin Wing You remined in China, married Louie See in 1905, and then prepared to join his father in Seattle in 1907. Since he was in China as a young child when the Chinese Exclusion Act was passed, he did not have a residence certificate. He did not have the required documentation to prove that he was born in the United States and was the son of a merchant, so he was required to have witnesses swear that he was the son of Chin Jim Wah and was born in Seattle.

Samuel L. Crawford was a witness for Chin Wing You in 1907. His affidavit stated that he had been a resident of Seattle for thirty years and he knew Chin Wing You's father, Chin Jim Wah, prior to 1887. Crawford confirmed that Chin Jim Wah was a merchant, partner, and bookkeeper for the Wa Chong Company and that he and his wife lived in the store and had several small children. Crawford was in the real estate business, and he was in the newspaper profession with the *Post Intelligencer* from 1875 to 1888. He knew all the Chinese businessmen and had dealings with them. He was acquainted with Chin Ching Hock, Woo Gen, Wan Lee, Chin Gee Hee, and Ah Wah. Crawford saw Chin Jim Wah, Wa Chong Company's bookkeeper, every month when he conducted business with the store, and he identified photos of Chin Jim Wah and Chin Ah Wing.[115]

Chin Ah Wing's marriage name was Chin Hui Quock. He was a U.S. citizen and resident of Seattle. He was born in Seattle on October 1, 1885, and his brother Chin Wing You was born at the Wa Chong Company store in Seattle on May 10, 1887. Chin Ah Wing left Seattle in 1888 and returned in 1900. He made another trip to China in 1904 and returned the next year through Port Townsend.

George Harman swore in his 1907 affidavit that he was a citizen of the United States and had been a resident of Seattle and Kitsap County for fifty-six years; that Chin Wing You was born in Seattle at the Wa Chong Company on the corner of South Third and Washington Streets where the Phoenix Hotel was standing in 1907; and that the family went to China in 1888 when Chin Wing You was about one year old. Harman testified that he had been in Washington Territory and then State since August 22, 1866, when he "got paid off in the navy yard from the navy." In 1907, he was living on a ranch about twelve miles south of Seattle. He worked in various places in the woods hauling out wood in 1885. He knew the Chinese workers at Wa Chong Company, especially the manager, Chin Ching Hock (Chun

Q How far out of the city were you engaged in logging operations?
A Possibly twenty odd miles to old Elder Creek.
Q What Chinese did you know in the city at that time?
A I didn't know anybody but the Wa Chong Company. In fact, Chin Ching Hockswife and my wife at that time were sisters; that is the reason I got acqauinted with them; I went there all the time.
Q You married an Indian wife then, did you?
A I have her yet; I have been with her thirty-two years; I have children and grandchildren.
Q How many of Chin Ching Hock's partners can you name?
A At that time Chin Ching Hock was always there, and I didn't inquire for the partners; I didn't have aby business with any of them.

Excerpt from interrogation of George Harman, 1907. *CEA case files, Chin Wing You, file 7030/13441, RG 85, National Archives at Seattle.*

Ching Hock), who at one time was a cook in a logging camp. Chin Ching Hock's wife and Harman's wife were sisters.

Chin Ching Hock's second wife was Chinese, and their children were born in Seattle. He was known to have been a witness for other unrelated Chinese people, but he stated that he had been a witness for only his nephews, the sons of Chin Ching Hock and his sister-in-law. The interrogator disagreed and told Harman he had affidavits showing Harman had been a witness for Woo Ah Moy in 1901 and Chin Ah Wing in 1900. Officials suspected that Harman might be a "professional witness."

After considering the evidence from the applicant and the witnesses, John H. Sargent, immigration inspector in charge, ordered that Chin Wing You be admitted to the United States on November 19, 1907, as a returning native-born American citizen.

Chin Wing You made another trip to China in 1912. When he returned, he had no proof of citizenship, so he produced a duplicate of his 1907 admittance to the Port of Seattle as an American-born Chinese. With this information, he received his certificate of identity. He made trips back to China in 1922, 1929, and 1941 and sired many children.

Lew Wa Hoo

When Lew Wa Hoo was getting ready to return from his trip to China in 1911, he wrote to Harold N. Smith, telling him he would be returning to Seattle soon.[116] Smith, who was a clerk for Puget Sound Mills and Lumber Company, then wrote to the "Chief Inspector of the Immigration Bureau" in Seattle to ensure that Lew's reentry into the United States went smoothly and without any unnecessary delays. Lew was a merchant and treasurer of Wa Hing Company at 214 Washington Street in Seattle.

Harold Smith, formerly an exchange teller for the National Bank of Commerce of Seattle, had been a witness for Lew Wa Hoo's application before he left for China four years earlier. Smith had known Lew for over fifteen years and had many positive business dealings with him.

In 1911, Lew Wa Hoo was forty-five years old and married, with the marriage name of Lew Jung Hen. He first entered the United States through San Francisco around 1881. By 1911, he had already made four trips back to China. He was registered under the name Sing Wa and was a member of the Sing (Sun) Wo Company in Olympia before moving to Seattle and becoming a partner of Wa Hing Company. He and his wife, Gong Shee, had five children in China: three sons and two daughters. The children were

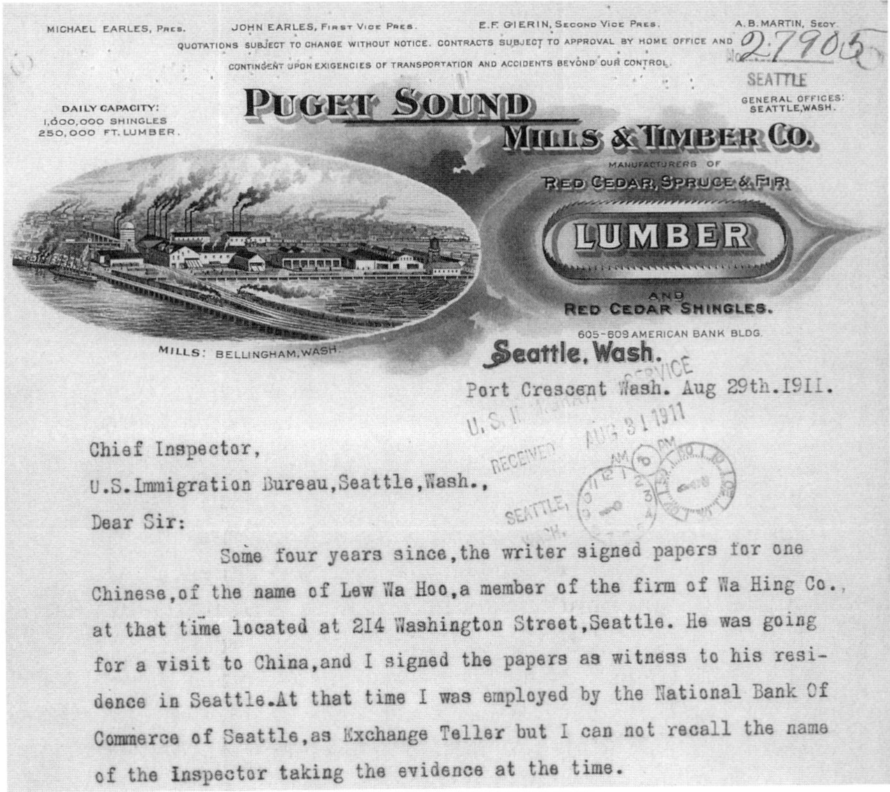

MICHAEL EARLES, PRES. JOHN EARLES, FIRST VICE PRES. E.F. GIERIN, SECOND VICE PRES. A.B. MARTIN, SEC'Y.

QUOTATIONS SUBJECT TO CHANGE WITHOUT NOTICE. CONTRACTS SUBJECT TO APPROVAL BY HOME OFFICE AND CONTINGENT UPON EXIGENCIES OF TRANSPORTATION AND ACCIDENTS BEYOND OUR CONTROL.

No. 2.7905
SEATTLE

DAILY CAPACITY:
1,000,000 SHINGLES
250,000 FT. LUMBER.

PUGET SOUND MILLS & TIMBER CO.

GENERAL OFFICES: SEATTLE, WASH.

MANUFACTURERS OF RED CEDAR, SPRUCE & FIR LUMBER AND RED CEDAR SHINGLES.

MILLS: BELLINGHAM, WASH.

605-609 AMERICAN BANK BLDG.
Seattle, Wash.

Port Crescent Wash. Aug 29th.1911.

RECEIVED AUG 31 1911 SEATTLE, WASH.

Chief Inspector,
U.S. Immigration Bureau, Seattle, Wash.,

Dear Sir:

Some four years since, the writer signed papers for one Chinese, of the name of Lew Wa Hoo, a member of the firm of Wa Hing Co., at that time located at 214 Washington Street, Seattle. He was going for a visit to China, and I signed the papers as witness to his residence in Seattle. At that time I was employed by the National Bank Of Commerce of Seattle, as Exchange Teller but I can not recall the name of the Inspector taking the evidence at the time.

Puget Sound Mills and Timber Company letterhead, 1911. *CEA case files, Lew Wa Hoo, file 35100/5245, RG 85, National Archives at Seattle.*

attending school in Bok Suk Village, Sun Ning District. Neither Gong Shee nor the children had been to the United States.

When Lew Wa Hoo applied to visit China in 1901, his witnesses were Fred Wilhelm, a carpenter who owned the building occupied by Wa Hing Company; G. Wyatt Upper, a teller at Commercial National Bank; and Lew King, manager of Wa Hing Company. According to Thomas M. Fisher, Chinese inspector, the firm had a fixed location with a good stock of merchandise, and the witnesses were reputable.

By 1922, Lew Wa Hoo was the manager of Wah Hing Company. Two of his sons had visited the United States and were back in China. One of his daughters was living in the United States, and the other was still in China. Lew Wa Hoo's paperwork was in order, and after every trip to China, he was readmitted to the United States without any problems or delays.

Lew Wa Hoo returned to China and died there in June 1927.[117]

OLYMPIA

Lock Ling (Lock Loon)

Olympia and Seattle Business Owner

On August 18, 1891, Rossell G. O'Brien, brigadier general of the Washington National Guard, signed an affidavit stating that Lock Loon (Lock Ling) of the Chung-Lee Company in Olympia wished to visit Victoria, British Columbia, before making a trip to China.[118] The document certified that Lock Ling was entitled to return to Olympia. James C. Horr, mayor of Olympia, added a note saying that he knew Lock Loon personally. Lock Loon signed his affidavit in Chinese characters. An undated form from the U.S. Treasury Department stated that Lock Ling was admitted.

O'Brien, a Union veteran of the Civil War, served in the territorial, state, and Olympia city governments after his arrival to Washington Territory in 1870.[119]

Lock Ling's file contains many pages and forms and covers the years 1891 to 1944. Sometimes the information is repetitive; frequently it is confusing and raises questions. The file and, therefore, this summary are not meant to be biographies. Immigration officials used a series of interviews, affidavits, witnesses, and other documents to evaluate whether they should admit someone to the United States. There were numerous restrictions, and the

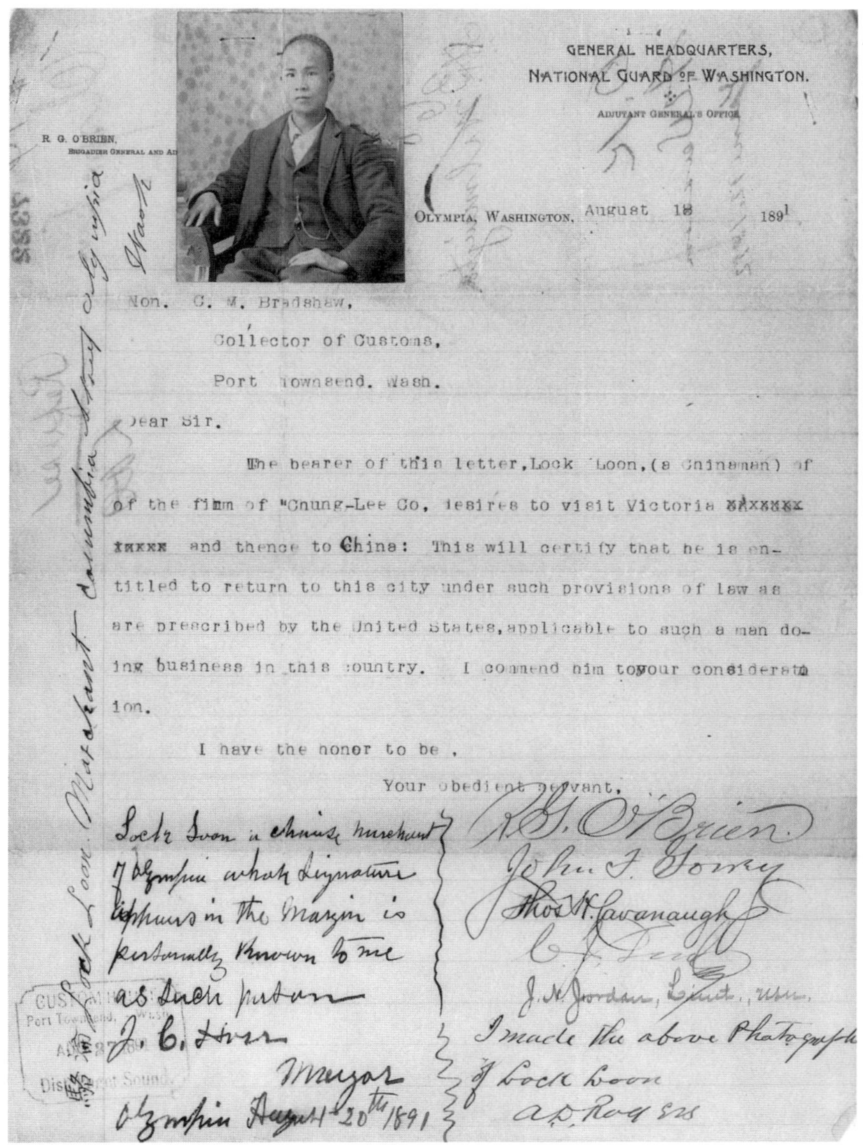

GENERAL HEADQUARTERS,
NATIONAL GUARD OF WASHINGTON.
ADJUTANT GENERAL'S OFFICE

R. G. O'BRIEN,
BRIGADIER GENERAL AND AD

OLYMPIA, WASHINGTON, August 18 1891

Hon. C. M. Bradshaw,
Collector of Customs,
Port Townsend, Wash.

Dear Sir.

The bearer of this letter, Lock Loon, (a Chinaman) of the firm of "Chung-Lee Co, desires to visit Victoria xxxxxx xxxxx and thence to China: This will certify that he is entitled to return to this city under such provisions of law as are prescribed by the United States, applicable to such a man doing business in this country. I commend him to your consideration.

I have the honor to be,
Your obedient servant,

R. G. O'Brien
John F. Gowey
Thos. H. Cavanaugh
J. H. Jordan, Lieut.

Lock Loon a Chinese merchant of Olympia whose signature appears in the Margin is personally known to me as such person
J. C. Horr
Mayor
Olympia August 20th 1891

I made the above Photograph of Lock Loon
A. P. Rogers

CUSTOM HOUSE
Port Townsend, Wash.
Dist. Puget Sound

Affidavit of Lock Ling (Lock Loon), 1891. *CEA case files, Lock Ling, file 7032/3676, RG 85, National Archives at Seattle.*

officials wanted to make sure they were not admitting laborers or anyone else deemed unacceptable under the Chinese Exclusion Act. It was a complicated system. The names Lock Ling and Lock Loon are used interchangeably throughout these documents, but Lock Ling will be used in this summary.

The Reverend Clark Davis and C.P. Stone of Seattle were witnesses for Lock Ling's trip to China in July 1897 and when he returned in September 1898. Sometime after 1898 Lock Ling moved from Olympia and was then working at Mark Ten Suie Company in Seattle.

In October 1902, Lock Ling wished to make another trip to China. He swore in an affidavit that he was thirty-six years old and had lived in the United States for twenty-one years. He was currently a merchant for Coaster Tea Company, which sold teas, coffees, and spices in Seattle. He wanted to visit his family in China and bring back his son, Lock Loui, who was fifteen and a student. He attached his photo and a photo of his son to his affidavit. Harold N. Smith and Clark Davis were his witnesses. His application was approved.

Section 2, S.21039 of the Chinese Exclusion Act was updated and made stricter in 1893. It was no longer enough for a witness to testify that an applicant had not engaged in manual labor for at least one year before his departure from the United States; the testimony had to specify the kind of work the applicant did during the entire year. This did not present a problem for Lock Ling. On his return trip in July 1904, he was admitted at Port Townsend. The record does not show if his son Lock Loui was with him.

In March 1910, Lock Ling declared in an affidavit that he was forty-four years old, had been in the United States for twenty-eight years, had been a resident of Seattle for sixteen years, had been a merchant for the last three years with Wing Long and Company, and had recently sold his interest in the business and become a member of Hong Chong Company. He wanted to visit his second wife, Lee See, in Sing Ning City, Canton. His first wife had died, and he wanted to bring his son Lock Kim, age thirteen and a student at Canton University, back to Seattle with him. He attached photos of himself and his son to his affidavit.[120]

P.K. Smith and George O. Sanborn, both citizens of Seattle, swore in affidavits that they had known Lock Ling for more than three years and that he was a merchant and performed no manual labor except what was necessary to conduct business as a merchant.

When Lock Ling was interviewed, he testified that he was married and had three sons—Lock Loy, Lock Yen/Ying, and Lock Kim—and a daughter. His son Lock Ying was admitted to the United States in 1908 and was presently living in Seattle. Lock Loy, who had been admitted at an earlier date, had been declared insane in a hospital in Steilacoom, Washington, and went back to China. The file does not give the date of Lock Loy's return to China.

I have a son by the name of Lock Kim, now of the age of thirteen years, who is now attending the Canton University, at the City of Canton, Empire of China; that I am duly registered under the Chinese Exclusion Law in the City of Portland, State of Oregon; that I make this affidavit for the purpose of more easily and readily being identified and of avoiding any difficulty in going to, or returning from my native country, China, where I am about to go on a visit, with the intention of returning to this city, and my absence will be from one to two years, after which I wish to return to this country and bring with me my said son, Lock Kim, now as stated of the age of thirteen years, to live with me in the City of Seattle and there to attend school and to learn and acquire the business duties and pursuits of a merchant; my said son, Lock Kim, has never heretofore been in the United States. That the first photograph attached hereto and upon which is written the name, "Lock Ling" is a correct likeness and representation of myself; that the second photograph hereto attached and upon which is written the name "Lock Kim", is a correct likeness and representation of my said son Lock Kim; that I have not during

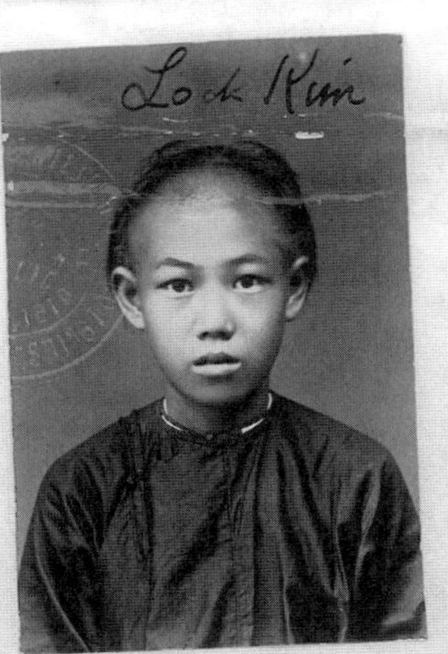

-2-

Photos of Lock Ling and son from Lock Ling's affidavit, 1891. *CEA case files, Lock Ling (Lock Loon), file 7032/3676, RG 85, National Archives at Seattle.*

Lock Ling had been back to China four times, once before the Chinese Exclusion Act was passed.

The immigration inspector made a note on Lock Ling's interview saying that Lock Ling was well known as a salesman for Wing Long Company. His new firm, Hong Chong Company, had forty partners. The firm sold drugs and general merchandise; he would be its treasurer. The company was incorporated according to Chinese custom, not under Washington State law. It had a four-year lease from Mrs. W.D. Hofius for its four-story brick building, which was still being built, for $950 per month.

Lock Ling's application was approved, and he left for China in March 1910. He returned in October 1912 and was interrogated when he arrived. He gave his marriage name as Yin Ling and his childhood name as Lock Lung. He was returning from his fifth trip to China with his third wife, Wong Shee; his son Lock Kim; and his daughter Lock Mee. He had three sons and a daughter with his first wife, who died around 1902. His son Lock Loy, age twenty-four, had been in the United States but went back to China around 1909, and his son Lock Yen, age nineteen, was in Seattle. His son and daughter Lock Gim and Lock Mee were in the detention house waiting for approval to enter the United States. Lock Ling's second wife, Lee Shee, had a son, Lock Goey, who was still living in China. When Lee Shee died, her son Lock Loy, according to tradition, carried the incense jar to the cemetery. Lock Ling then married Wong Shee. According to Chinese custom, she did not wear a veil for the ceremony, but the tassels from her coronet hung down over her face. She was brought to his house in a regular red, blue, and green sedan chair.

In 1912, Lock Ling described his property in China: a house and rice land worth the equivalent of $3,000 in Chinese currency and a building in Hong Kong worth the equivalent of about $15,000 in Hong Kong currency. He boasted that he went to China five times and a child was born as a result of each trip. In January 1943, Lock Ling, age seventy-five, applied for a laborer's return certificate to visit Vancouver, British Columbia. He qualified because he owed his daughter, Lock Mee Oye, born and residing in Seattle, more than $1,000. He presented the immigration authorities with his certificate of residence, which was issued in Portland, Oregon, in 1894. It showed that he was born on May 11, 1868, in China and entered the United States with his father around 1882 at San Francisco when he was fifteen. He had lost his original certificate of residence, so he presented his replacement certificate. His application was approved, and his current photo was attached to the document. Lock Ling and his wife went to Vancouver and returned to Seattle four days later.

Lock's reference sheet shows that three files were brought forward and gives file numbers for his wife, four daughters, and two sons.

According to Hao-Jan Chang, Chinese Exclusion Act volunteer at the National Archives at Seattle and Locke family expert, Yen Ling Lock and former Governor Gary Locke are distantly related. They have common ancestors, starting from the first generation to the third generation. Yen Ling Lock is of the nineteenth generation; Gary Locke is of the twenty-fifth generation.

Port Townsend

Ng Ah Yun

Ng Ah Yun was born in Port Townsend, Jefferson County, Washington, on August 23, 1889.[121] He was the son of (Ng) Yee Kong and Wong Shee. Yee Kong had come to the United States from China around 1877 and married Wong Shee in San Francisco in 1882. Shortly after they married, they moved to Port Townsend and resided at the corner of Madison and Water Streets. Their first son, Ah Don Ng, was born there in 1885 or 1886.

Yee Kong operated the Yee Wah Laundry. Its original location was across the corner from the sailors' boardinghouse. In December 1888, Yee Kong's cousin, Charley Quong, who was born in California, joined them in Port Townsend. Charley's father and Yee Kong's father were brothers. Around 1890, the laundry burned down, and the building was replaced. Eventually that building also burned and the family moved over to the King Tai Company building. Around 1892, discouraged after twice losing their business, Yee Kong, his wife, and their two sons moved back to China.

In June 1907, the two brothers, (Ng) Ah Don and (Ng) Ah Yun (sometimes their names appear in documents as Ng Ah Don and Ng Ah Yun and sometimes as Ah Don and Ah Yun), returned to Port Townsend on the SS *Shawmut* and applied to be admitted to the United States as U.S. citizens. Over a ten-day period, they were interrogated and eventually admitted.

The file does not indicate where they stayed during those ten days. The Port Townsend U.S. Customs House may have made some arrangements for them. Charley Quong, another Chinese man, and two Caucasian witnesses swore in affidavits about their knowledge of the brothers. They were shown photographs and asked to identify each one. Frank A. Bartlett said he had been a resident of Port Townsend for more than forty-two

Townsend, Washington, and affiant alleges that from his acquaintance with said family and from knowledge of their residence and whereabouts, he is satisfied beyond doubt, that the said Ah Don must have been born in Port Townsend, Washington; that the said boys, Ah Don and Ah Yun, went with their parents to China about fifteen years ago; that about fourteen years ago affiant was in China and again five years ago; that affiant saw the said children on both trips, and knows them and can recognize them now, and that the photographs hereto attached are good likenesses respectively of the said children, as marked.

Ah Yun Ah Don Charlie Quong

Subscribed ad sworn to before me this 14th day of March 1907.

W.D. Granger
Notary Public in and for the State of Washington, residing at Port Townsend, Wash.

Affidavit photos of Ng Ah Yun (*left*) and Ah Don (*right*), 1907. *CEA case files, Ng Ah Yun, file 7030/6363, RG 85, National Archives at Seattle.*

years. He was a member of C.C. Bartlett and Company, his father's general merchandise store, and sold laundry supplies to Yee Kong. C.C. Bartlett also rented a lot and a building to Yee Kong. After the building burned down, Yee Kong rented the land from Bartlett and built a two-story frame building for his laundry business. The Bartletts had a good working relationship with Yee Kong, and they both remembered seeing his young sons playing around the laundry.

Joseph Steiner also swore in an affidavit that he was acquainted with Yee Kong. Steiner owned a cigar store and had been a resident of Port Townsend since February 1888. Steiner patronized the Yee Wah Laundry, and Yee Kong brought his sons with him to the cigar store when he came to collect Steiner's laundry fees and visit with him.

Eng Yee Tung testified that he was forty-four years old and was born in Pen On, Har Pang county, Sunning district, province of Canton, China. He was the manager of the Yee Sing Wook Kee Company in Port Townsend. Around 1885, there were about one hundred Chinese people in Port Townsend. Eng Yee Tung testified that he and about thirty or forty other Chinese attended a "shaving feast" to celebrate the birth of each of Yee Kong's sons. This was a Chinese ritual in which a barber would shave off all but a small tuft of hair on the front of a male baby's head about a month after the birth, and then family and friends would gather to celebrate.

Ah Don, age twenty-one, was interviewed on June 13, 1907. Even though he was only five or six years old when he left Port Townsend for China, he was asked many of the same questions asked of the adults. He testified that his uncle Charley Quong, whose Chinese name was Bing Quong, lived next door to his father's house in China and that Charley's father was Jet Hock, the brother of Hen Hock. In the interview, Ah Don described his house: it had two sleeping rooms, two kitchens, and a worship room. His mother had a brother named Wong Sai Chuck, a farmer in China. The interviewer then gave Ah Don a genealogy lesson. He explained that Charley and Ah Don's fathers were first cousins; therefore, Charley could not be his uncle. When asked if he had any first cousins, Ah Don responded: "Under the Chinese custom I call Bing Quong my uncle, but according to the American custom he is my cousin, but not my first cousin." He had learned his genealogy lesson and how to deal with interviewers. He had no other cousins. His father had given him about $1,000 to come to the United States.

Ah Yun, age eighteen, was interviewed the next day, ten days after the brothers had arrived in Port Townsend. He was only three or four years old when he left the United States for China. He told the interviewer that the family name was Ng, although it was not always used. When Ah Yun called Charley Kong (Quong) his uncle, Mr. Monroe, the interviewer, gave him the same genealogy lecture he had given his brother. Ah Yun gave the same answers to the interview questions as his brother had. As one would expect, they both correctly identified the photographs of each other and of Charley Quong.

Charley Quong had married in San Francisco. He had made two trips to China, once in 1895 and again in 1901. He had registered each time before he left the country. The interviewer asked him why he had registered, since he was born in the United States. He replied, "Because every Chinaman was registering, and I thought I would do the same." It was odd that the interviewer asked Quong why he had registered, because in 1892, the Geary Act was passed, which expanded the 1882 Exclusion Act. All Chinese were now required to register and obtain a certificate of identity as proof of their right to be in the United States and to safely return when they left the country.

The interviewer asked Quong many questions about his family in China. Charley Quong and his cousin Yee Kong had lived in the village of Song Cheong, sometimes called Song Clen, Song Lung, or Song Leung. There were only two houses in the village, and they each owned one of them. Quong lived there with his wife, his stepmother (his father's first wife), and his two sons.

Caucasians were considered more credible witnesses than Chinese people, so it was important for returning Chinese to have white witnesses who could swear that they were respectable citizens. Even though information on Caucasians in the files is incidental and rarely indexed, there are sometimes tidbits of information about those who had working relationships with Chinese people. Sometimes a witness might tell officials where a Caucasian was living in the 1890s, when no census records were available. Unfortunately, because most Caucasians mentioned in the files are not indexed, it is extremely difficult for researchers to find information about minor figures in the records.[122]

Three months after Frank A. Bartlett and Joseph Steiner gave sworn statements about their knowledge of Ah Don and Ah Yun, the affiants gave witness testimony. Mr. Monroe asked Steiner how long he had lived in Port Townsend, and Steiner replied that it had been a little over twenty years. Monroe came back with, "How much over twenty years?" Steiner replied that it had been twenty years in February. Monroe may have felt that he was wasting his time trying to disprove that the brothers were U.S. citizens.

Steiner was asked to give the names of any Chinese people he remembered; he named six. He said he had never been to Yee Kong's laundry because Yee Kong always called for his items and delivered them back to him when ready. When Yee Kong's former landlord, Frank A. Bartlett, was interviewed, he reported his occupation as both bookkeeper and merchant. He recounted that Yee Kong had paid various amounts in rent to him for his laundry, starting out at $15 a month, then $25, and finally $100, the latter being paid during boom times in Port Townsend. The first laundry was in a one-story building that was about twenty feet wide by thirty feet long. According to Bartlett, that building burned down around 1886. Bartlett then leased the land to Yee Kong for $100 a month, and Yee Kong built a new laundry. He was there about five or six years until that building also burned down. The dates given were not always consistent from one person to another, but that did not seem to matter to the interviewer.

After considering the evidence, Henry A. Monroe decided that Ah Don and Ah Yun were born in the United States. They were admitted to the country on June 14, 1907, ten days after their arrival, as returning native-born Chinese persons.

In October 1913, (Ng) Ah Yun filed an "Application of Alleged American-Born Chinese for Preinvestigation of Status" to visit China. His photograph was taken, and his description was listed: age twenty-four; height five feet, six inches; occupation canneryman; mole on chin below lower lip; left ear pierced; "pit—right forehead." He said his correct name was Young, not Yun, and that he lived at the Wa Young Company store on 416 Eighth Avenue South in Seattle. He was probably living above the store. Ah Yun considered himself a general laborer. Although he worked in the cannery, he also worked as a cook and sometimes in laundries. Even though these Chinese people were born in the United States, they had to go through the whole investigation process every time they left or reentered the country.

(Ng) Ah Yun returned from China on the SS *Ixion* in April 1915. While in China, he married Wong She, and they had a son, Bak Sing. Ah Yun was asked about his brother Ah Don. He told the interviewer that Ah Don had married Lin She, who had natural feet. They had one son, age two. A Chinese man was usually asked if his wife or mother had bound or natural feet. This was probably one of many questions asked to see if his answer was consistent each time he left or entered the United States.

In May 1915, (Ng) Ah Yun received his certificate of identity. This certificate contained his photo, was made of sturdy paper, and, at four by nine inches in size, fit into a durable storage sleeve, making it much easier and safer for him to carry than court discharge papers. He was required to carry the certificate with him at all times.

In June 1917, Ah Yun registered for the military draft in Hartford, Connecticut. His registration lists him as "Wah Young," although he signed his name "Wu Ah Young," and he gave his date of birth as October 29,

1889, instead of August 23, 1889. The rest of the information agrees with previously stated facts about him. At that time, he was working as a waiter at a Cantonese restaurant and living at 257 Asylum Street. The physical description of him says that he had lost a toe.[123]

His draft registration card is not included in his case file, but the registration number is referred to in his file. Without knowing when and where Ah Yun registered for the draft, it would been almost impossible to find his draft registration card. The 1919 interrogation is the only document in his file that tells us that he was living in Connecticut when he registered. Because of the differences in the spelling of his name and in his date of birth, it would have been extremely difficult for a researcher to make the connection between Ah Yun in the file and his draft registration. There is no additional information given about his missing toe.

In November 1919, Ng Ah Yun again applied to leave the United States. He went through an interrogation process similar to his interview in 1913. New information revealed that his father, Yee Kong, had died in 1912 in Song Leung village; his mother's brother Si Chuck, who lived in Gow Ngok Won, had also died. Ng Ah Yun said he had married in 1913 and his son, Ng Bok Sen, was born in 1914. His marriage name was Ng See Tong. He stated that he was in poor health at that time.

Ah Yun was in New York City at the time he applied for his passport. James V. Storey, customs broker at Willim A. Brown and Company, was his identifying witness. Ah Yun paid a two-dollar application fee.[124]

In December 1919, Ng Ah Yun received his passport so he could go to Hong Kong to visit his mother and family. The passport had a current photo and gave his age and a physical description. Ng Ah Yun returned to the port of Seattle on the SS *Bay State* in May 1922. His life had changed. He had a second son, Ng Bok Chung (Teung), and his wife had died, possibly in childbirth. He had remarried, to a woman named Chin She, who also had natural feet. She remained in China.

Ng Ah Yun applied for his third trip back to China in August 1926. His third son, Bok Wong, was born a few months after his return to Seattle in 1922, and he was probably anxious to see him. Ng Ah Yun returned to the United States through Seattle in July 1927, on the SS *President McKinley*.

At age forty-five, Ng Ah Yun once again went to visit his family in China. He was still living in New York City and working as a laundryman. His oldest son, Ng Bok Sing, had been living in the United States as well, but he went back to China through Seattle in 1933. His other son by his first wife, Bok Chung, was living in Song Lung village in China. Ng Ah Yun's second wife had given birth to another son, Bok Teung, who was born in 1927 after his last visit. Bok Teung was almost seven years old before his father met him for the first time. Ng Ah Yun returned to Seattle on the SS *President Jackson* in November 1936. He now had six children, all sons, living in China. His son Ng Bok Sing was no longer living in the United States.

Not all Chinese Exclusion Act case files give this much information, although some give even more. This case file provided information for a four-generation genealogy chart and contained six photos of Ah Yun from 1907 to 1934, a photo of his brother in 1907, addresses where Ah Yun had lived over the years, information about his extended family in China, and a 1919 passport. More family information could be obtained from Charley Quong's case file and the files of his siblings who were born in the United States. The file refers to other documents: passenger lists, World War I draft registration information, and the file of the son who was living in the United States. His file has a wealth of genealogical information and gives clues to finding much more information on the extended family.[125]

Spokane

In the 1880s, Spokane had a Chinatown. It was centered on Front Avenue, later called Trent Avenue or Alley (now called Spokane Falls Boulevard). The Chinese had moved up from California and Oregon to help build the railroads and work in the mines. Many held support jobs in grocery stores, fish markets, restaurants, pool halls, and laundries. In the outskirts of Spokane, Chinese people worked as farmers and gardeners. Gradually, the Japanese moved into the area, and it became known as the international district. Most Asians moved away after World War II, and the area was razed for Spokane's 1974 World's Fair.[126]

Ah Kong

Oriental Café

Ah Kong was born in Seattle, moved with his parents to Port Townsend, lived for a short time in Port Discovery, and spent his childhood in China before returning to Spokane.[127] This follows the pattern of many Chinese people who moved to Washington State in the late 1800s to early 1900s:

moving from city to city seeking employment and sometimes making a trip to China.

In 1908, Eng Gin, a merchant, had been living in Port Townsend for forty-three years. He wanted to bring his American-born son, Ah Kong, over from China to live with him and help him in his business. He started the process of gathering the information needed to fulfill the requirements of the Chinese Exclusion Act.

Eng Gin swore in an affidavit that he and his wife, Yet Yue, had a son, Ah Kong, in March 1877, born at his place of business and their residence in Seattle. In 1885, they sent eight-year-old Ah Kong to live with his Chinese relatives in Her Ping village, in the district of Sun Ning, Canton province, China, to be educated. His mother died two years after he left. Ah Kong had completed his studies by 1907, and his father wanted him to join him in Port Townsend. A photo of Ah Kong was included on his father's affidavit.

In January 1908, Ah Kong applied for admission to the United States at the Port of Seattle as a returning native-born Chinese. He was questioned after he arrived. He gave his name as (Eng)Yee Quay and said he was thirty years old and born in Seattle. He stated that when he was about seven years old, he traveled to China from San Francisco with a distant cousin, Eng Fong Hock.

Ah Kong had one Chinese witness and the required two Caucasian witnesses who had known him for over one year. They were all required to swear to the facts stated in Ah Kong's affidavit. Witness Ah June's statement was seven pages long. He gave the following information: He was forty-four years old and a merchant, the manager of Zee Tai Company in Port Townsend. He came to the United States in 1876. He had lived in Port Townsend since his arrival except for nine years in Boise, Idaho (1894 to 1903). He made three trips to China during that time. On his third trip in 1904, he visited Ah Kong and his family and gave Ah Kong one hundred Mexican dollars from his father. He was required by the Chinese Exclusion Act to state whether he had visited the applicant's family in China and whether he had given the applicant any money.

Ah June had known Eng Gin since 1882, when Eng Kong was about five or six. They were living in Port Townsend at the Zee Tai's store on Water Street. Shortly after Ah June met the family, they moved to Port Discovery, where Eng Gin was employed as a foreman in a sawmill. They stayed there for about two years and then moved back to a house on Quincy Street in Port Townsend.

Aloysuis Harker was a Caucasian witness for Ah Kong. He was in the produce and commission business and had lived in Seattle since 1871, for over thirty years. He was well acquainted with many Chinese people and knew the prominent Chinese residents of Seattle: Chin Ching Hock, Chin Gee Hee, Lu Woo, Eng Gin, and many others. He was asked in detail about the addresses of several Chinese businesses. Some of the street names had changed since the Seattle fire of 1889, so he drew a map to show where the businesses were and to explain the new street names. Although Harker had not seen Ah Kong in many years, he thought the photo of Ah Kong on his identity card looked like the boy he had known twenty years ago.

C.E. Carleton also testified for Ah Kong. Carleton was a painter who came to Seattle in 1881. He got to know Eng Gin when he painted the store Eng managed, Quong Yuen Long Company, on Washington Street. He described Eng Gin's wife as short, thickset, fat, and good-looking, with big feet. Sometimes "big feet" meant feet that had never been bound. Ah Kong was a young boy when Carleton met him. To the best of Carleton's memory, the young man in the case file photo resembled the boy he met many years ago.

Ah Kong's Caucasian witnesses were considered credible even though they had not seen him since he was a young boy. Based on the accumulated evidence, Ah Kong was admitted at the Port of Seattle.

In April 1912, Ah Kong submitted his Form 430, "Pre-investigation of Status as an American-born Chinese." He wanted to make a trip to China. Ah Kong was a restaurant keeper at the Oriental Café at 412 Riverside Street in Spokane. He gave his name as Ah Quong (usually spelled Kong) of the Ng (Eng) family. His married name was Yee Quay. He was thirty-five years old and was born in Seattle. He married Louie See of Wong Mo Hin village, Sunning district, China. She had bound feet. Their two sons and one daughter, ages eight to twelve, were born in Sai On village, Sunning district, China. The immigration interviewers would usually ask specific questions, such as if the wife or mother had bound feet, how many steps to the well, or where the cemetery was located. They wanted to make sure

Ah Kong's Form 430 photo, 1912. *CEA files, Ah Kong, file RS 29169, RG 85, National Archives at Seattle.*

the applicant and the witnesses gave the same answer no matter how many years had passed since their last interview or trip. Ah Kong's application states that the officer in charge was prepared to approve his application. There is nothing in the file that shows that Ah Kong left the United States in 1912 or returned at a later date.[128]

Yee Gim

1905 Spokane Merchant

Riverfront Park is now located where Front Avenue/Street in Spokane's Chinatown was in the early 1900s.

When the Chinese Exclusion Act was renewed in 1892, Chinese people in the United States were required to register in the form of a certificate of residence or a certificate of identity. Yee Gim did not have his papers because he was in China at the time of registration.[129] It was possible that he might not be able to reenter the United States because of this. The interviewer asked to see Yee Gim's "chak chi," or certificate of residence or identity.

In 1905, Yee Gim, age forty-six, was a merchant, a partner at Yee Yuen Hong Kee Company at 516 Front Street in Spokane. He was the bookkeeper and in charge of buying and selling goods for his firm. He had been in the United States for twenty-seven years: nineteen years in Port Townsend at King Tai Company and eight years in Spokane. He was returning via Port Townsend from his third trip to China. His wife, three sons, and three daughters were in China. There were seven partners in his Spokane firm. They sold Chinese goods, nut oil, rice, sugar, and tobacco. Hock Geng was the manager. A witness for Yee Gim was W.D. Vincent, a cashier at the Old National Bank, who had known him for over eight years. He swore that Yee Gim had never worked anywhere else except as a merchant and that Yee Gim had a personal account and a business account with the bank.

Yee Gim's affidavit, 1905. *CEA case files, Yee Gim (Ah Tai), file RS 939, RG 85, National Archives at Seattle.*

Mose Oppenheiser, who was in the insurance business, swore that he had known Yee Gim for about four years, that Yee Gim paid bills for the firm, and that he had never seen Yee Gim behind the counter. If he had been working behind the counter, it would appear that he was a laborer. The Chinese Exclusion Act was passed to keep out laborers; therefore, it was important that Yee Gim's status as a merchant was clearly stated. James McGougan signed an affidavit swearing that Yee Gim was "neither a huckster, peddler, laundryman or laborer."

In spite of the fact that Yee Gim did not have his certificate of residence, the testimony of his witnesses was strong enough to allow him to be admitted by A.F. Richardson, Chinese inspector at Port Townsend.

The following is an excerpt of the Chinese Exclusion Act included in Yee Gim's file pertaining to "creditable witnesses" and "not performing any manual labor":

> *Provided as follows, to-wit: "When an application is made by a Chinaman for entrance into the United States upon the ground that he was formerly engaged in this country as a merchant, he shall establish by the testimony of two creditable witnesses other than Chinese, the fact that he conducted such business as herein before defined, for at least one year before his departure from the United States, and that during such year he was not engaged in the performance of any manual labor except such as was necessary in the conduct of his business as such merchant, and in default of such proof shall be refused landing.*[130]

Hui Hin

Minor Son of Merchant or Laborer

In 1936, Hui Cheung, Hui Hin's father, wanted his son to visit China for a few months before returning to Spokane. His status would be "son of a merchant." As the laws pertaining to Chinese immigration became stricter, it became harder for merchants to prove their status as such. Although in many cases, Hui Hin's father, Hui Cheung, would probably have been thought of as a merchant, a strict reading of the Chinese Exclusion Act put him in the manufacturing category and therefore made him a laborer. Hui Cheung's being a merchant would have most likely ensured his son's readmittance to the United States.

Hui Hin was originally admitted to the United States at the Port of Seattle on December 12, 1927, as a student and the minor son of Hui Cheung, a

UNITED STATES OF AMERICA)
:
STATE OF WASHINGTON,) ss.
:
COUNTY OF SPOKANE.)

HUI CHEUNG, being first duly sworn, deposes and says: that he is a Chinese resident of the City of Spokane and has been such resident for ten years last past, and is the person who makes application herein for permission to bring his son, Hui Hin, into the United States; that for more than ten years last past affiant has at all times been and now is a merchant doing business in the City of Spokane, County of Spokane, State of Washington, at No. 126½ North Wall Street, under the firm name and style of Wing Wo Medicine Company, dealers in general merchandise and drugs, and at all of said

Hue Cheung's affidavit with photo of Hui Hin, 1927. *CEA case files, Hui Hin, file 7031/636, RG 85, National Archives at Seattle.*

merchant at Wing Wo Chinese Medicine Company in Spokane.[131] Hui Hin was nine years old. He settled in, was called by the American name Bill Huie, and attended school at Hawthorne School, Washington School, and Lewis and Clark High School in Spokane.

Hui Cheung started the paperwork to get approval for the trip to China. Two white witnesses swore that Hui Cheung was a merchant. Hui Hin's application for predetermination of his status as the minor son of a merchant was disapproved, and his right of appeal to the local secretary of labor was disapproved by the district director of immigration and naturalization at Seattle on the grounds that Hui Cheung was not a merchant as defined by the law and regulations but was engaged in manufacturing. Hui Hin did have the right to appeal to the secretary of labor in Washington, D.C.

On the day immigrant inspector Herbert Nice stopped in to observe the Wing Wo Chinese Medicine Company, he found Hui Cheung washing medicine bottles in the sink. Cheung said it was because the regular clerk was at lunch. The inspector verified that it was lunchtime. Next, Inspector Nice found herbs cooking on the stove in the kitchen. Cheung said that was also the duty of the clerk who was at lunch. Nice asked Hui Cheung to explain the company's process of making the medicine. Cheung said the medicinal herbs were sent from China to San Francisco and then shipped to Spokane. One of the clerks cooked the herbs to make the medicines. Dr. Hui Yut Seng, the other partner in the company, saw patients and prescribed the medicine. The clerk prepared the medicine and gave it to the patient. Inspector Nice concluded that Hui Cheung was engaged in manual labor and that his application should be denied.

Hui Cheung swore in an affidavit that he was one of the partners and owners of the Wing Wo Chinese Medicine Company on Wall Street in Spokane. He had been a partner since 1918 and had not engaged in manual labor of any kind.

Hui Hin was interviewed twice in 1936 about his life in his village in China before he came to the United States when he was nine years old. There were six pages of questions in his file about his deceased grandparents, where they were buried, the number of houses in his village, where the front door of their house was located, the size of the doors, and what were they made of. He was asked to draw a diagram of his village and tell officials how many rooms were in his house; what color was the tile floor; whether there was a courtyard, any skylights, a rice mill, a rice pounder, any pictures, a balcony, or any clocks; where everyone slept; who lived in the houses in the village; who lived in the first house in the fourth row; how far away was the school; were there gardens or farms; what did they grow; was there a river or steam; were there any bridges; where was the market; how old was he when his father visited (he was seven or eight); and about three more pages of questions. He did not know many of the answers. His answers were compared to his 1928 interview. The immigration inspector also had some doubts that Hui Hin was Hui Cheung's son. Hui Hin could not remember his mother's name, the names of his grandparents and various neighbors, or details about his home and village. Hui Hin was nine when he entered the United States, and it was now eight years later. He may have been nervous about the interview. He knew how important it was to get everything correct. It was understandable that he would not remember his village and classmates in great detail.

Immigration officials reviewed Hui Cheung's file. Hui Cheung had made two trips to China as a laborer. The interviewer noted that one of his trips showed him being admitted to the United States in April 1918, which would have "render[ed] his paternity of the applicant possible."

When Hui Cheung returned from his 1927 trip to China, he and his witnesses were interrogated at length. Clearly, immigration officials were not confident about Hui Cheung's current status as a merchant or the fact that Hui Hin was his son. Cheung's answers were not always consistent from one trip to the next. In 1918, he stated that he had two sons and a daughter. In 1927, he said he never had a daughter or any children who died.

Hui Hin did not make his 1936 trip to China. His application was disapproved, and no appeal was filed. Perhaps Hui Cheung did not want his son visiting China when that country was suffering an invasion by Japan, or maybe they were exhausted from the interviewing process. Hui Hin's file contains over seventy pages of interviews.

Nelson Wah Chan King's Plans to Go to Canada

No one asked Nelson Wah Chan King why he wanted to go to Canada or what he was going to do while he was there.[132] It would be a quick excursion, but the paperwork involved was twenty-one pages, including a notarized copy of Nelson's 1911 Utah birth certificate. The interrogation and documentation process was the same whether a Chinese person was going to Canada, China, or anywhere else outside of the United States.

In July 1938, Nelson Wah Chan King, age twenty-seven, applied to the U.S. Department of Labor Immigration Service for a two-day visit Vancouver, British Columbia. His application created much paperwork and eventually was approved by Tom L. Wychoff of the Spokane immigration office but never used. Nelson canceled his trip to Canada because he was transferred from his job in Spokane to New York City. This image on the following page is a list of the documents that were in his file.

Nelson Wah Chan King was born on June 10, 1911, in Salt Lake City, Utah, the son of Harry N. King and Lily Dorothy Mowlan Shem. His parents were both born in San Francisco. His father owned the Kwong Nom Low Restaurant in Salt Lake City, Utah, before moving to Los Angeles to become a merchant. Although Nelson's grandparents were born in China, Nelson, his parents, and his brother had never been there. Nelson's only sibling, Paul Ming King, was born in 1918 in Salt Lake City and by 1938 was a student at the University of California in Los Angeles.

Nelson was working as a floor manager for the National Dollar Stores in Spokane, making $90 a month in 1938, a little over $2,000 in today's dollars. He had a grandmother, an uncle, and cousins living in San Francisco and

In the case of the application of NELSON WAH CHAN KING, alleged American citizen of the Chinese race for preinvestigation of status who desires to reenter the United States at Seattle after a temporary visit to Canada, there are enclosed herewith the following documents:

Form 430, original and triplicate.
Certificate of birth.
Two copies each of sworn statements of the applicant, the witnesses Walter G. King, Ruth King Chang, Anna C. Stevenson and report of Immigrant Inspector Gilbert F. Gower, appended thereto.
Two copies each of the sworn statements of the alleged parents of the applicant.
Two copies of letter from Board of Education at Los Angeles.
Two copies of a certificate of the Registrar of the University of Southern California.
Two copies of the report of the examining officer.

It is recommended that the application be approved.

TOM L. WYCKOFF
Acting District Director
Spokane District.

List of documents on file for Nelson Wah Chan King, 1938. *CEA case files, King Wash Chan Nelson, file 7030/11344, RG 85, National Archives at Seattle.*

more cousins in Salt Lake City: a reporter for the *Salt Lake City Tribune*, a U.S. Army sergeant associated with a Civilian Conservation Corps camp (the CCC was a program to provide jobs for young men during the Great Depression in the 1930s), a newspaper photographer, and a physician.[133]

Nelson Wah Chan King graduated with a Bachelor of Science degree in pharmacy from the University of Southern California in Los Angeles in 1933. Nelson's parents, Harry N. and Lily S. King, both gave detailed family information in sworn statements. His father was an art dealer with the Tom Gubbins Company. Anna C. Stevenson also testified on Nelson's behalf in 1938. She was a seventy-year-old widow who had lived in Salt Lake City for thirty-five years and had owned the apartments on Vissing Court where the King family lived. She stated that Nelson's mother was brought up in a Methodist home in California. Anna had last seen Nelson in 1936 on her birthday. He brought her a present from the King family.

On August 23, 1938, Nelson Wah Chan King notified the immigration office in Seattle that because of his transfer to New York City, he would not be making his trip to Canada. This is the last document in his file.

Although Nelson Wah Chan King and his parents were all born in the United States and never left, his grandparents were Chinese immigrants, and therefore, Nelson was subject to the Chinese Exclusion Act. On the positive side, there is a tremendous amount of family information in the file. The reference sheet in Nelson's file lists file numbers, names, and relationships for five of Nelson's cousins.

Goon Fon

Port Townsend and Spokane

Goon Fon was born in Hom Quon village, Sun Woi district, China, on January 14, 1883.[134] He came to the United States with his father, Goon Sam, arriving at the Port of San Francisco around 1894. From there they went to live in Port Townsend. His father returned to China in 1902 and died there.

On July 2, 1904, A.F. Learned, postmaster; William P. Wyckoff, customshouse official; and H.L. Tibbals of Port Townsend, Jefferson County, Washington, swore in an affidavit that they had been residents of Port Townsend for more than twenty years and were U.S. citizens. They testified that Goon Fon's father, Goon Sam, was a bona fide merchant for more than twelve years and a member of the Wing Sing Company on Washington Street near Quincey Street in Port Townsend. Before leaving for China in 1902, Goon Sam gave his son a $500 share in the business.

The Wing Sing Company closed around 1906, and Goon Fon lost his investment. After his father left, Goon Fon went to New York City and worked in the Mon Fong Restaurant on Pell Street and then in a laundry. He came back to Seattle and worked in a cannery in Alaska for Goon Dip and then moved to Spokane.

In 1924, Goon Fon applied for a return certificate as a laborer. His only proof of his status was the 1904 affidavit. He secured a $1,000 bond for the required proof of the necessary debt owed to a laborer to enable him to

State of Washington, SS July 2, 1904.
County of Jefferson,

A. F. Learned, Wm. P. Wyckoff, and H. L. Tibbals, all three of the city of Port Townsend, Washington, County of Jefferson, State of Washington, on honor deposes and says, each for himself and he not for the other; that they are citizens of the United States of America, over the age of 21 years, and a resident of the city of Port Townsend, Washington, that he has resided therein for more than twenty years that he is well and truly acquainted with Goon Sam, and know him to be a bonafide merchant and member of the mercantile firm of Wing Sing Company, Washington Street, Port Townsend, Washington, where he has been such merchant for more than twelve years last past, that during all of said time Goon Sam has not engaged in any laboring work of any kind, but is a merchant buying and selling goods at this fixed place of business; that we and each of us are well acquainted with Goon Fon, the son by blood of Goon Sam who is now 82 (22) years of age as reckoned by the United States counting, he having been born 1883; that Goon Fon has been a resident of Port Townsend, for more than 12 years last past and residing with his father at the Wing Sing Company in Port Townsend, Washington; that Goon Fon is in no way a laborer, staying in his fathers said store where he has now acquired an interest of five-hundred dollars; that during all of the twelve years last past we and each of us have been well and personally acquainted with said Goon Fon; that we make this certificate so that the Customs and Immigration Inspectors of the United States Treasury Departments may not hinder the free movements of Goon Fon; we hereby attach our initials to the photograph of Goon Fon attached to this certificate to better identify Goon Fon; we and each of us further certify that Goon Fon is not married and is a resident of Port Townsend who engages in no gambling or other unlawful enterprise; that Goon Fon has never been arrested to our personal knowledge or charged with any crime; should the said Goon Fon be apprehended at any time by the officials of the Department of Commerce and Labor or the Treasury Officials of the United States Government that we and each of us be immediately notified so that we and each of us may assist in the identification of said Goon Fon.

A. F. Learned
W. H. Wyckoff
H. L. Tibbals

Goon Fon's affidavit photo, 1904. *CEA case files, Goon Fon, file 7032/3500, RG 85, National Archives at Seattle.*

return to the United States. His application was approved. While he was in China, he married and had a son. When it was time for him to return to the United States in 1925, he obtained a "Nonquota Immigration Visa" with his photo from the American consular service in Hong Kong. He was admitted at the Port of Seattle, obtained his certificate of identity, and went to live in Troy, New York, where he was a dishwasher at a restaurant.

In 1937, Goon Fon was living at Noodles Café at 512 Main Street in Spokane, and he wanted to make another trip to China. According to his application for his "Return Certificate for Lawfully Domiciled Chinese Laborer," he had a $1,000 loan due from Hui Cheung, who was living at 126½ North Wall Street in Spokane. The interrogation was thorough. Goon Fon was asked about his early life in Port Townsend: the Chinese businesses and their exact locations, the business owners, and the whereabouts of other businesses. Hui Cheung was his witness; his and Goon Fon's answers agreed.

The Seattle immigration office wrote to San Francisco immigration to verify when Goon Sam and his son entered San Francisco in 1893. San Francisco could not find any record of Goon Sam in its indexes of ship manifests or other records. On July 9, 1937, the Seattle office disapproved Goon Fon's application for a laborer's return certificate, but he had the right to appeal. Based on the 1924 statement by the examining inspector, it was believed that since Goon Fon was eleven years old when he entered the United States in 1893 and living with his father, he was not required to obtain a certificate of residence. The immigration inspector reviewed Goon Fon's 1904 affidavit and believed the signatures of the affiants and the photo of Goon Fon were genuine. The appeal was sustained, and Goon Fon left for China. He returned in July 1938.

TACOMA

Ah Fook Family

Left Tacoma During Anti-Chinese Riots in 1885

Ah Fook and his family went back to China after the Chinese were run out of Tacoma in 1885. In 1907, their son (Wong) Ah One applied for admission to the United States as a native-born Chinese person.[135] He was the son of Ah Fook and Lem Shee and was born in Tacoma. He had gone back to China with his parents and younger brother, Ah Wah, when he was about four or five years old, around 1888 or 1889. They lived in Chung Chi village and then Hong Kong.

Ah Lung, a witness for Ah One, was a laundryman in Seattle and a good friend of Ah One's father. He came to the United States around 1867. He lived in Tacoma for about ten years and met Ah Fook there; they were friends but not related. At that time, the Chinese businesses in Tacoma were all located near the Hatch sawmill. Ah Lung remembered that Ah Fook left Tacoma after the anti-Chinese riots in November 1885 but a few months before the Chinese fire. The fire took place almost immediately after the expulsion, so Ah Lung may not have remembered all the details correctly. Ah Fook went to Portland and then came back to Tacoma briefly before moving to Seattle. He took his family to China around 1888 after he received reparations from the government for damage done to his property during the riot in Tacoma. It is not known how much Ah Fook received, but in October 1888, Congress authorized a payment of over $270,000 to China—not individual Chinese people—as compensation for the Tacoma expulsion and other West Coast anti-Chinese violence.[136]

F.W. Southworth, a physician for most of the Chinese in Tacoma, had lived there since around 1887 and testified that Ah One was born in Tacoma. In 1907, Dr. Southworth swore that he was well acquainted with Ah One's father, Ah Fook, a merchant. He believed that Ah One was his son.

S.J. Murphy was another witness for Ah One. He testified that he was a deputy sheriff and had been living in Tacoma for thirty-one years, since about 1876. He was a teamster in 1885: someone who drove a team of horses, usually for hauling freight. He remembered that Ah Fook was the proprietor of Quong Yen Company, which was located near the commercial dock in 1907 or near the old Hatch sawmill.

A.S. Fulton, the immigration inspector, asked Murphy what became of Ah Fook "after the so-called Chinese riots in Tacoma." Murphy said Ah Fook and his family left the city immediately and may have gone to Portland or come back briefly. Ah Fook's business was burned out during the Tacoma riots. Murphy said that Ah Fook was "a friend of his in those early days and frequently used to invite him into his store and pass him a cigar and talk about his business and his boy Ah One."

Immigration authorities considered the evidence and decided that Ah One was born in the United States and had been satisfactorily identified. Ah One was admitted to the United States in 1907. Ah One made several more trips to China. In 1911, Ah One testified that he owned a tideland lot in Tacoma. He bought the property from Mr. Harmon and had a contract at

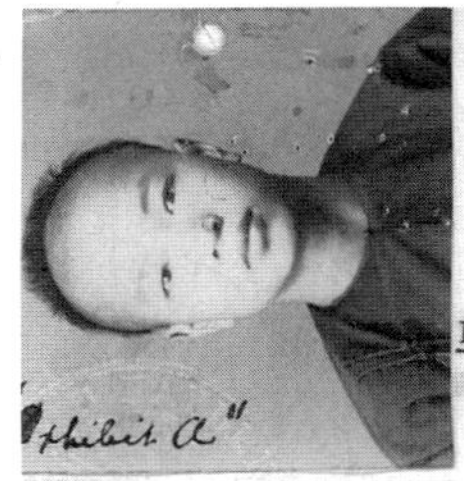

RE CITIZENSHIP OF AH ONE.

* * * * * *

State of Washington,)
County of Pierce.) SS:

F. W. Southworth, being first duly sworn deposes and says:

That he is a practicing physician in and a resident of the City of Tacoma, and has been such for the last seventeen or eighteen years.

That he was well acquainted about eighteen years ago with a Chinese Merchant living in Tacoma, by the name of Ah Fook, and that at that time Ah Fook spoke to him frequently about his boy and in affiants' presence would place his hand on the head of his child and speak to him as his son; that the boy was then four or five years old. Affiant is unable to recollect the circumstances in detail which caused him to then form the belief that the child was born in America and was the son of Ah Fook, but that from his acquaintance with Ah Fook and conversations with him, and the circumstances surrounding the relationship, he believes Ah Fook was the father of the child and that the child was born in America. Affiant further says that he does not now recollect having seen the childs' mother, but his belief was and still is that Ah Fook was married and that the child was the issue of that marriage. Affiant further states that he distinctly remembers the appearance of the child and he is of the belief that the attached photograph marked Exhibit "A", is a picture of the same child, although said picture represents a grown-up young Chinaman and he cannot swear positively from the picture, that it is a picture of the child he saw when four or five years old. Affiant further says, that he acted as physician for Ah Fook about ~~seven~~ nineteen teen or eighteen years ago.

F. W. Southworth

Subscribed and sworn to before me, this 15th day of February, 1907.

W. H. Hayden

Notary Public in and for the State of Washington, residing at Tacoma, Pierce County, in said State.

Affidavit of F.W. Southworth with photo of Ah Fook, 1907. *CEA case files, (Wong) Ah One, file 7030/13432, RG 85, National Archives at Seattle.*

the Pacific National Bank of Tacoma. He showed the interrogator some of his payment receipts. He paid $705 for the lot. He also had a $650 interest in the Shanghai Café, where he was the manager.

In 1912, Ah One testified that he was born near the old Flyer Dock in Tacoma at Second and Pacific Avenues. He learned to speak English at Sunday school. When asked if he paid his witnesses to testify for him, he denied it. He said they testified because they knew him, and they were acquainted with his father. Ah One had saved about $600 for this trip to China. He was going back to China to get married.

In 1917, Ah One testified that his marriage name was Chun Wong. He had a brother, Ah Wan. His parents, Ah Fook and Lum Shee, both died before 1917. He was married to Chin She, and they had one son, Ah Him, born in 1913. They were living in Jung Sai, Sun Ning, China. Although Ah One had entered the United States successfully on previous trips, this interrogator wanted more witnesses to prove that Ah One was born in the United States and that he was the same person who left for China when he was four or five years old. This is part of the testimony:

Q. "Do you mean then that you are relying simply on your two former admissions at this port to prove your right to readmission on your return from China?"
A. "Yes, and I have a certificate of identity as a native."
Q. "Have you ever voted in this county?"
A. "Yes, I voted for mayor in Seattle, I voted for Hi Gill when he last ran."

Hiram Gill was mayor of Seattle from 1911 to 1912. Ah One stated that he attended a mission school in Tacoma for a few months. After he returned from China when he was twenty-three, he worked as a cook for four or five years and then worked as a foreman at the Deep Sea Salmon Cannery Company in Alaska. Since September 1916, he had been the foreman of the Chinese workers at a company at Richmond Beach, north of Seattle.

In 1923, he was living at 1346 Broadway in Tacoma and was a merchant at the Kwong Fat Lung Company in Seattle. In 1928, Ah One (Wong Ah One) had a problem with his eyes and could not see to write. His final trip to China was in 1941. Although Ah One's earlier trips required several witnesses, affidavits, and testimony, his later reentries into the United States went smoothly.

Walla Walla

Gim Bing, Gardener

In October 1898, Gim Bing started the process with immigration services to make a trip back to China.[137] It would be his first trip to his home village since he arrived in San Francisco in 1882. Because he was a Chinese laborer, he needed to be registered; to have two witnesses, preferably Caucasian, to swear that they had known him for over a year; and to be owed at least $1,000 as an assurance that he and not someone who had assumed his identity would return to collect the money due him.

E.L. Brunton, U.S. postmaster, and George H. Barber swore in an affidavit that they were both over the age of twenty-one and citizens of the United States, that they had been well acquainted with Gim Bing for over three years, and that he was a gardener in Walla Walla. They knew that Gim Bing was owed $1,374.48 by Hoy Loy, a longtime Walla Walla resident.

Gim Bing's affidavit said that he had obtained a certificate of residence and had been a resident of Walla Walla for more than seven years. Hoy Loy owed him $1,374.48 for work performed before February 1, 1898, and Gim Bing would collect the amount due him on his return. Gim Bing's photo was attached to the affidavit. Hoy Loy also swore that he owed Gim Bing $1,374.48 for labor he had done for him. Gim Bing left in 1898. He returned and was admitted at Port Townsend in 1899.

In late September 1903, Gim Bing started the paperwork for his next trip to China. He filed an affidavit and attached his photo. He was listed as a Chinese laborer, registered, residing in the United States, and wishing to

Name, Gim Bing,
Present age, 43 years.
Local residence, Walla Walla, Washington.
Occupation, Gardener,
Height: 5 feet, 4 1/2 inches. Weight, 125 lbs.
Color of eyes, Dark, Complexion, Dark,
Physical marks or peculiarities for identification:
Scar on top head.

Gim Bing, Statement of Registered Chinese Laborer (with photo), 1908. *CEA case files, Gim Bing, file 9347/9-3, RG 85, National Archives at Seattle.*

leave for China and return within one year. He had debts of a total of $1,000 from Hoe Sing and Lee Chung, both from Walla Walla, who owed him $500 each. The Bureau of Immigration compared Gim Bing's application to the original information in its files and found that everything agreed. Chinese inspector R.B. Scott reported that Hoe Sing and Lee Chung were indebted to Gim Bing for $500 each.

On November 5, 1904, Gim Bing arrived at Port Townsend. He was questioned again to make sure he was the same person who left one year earlier. He testified that he had leased a garden for the last six or seven years from Mr. Hill in Walla Walla. He was paid $600 a year. Hoey Sing owed him $550 for wages from three or four years ago. Lee Shung also owed him $300 for wages and a loan of $200 from five years ago.

Gim Bing's next trip to China was in September 1908. He filed a "Statement of Registered Chinese Laborer About to Depart from the United States with the Intention of Returning Thereto." It included photos of Gim Bing, front and side view, showing his queue—hair on top of the scalp that was grown long and often braided, while the front portion of the head was shaved. Gim Bing stated that he was forty-three years old, from Walla Walla, a gardener, and was owed $550 from Young/Yung Foo and $480 from Moy Kee, both from Walla Walla.

A few weeks later, Gim Bing was interviewed again and said he was born in Num Mon village, Sun Ning district, Kwong Tung province, China. He had been living in the United States for twenty-six years, since 1882. He was asked if he knew anyone from his village in China who was living in Walla Walla. Jim Dune, a cook from his village, was living nearby in North Yakima. Yung Foo and Moy Kee were interviewed, and their statements agreed with Gim Bing's. Gim Bing returned on June 4, 1909, and was readmitted to the United States.

Gim Bing applied to visit China again in October 1912. He had made three trips to China, and every time he completed the same paperwork with updated information about who owed him money. Wong Chew, a gardener, owed him $1,000 for his interest in Mrs. Villa's place.

In January 1921, Gim Bing applied for a return certificate as a merchant of the Kwong Chung Sing Company in Walla Walla. He gave his marriage name as Gim Sing Wing, and he was fifty-five years old. He said he was born in Lung On village. In 1908, he said he was born in Num Mon village, but the interrogator did not question him on this discrepancy. He was questioned about his previous four trips to China. He and his wife, Pon Shee, had four children. He was now a partner and salesman with a $1,000 interest in his store. It sold about $13,000 to $14,000 in Chinese goods every year, mostly tea, tobacco, cigars, rice, and canned goods.

One of Gim Bing's white witnesses was William George Sargent, a citizen of Great Britain, who had filed his first papers for his citizenship after living in Walla Walla for about nine years. Sargent was asked if he had seen Gim Bing selling vegetables in the last year. He had not.

Gim Bing's other Caucasian witness was James E. Ward, who had lived in Walla Walla for over twenty-two years. Ward was a meter reader for the Power and Light Company. Lee Yun Nam was also a witness for Gim Bing. He arrived in the United States in 1915 at San Francisco as a student but soon came to Walla Walla and became a partner at Kwong Chung Sing Company with a $1,000 interest. The interrogator asked if Gim Bing had been working as a gardener or in a laundry in the last year. Lee said that Gim Bing had not worked as a laborer.

The acting commissioner approved Gim Bing's application but asked that it be noted that the application had not been properly filled out and that at one time in the past Gim Bing was found to be a laborer when he claimed to be a merchant.

In early September 1927, Gim Bing, now age sixty-two, filed for a return certificate for his sixth trip to China. Once again, he was applying as a laborer, so he needed to prove that $1,000 or more was owed to him. Wong Chew still owed him $1,000 from when Gim Bing sold him his interest in the McCool's Garden. Gim Bing sold him the garden, the implements, tools, a truck, wagons, horses, and crops for $2,000. Wong Chew's testimony agreed with Gim Bing's.

Gim Bing returned and was admitted at the Port of Seattle on August 13, 1928. It is the last document in his file. There is a photo of Gim Bing for each one of his six trips to China, from age forty-three to his final trip at age sixty-two. His file chronicles his life, mostly his business activities, for two decades.

Yakima and Other Communities

Chin Yick Thlew

Daughter of U.S. Citizen, Bellingham

Chin Yick Thlew was fifteen years old when she took the long journey from China without her family on the *Princess Marguerite*, arriving at the Port of

Seattle on January 11, 1941.[138] She would be living with her parents, Chin Yock Can and Dong Shee, at 1211 Cornwell Avenue in Bellingham. Her father swore in an affidavit that he was the son of Chin Tong, an American-born citizen. Therefore, he was considered a U.S. citizen and so were his children. Their older son was living in China with his grandparents. Their son Chin Yick Goon and daughter Fee Lon, who were born in China, and two younger children born in Washington State were living with them in Bellingham. Attached to Chin Yock Can's affidavit were photos of himself and his daughter Chin Yick Thlew.

Chin Yick Thlew's file contains a long letter she wrote to her parents in Chinese before she left China, along with an English translation. She wanted her parents to know that she missed them and that her education was extremely important to her. She told them several times that she was not ready to get married and she wanted to join them in the United States. She signed her letter, "I am, your little daughter."

Chin Yick Thlew was admitted despite the district director of Seattle immigration R.P. Bonham's claim that there was some unsatisfactory testimony. Several of the family members changed their interview answers so that everyone's story agreed. Their attorney, Henry A. Monroe, explained that the parents were afraid that if their testimony did not agree completely with their daughter's, she would be sent back to China. Chin Yick Thlew was held in detention for over five weeks. She misidentified a family member in one of the photographs presented during the interrogation. Her parents

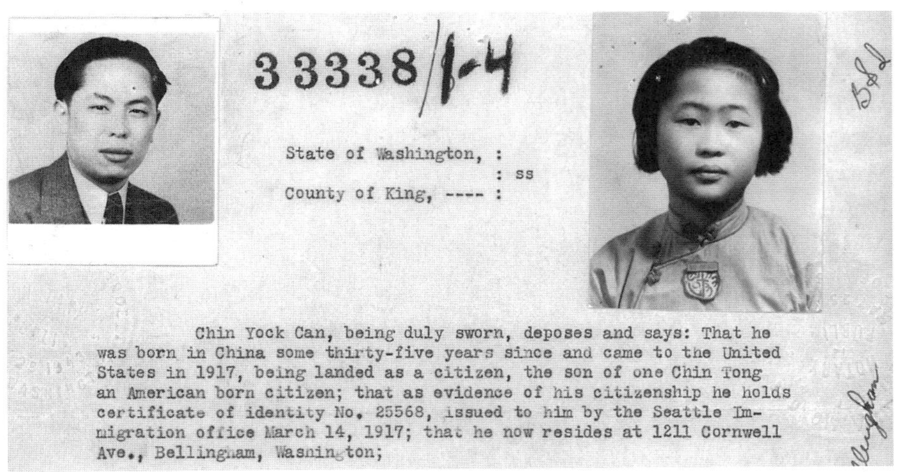

33338/1-4

State of Washington, :
: ss
County of King, ---- :

Chin Yock Can, being duly sworn, deposes and says: That he was born in China some thirty-five years since and came to the United States in 1917, being landed as a citizen, the son of one Chin Tong an American born citizen; that as evidence of his citizenship he holds certificate of identity No. 25568, issued to him by the Seattle Immigration office March 14, 1917; that he now resides at 1211 Cornwell Ave., Bellingham, Washington;

Affidavit photos of Chin Yock Can (*left*) and Chin Yick Thlew, 1940. *CEA case files, Chin Yick Thlew, file 7030/13465, RG 85, National Archives at Seattle.*

Group photo of Chin Yick Thlew's family, circa 1926. *CEA case files, Chin Yick Thlew, file 7030/13465, RG 85, National Archives at Seattle.*

were distraught and decided that whatever their daughter said, they would agree with it in their testimony. They presented several family group photos to their immigration interrogators, hoping this would appease them. Everyone involved was questioned over and over. Finally, Monroe, who had been working with Chinese immigrants for thirty-five years, stepped in. He got everyone to tell the truth and straightened out all the misunderstandings.[139] Above is one of several photos they submitted.

There were over thirty pages of interrogations of Chin Yick Thlew, her father, her mother, and her brother, Chin Yick Goon. Files for her father, her mother, her grandfather, two great-uncles, three uncles, a brother, and a sister were reviewed, and their file numbers are listed in Chin Yick Thlew's file. Chin Yick Thlew was admitted as a U.S. citizen, the daughter of a U.S. citizen, on February 19, 1941, thirty-nine days after her arrival.

Huie Taong

Ellensburg

Huie Taong arrived in the United States at the Port of San Francisco in 1872.[140] From there, he went to Ellensburg, where he worked as a cook and ran a laundry. According the 1892 Geary Act, which renewed the 1882 Chinese Exclusion Act, as a laborer he was required to obtain a certificate of residence. His certificate described him as a laundryman, thirty-seven years old, and 5 feet, 3¾ inches, with a scar in the center of his forehead. It was signed and dated May 3, 1894, by Henry Blackman, the collector

Ex Charles E. Metz. Oct 24/94

No. 127194

ORIGINAL.

No. 30,088 SEATTLE

UNITED STATES OF AMERICA

Certificate of Residence.

Issued to Chinese LABORER*, under the Provisions of the Act of May 5, 1892, as amended by the Act approved November 3, 1893.*

This is to Certify THAT Huie Taong, a Chinese LABORER, now residing at Ellensburg Wash has made application No. 10291 to me for a Certificate of Residence, under the provisions of the Act of Congress approved May 5, 1892, as amended by the Act approved November 3, 1893, and I certify that it appears from the affidavit of witness submitted with said application that said Huie Taong was within the limits of the United States at the time of the passage of said Act, and was then residing at Ellensburg Wash, and that he was at that time lawfully entitled to remain in the United States, and that the following is a descriptive list of said Chinese LABORER, viz:

NAME: Huie Taong AGE: 37 Years

LOCAL RESIDENCE: Ellensburg Wash

OCCUPATION: Laundryman HEIGHT: 5 feet 3¾ COLOR OF EYES: Dark

COMPLEXION: Dark PHYSICAL MARKS OR PECULIARITIES FOR IDENTIFICATION: Scar on center forehead

And as a further means of identification, I have affixed hereto a photographic likeness of said Huie Taong

GIVEN UNDER MY HAND AND SEAL this 3rd day of May, 1894, at Portland, State of Oregon.

[SEAL.]

Henry Blackman

Collector of Internal Revenue,

District of Oregon.

Huie Taong, Certificate of Residence No. 127194, 1894. *CEA case files, Huie Taong, file 31-223, RG 85, National Archives at Seattle.*

of internal revenue in Portland. Huie Taong's photograph was attached to the document.

In 1905, Huie Taong applied for a return certificate so he could go to China and legally return to the United States. He swore that he had property worth more than $1,000. It consisted of a one-fourth interest in the California Restaurant in Ellensburg, Kittitas County, Washington, valued at about $2,000. His interest was $500. Suey Gin owed him about $700, and Lew Fong owed him $500.

The information in affidavits by Suey Gin and Lew Fong agreed with the information provided by Huie Taong. Eight Ellensburg residents signed a statement certifying that they knew Huie Taong and believed his statement was true. They were O. Henman, an employee of the post office; L.R. Thomas, sheriff; M.E. Flynn, mayor; J.C. Hubbell, manager of a water company; P.H.W. Ross, banker; E.H. Snowden, banker; B.F. Reed, creamery proprietor; and Austin Mires, city attorney.

The Chinese inspector, A.F. Richardson, visited the California Restaurant several times and was impressed with the people and the place. The restaurant was leased to Wing Yick Tong Company from J.E. Farrell for fifty dollars a month. Because it was doing such good business, Richardson recommended that Huie Taong's return certificate be approved.

Huie Taong returned from his trip to China and was admitted at Port Townsend as a laborer on March 31, 1906. He was forty-six years old, weighed 154 pounds, and was stout, with a large brown mark inside his left forearm, a large scar about two inches long in the center of his forehead, and moles on his jaws and temple. Lew Fong and Suey Gin still owed him over $1,000. He did not have an official bank note, but he kept a small book where he recorded the amounts owed him.

On October 24, 1908, Huie Taong applied to go to China again as a laborer. He gave his baby name as Huie Doo Taong and his marriage name as Huie Tai Ball. He still had a $500 interest in the California Restaurant and debts due from Suey Gim and Lew Fong. He attached a current photo of himself to the application. The interrogator warned Huie Taong that he must return to the United States with one year and that during his absence his property must not be disposed of or his debts collected.

Huie Foy was a witness for this trip. He was forty-five years old, was born in China, had a certificate of residence, and owned the Loy Lee Laundry in Ellensburg. He came to the United States in 1882 and bought his laundry from Hop Lee in 1907. He had been back to China twice. He had known Huie Taong for about twenty years and owed him $500.

Sam Wah was also a witness for Huie Taong. He was in the hop business and a partner in the California Restaurant, which he described as the best business in town. Because for the two previous years the price of hops was so low, he borrowed $700 from Huie Taong.

Huie Taong's application was approved in late November 1908, and a few weeks later, he left for China. He returned to Ellensburg in November 1909. In his interview for admission, he said that while he was in China, he and his wife adopted a seven-year-old boy named Huie Hong Jack, whose birthplace in China was not known.

Huie Taong applied for another trip to China in November 1912. He based his application on having a $1,000 deposit at the Washington National Bank of Ellensburg. His return certificate was approved. Huie Taong returned to China in October 1913. His wife had died, and he remarried. His current wife and adopted son were in China.

In July 1920, Hui Taong—now using his complete name, Huie Doo Taong—was the chief owner and manager of a large restaurant and wanted to change his status from laborer to merchant so he could bring his family to the United States. He asked his lawyer, Mr. E.E. Wagen, to help him. Wagen told him that since he managed a large restaurant and did no manual labor, he should be considered a merchant under the Chinese Exclusion Act. The New York Café did between $40,000 and $50,000 in business per year.

Wagen checked with the Honorable Henry M. White, commissioner of immigration, who told the attorney the rules and documents needed:

> *The practice is for the father to have drawn up an affidavit by himself in which his present status is described and information given as to his right of domicile in the country. In this affidavit he should mention something about his family in China, especially the son he purposes having join him in this country. To this affidavit there should be attached a photograph of both the father and the son. The foregoing paper should be supplemented by the joint affidavit of two white persons who know the status of the father as a merchant during the last past year. These men should be prepared to state definitely what the particular daily work of the applicant has been during the year. The practice is to prepare the affidavit in duplicate, to send the duplicate to this office for filing and future use, and the original to the boy in China to be used by him in obtaining transportation to the country.*
>
> *Under the supreme court decision which permits the minor sons of exempts to come to this country, it is particularly stated that they are admitted to assume the exempt status of their resident parent. Under the*

> *law, therefore, such persons cannot become laborers while in the United States. It would be contrary to the law for Huie Doo Taong to bring his son to this country to place him in school for a short time, and then to have him work as a laborer, no matter if working for him in his own restaurant.*[141]

After hearing that he qualified as a merchant, Huie Doo Taong started the process of bringing his son, Huie Hong Jack, to the United States to continue his education. Attorney Wagen swore in an affidavit that he knew Huie personally, that Huie had done no manual labor in the last year, and that he had filed Huie's income tax return with an income of more than $90,000 for the café for the year 1919. Huie filed an affidavit with all the pertinent information and included photos of himself and his son. The paperwork was approved, and Huie sent it to the consulate in Hong Kong.

Huie Hong Jack arrived at the Port of Seattle on January 6, 1921. He completed the interrogation process but was found to have hookworm. He received hospital treatment, and when he was certified disease-free, he was admitted to the United States as the minor son of a domiciled Chinese merchant on January 28, 1921.

Huie Taong made his final trip to China in December 1923, and there is no indication from his file that he returned to the United States.

National Archives CEA volunteer Lily Eng indexed this file. Lily's grandfather worked at the New York Café as a waiter and became a partner in the early 1930s. Her father worked there when he first immigrated to the United States until he started his own restaurant in Yakima in 1951.

See Jan (Gong Yen/Ah Yen)

Port Ludlow

In 1903, Ah Gooey (married name Yee Fon) applied to Judge Kuhn, U.S. commissioner in Jefferson County, to obtain the proper documents for him, his wife, and their seven children to travel to China and be admitted to the United States on their return. The file is for his son See Jan, but it has information on the whole family.[142] They had a family group photograph taken at that time. The eyes of the infant in the photo are faint, but the irises of the eyes stand out; someone may have doctored them a little. In an extremely rare event, Judge J.A. Kuhn attached his own photograph to the court papers to be sure of the identification.

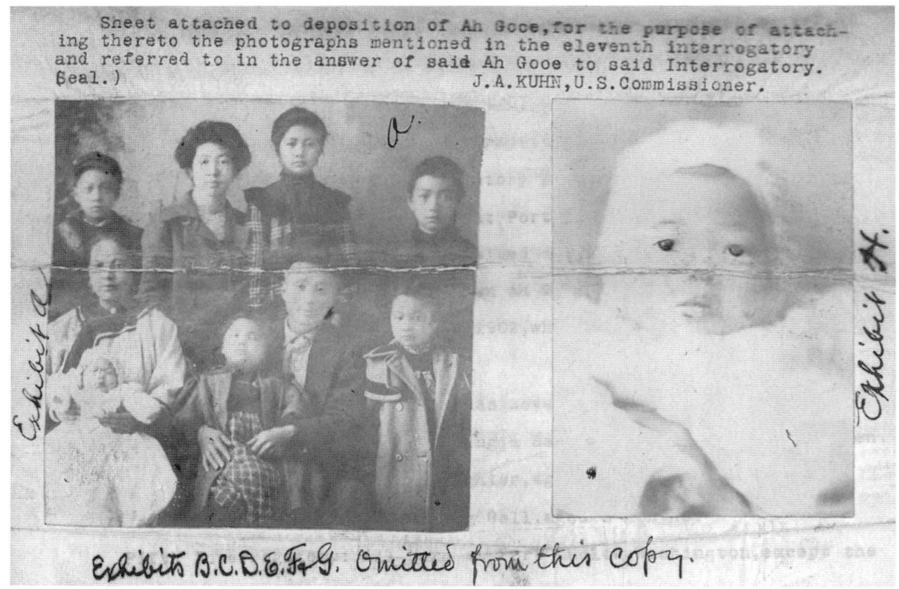

Ah Gooey's family portrait (*left*) and photo of unidentified infant, 1903. *CEA case files, See Jan, RS 1392, RG 85, National Archives at Seattle.*

Ah Gooey and Kee Toy's children were Ah Lun, Ah Yen, Ah Len, Suie Yen, Fung King, and Fung Sing, all born in Port Ludlow, and a daughter, Fung Gall, born in Irondale, Jefferson County. The three eldest children attended public school in Port Ludlow. They could read, write, and speak English. Ah Gooey was a steward at the Puget Mill Company's cookhouse in Port Ludlow, and he had a brother, Ah Loy, living nearby.

Several people, both Chinese and Caucasian, in the community knew of Ah Yen's birth in Port Ludlow. C.H. Hanford, judge of the U.S. District Court, District of Washington, issued a commission to Judge Kuhn to take their testimony and report back to him. H. Hallinger was their attorney. Louis Poole and Mrs. Charles Guptill were witnesses.

Louis Poole was fifty-seven years old in 1903 and had resided in Port Ludlow for thirty-eight years. He had known Ah Gooey since 1875. He testified that because he was in the mercantile business, he had seen Ah Gooey and his growing family almost daily as customers, especially the children, who bought candy at his store. Mrs. Charles (Elthea S.) Guptill, age sixty, a resident of Port Ludlow since 1873, was also a witness for Ah Gooey. She was present at the birth of his three oldest children. She saw all the children almost daily until they moved to Irondale in 1902.

Ah Yen was born in Port Ludlow on April 9, 1888. His father, Ah Gooey, died in China in 1905. In June 1907, Yen (or Ah Gong Yen, married name See Jan) returned to Port Townsend by himself and was admitted to the United States after the court declared that he was a returning native-born Chinese person, son of Ah Gooey and Kee Toy. See Jan's file has at least three different names for him. The name on his case file is See Jan. The file says his marriage name is Gong Yen, but sometimes it says it is See Jan. He was also known as Ah Yen. Ah can be used as the equivalent of "Mr." in English. This makes it difficult to research Chinese people.

Lock Yet

Olympia to Hoquiam, Laborer to Merchant

In 1901, Lock Yet, a Chinese laborer from Olympia, wanted to visit his family in China, stay for one year, and bring his son back to the United States.[143] He filled out all the necessary paperwork according to the 1882 Chinese Exclusion Act. He wanted to ensure that he would be able to return to the United States with his son. In an affidavit, Lock Yet stated that he had been a resident of Olympia since 1894. He applied for and received a certificate of residence. He described himself as thirty-eight years old, with shallow complexion, brown eyes, and very large, thick lips. The Chinese Exclusion Act required a laborer wanting to leave to be owed more than $1,000 that could be collected only on his return. Lock How, Lock Wing, and Lock Sing, all from Olympia, each owed Lock Yet more than $400, fulfilling the requirement. Lock Yet completed his affidavit by attaching a photo of himself.

P.J. O'Brien and W.W. Bellman were Lock Yet's witnesses. Their testimony agreed with Lock Yet's. A notary public also swore in an affidavit that he had personally known the witnesses for the past five years, they were reputable businessmen living in Olympia, and their statements were truthful. Lock Yet hoped to leave from Port Townsend. There are no documents in his file showing whether his paperwork was approved or whether he left for China and returned with his son.

In August 1913, Lock Yet started the process again. He left Olympia by train, destination Hoquiam, Grays Harbor, Washington. Somewhere on the trip, he lost his certificate of residence. He applied for a new one and attached a current photo of himself in American clothes. His attorney sent a

United States of America, *
State of Washington, * SS.
County of Thurston. *

I, Lock Yet, a laborer and native of China, now residing at Olympia, Thurston County, State of Washington, desiring to avail myself of the provisions of Article 2, of the Treaty with China, promulgated December 8- 1894, and of Sections 6 & 7, of the Act of Congress of September 13th, 1888, and to depart from the United States of America, for the purpose of visiting China, and to afterwards within one year return unto the said United States of America, do now state and declare upon oath as follows, to-wit:

My name is Lock Yet. That the attached photograph is a picture of myself. That I am a resident of Olympia, Thurston County, State of Washington, and have there resided since 1894, and prior thereto. That I am a recorded Chinese Laborer. That I was registered at Olympia on the 18th, day of January 1894, and received and now hold Certificate No., 43944, that I herewith present. That my tribal name is Lock and I am a native of Sen Nan of Providence of Canton China. That the following is a full description of myself to-wit: Name Lock Yet. Age 38 years. Height 5 feet 3½ inches. Local residence Olympia, Thurston County, Washington. Occupation Laundryman. Color of eyes Brown. Complexion Sallow. Weight ____ pounds. That I have on my person the following distinguishin mark and peculiarities for identification, Mouth very large, thick lips.

That I desire to depart from and return to the United States of America via, the Port of Port Townsend, State of Washington.

That I claim the right to so depart from and return to the United

Lock Yet's affidavit (page 1), 1901. *CEA case files, Lock Yet, file RS32260, RG 85, National Archives at Seattle.*

letter to the immigration office in Seattle explaining the situation. Lock Lad, owner of the Foo Lee Laundry in Hoquiam, testified that he had known Lock Yet for twenty-five years and had seen his original certificate in the past but neither of them could find it. Parker Ellis, immigrant inspector, wrote a letter in October 1913 regarding the lost certificate. Ellis mentioned Lock Yet's 1901 visit to China. Ellis DeBruler, immigration commissioner at Aberdeen, wrote back saying that Lock Yet was admitted through the Aberdeen port in late 1902 and had his certificate with him at the time. Lock Yet's certificate of residence was officially declared lost and a duplicate was issued to him.

In October 1914, Lock Yet applied for a return certificate. He swore in an affidavit that he was fifty years old and had been a resident of Hoquiam for the last year, after living in Olympia for twenty years. He had no relatives in the United States. His marriage name was Jung Lun. His wife and son, Lock Sang, age thirteen, were living in his native village. He stated that he made a trip to China in 1901 and returned in 1902. This trip is not recorded in his file. Liw Ting swore that he owed Lock Yet $1,000. Liw Ting, the owner of Nanking Noodle House in Hoquiam, was fifty-three years old and had known Lock Yet for fifteen years. Lock Yet's application was approved, and he left for Git Lung, Sunning district, China. When he returned in November 1915, he told immigration authorities that a new son, Lock Ying, was born shortly before he left China to return to the United States.

In 1918, Lock Yet wanted to change his status from laborer to merchant so he could bring his older son over from China to live with him. He now had a $300 interest in the Kung Yick Company and was working as a salesman. His salary was $25 a month. In October, Lock Yet applied for a "Preinvestigation of Status as a Merchant." Immigration inspector G.H. Mangels interviewed Lock Yet at the store, in his sickbed. He was very ill with influenza. He denied working as a laundryman, oyster fisherman, or canneryman, or doing any other kind of manual labor during the last twelve months. He stated that he had been to China twice. In 1901, he left from the Port of Seattle and returned in 1902 through Port Townsend. This is the 1901–02 trip mentioned earlier that is not documented in the file. His second trip was in 1913, when he went through Seattle and returned in 1914. His status was laborer both times.

According to the Chinese Exclusion Act, it was necessary for two white witnesses who were U.S. citizens to swear in an affidavit that the Chinese person wishing to be classified as a merchant had been a merchant during the last full year and had done no manual labor. White witnesses were considered more credible than Chinese witnesses.

Grant Talcott, a fifty-four-year-old jeweler who had lived in Olympia since 1873, was interviewed by immigration inspector G.H. Mangels. Talcott said he was acquainted with most of the Chinese people in Olympia, and he recognized a photo of Lock Yet. Even though he had known Lock Yet for twenty-five to thirty years, he didn't know his name. He called him "boy." Talcott had seen Lock Yet in the vicinity of the Kung Yick Company, so he assumed he had some business there. The inspector questioned whether Talcott knew much about Lock Yet. Talcott admitted that he signed the affidavit Tom O'Leary prepared without inspecting it closely.

Joseph Zamberlin was also a witness for Lock Yet. He swore that he was fifty years old and a fish dealer who had lived in Olympia for over thirty years. He had known Lock Yet for about one and a half years. He had seen him working in the store many times. George G. Mills testified that he had lived in Olympia for fifty-two years, since he was an infant. He was a hardware merchant. He was acquainted with all the Chinese people in Olympia. He rambled on about how he had probably seen Lock Yet in town or at the store.

Inspector Mangels interviewed Lock You, the manager of Kung Yick Company. Mangels noted that immigration officials had Lock You's family history from when they interviewed him when his son was admitted. There were ten members of his firm; four were active. The company sold Chinese general merchandise and had about $1,400 in inventory. Lock You also ran the Lew Café, where he employed six people, including two white women. Mangels reviewed the partnership and salary books.

Inspector Mangels wrote up a summary of the interviews for the Seattle immigration office. He said Mills and Talcott were both men of high standing and that they positively identified Lock Yet's photo. He did not place as much confidence in Zamberlin's testimony. After reading Mangles's reaction to Talcott's testimony, it was surprising that he said he had more confidence in Talcott's testimony than in Zamberlin's. Mangels was impressed with Lock Yet's knowledge of the store's goods and prices and the fact that, despite Lock Yet being very ill, he testified to obtain his certificate. He thought Lock Yet had become a merchant just so his son could enter the country and then would probably go back to being a laborer.

In spite of this, Lock Yet's status as a merchant was approved. There is no information in the file to show when or if Lock Yet left for China and returned to the United States.

Gee Moon Jew

Vashon Island Farmer

Gee Moon Jew was a poultry farmer on Vashon Island, Washington, in 1930.[144] He was born around 1897 in Hong How village, Sunning district, China. He came to the United States in 1909, at the age of fourteen, arriving in San Francisco. Although he was a laborer, he was considered a U.S. citizen because he was the son of a U.S.-born citizen. His father, Gee Fee Yee, was born in San Francisco. His mother was living in China. He had three brothers and one younger sister. His older brother, Gee Moon Ben, and his younger brother Gee Moon Taw were both living in California. Gee Moon

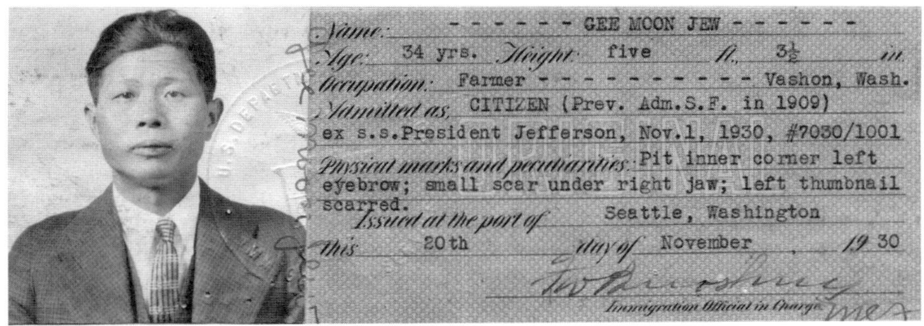

Name: ------ GEE MOON JEW ------
Age: 34 yrs. Height five ft. 3½ in.
Occupation: Farmer ---------- Vashon, Wash.
Admitted as: CITIZEN (Prev. Adm.S.F. in 1909)
ex s.s.President Jefferson, Nov.1, 1930, #7030/1001
Physical marks and peculiarities: Pit inner corner left eyebrow; small scar under right jaw; left thumbnail scarred.
Issued at the port of Seattle, Washington
this 20th day of November, 1930
Immigration Official in Charge.

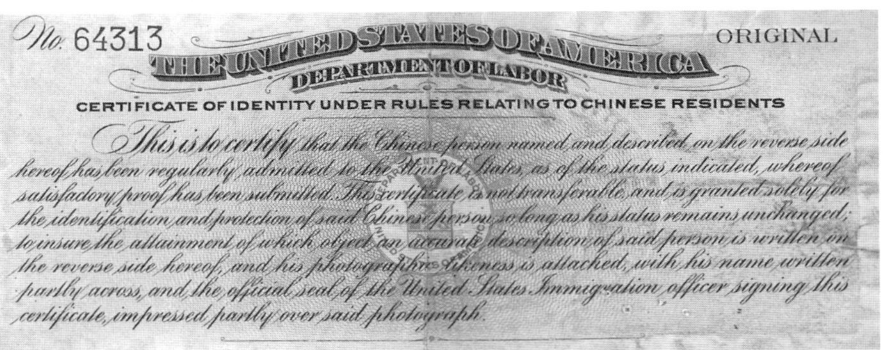

No. 64313 ORIGINAL

THE UNITED STATES OF AMERICA
DEPARTMENT OF LABOR

CERTIFICATE OF IDENTITY UNDER RULES RELATING TO CHINESE RESIDENTS

This is to certify that the Chinese person named and described on the reverse side hereof has been regularly admitted to the United States, as of the status indicated, whereof satisfactory proof has been submitted. This certificate is not transferable, and is granted solely for the identification and protection of said Chinese person so long as his status remains unchanged; to insure the attainment of which object an accurate description of said person is written on the reverse side hereof, and his photographic likeness is attached, with his name written partly across, and the official seal of the United States Immigration officer signing this certificate, impressed partly over said photograph.

Gee Moon Jew, certificate of identity (CI), 1930. CIs were made of sturdy, high-quality paper and housed in a protective sleeve. Chinese people were required to carry their CI with them at all times or risk prison or deportation. *CEA case files, Gee Moon Jew, file 7030/1001, RG 85, National Archives at Seattle.*

Jew married a Caucasian woman, Charlotte Irene Rogers, in Vancouver, Washington, in November 1918. After marrying, he took the name George W. Jenn. George and Charlotte had six children: Mary Frances, George Walton, Alice Martha, William Lawrence, Eugene (also called Wee Jee), and Helen Elizabeth Jenn, born between 1919 and 1927. Mary Frances was born in Seattle, and the other children were born in Vashon.

Gee Moon Jew gave his age as thirty-five in 1930 when he applied for a return certificate to allow him to make a trip to China, and he received his certificate of identity.

In 1909, certificates of identity were required for Chinese Americans and Chinese nationals entering any U.S. port. A certificate was issued to all exempt classes of Chinese people as proof of their legal admission into the United States. It replaced the certificate of residence that was required in 1892 by the Geary Act. The McCreary Amendment of 1893 made it necessary for a photograph of the owner to be attached to the document.[145]

Gee Moon Jew was taking his two eldest children, Mary Frances and George Walton, to China so they could attend a private Methodist school in Canton City. He was also going to visit his mother and other relatives and expected to be away for about three or four months. The children would probably stay for three years.

Immigration authorities also interviewed Gee Moon Jew's wife. Charlotte Irene Ward was twenty-eight years old and born in Larned, Kansas. She wanted her children to go to school in China, and they could not afford to take the whole family, so she was staying home with the younger children. Her mother was coming from California to stay with her. Because Mary Frances and George Walton were only eleven and nine years old, their interviews were brief. They both signed their own names and identified their parents. Their certified birth certificates were examined and returned to their parents.

Roy M. Porter, the immigrant inspector, examined Gee Moon Jew's 1909 San Francisco file, which included his father's 1909 affidavit. His father, Gee Fee Yee, had a Seattle file showing that he was admitted at Port Townsend in 1897. He also had a San Francisco file with a discharge statement showing that he was a native-born U.S. citizen. Porter approved the application for a return certificate for Gee Mon Jew and his children.

The reference sheet in the file includes the case numbers for the files of Gee Moon Jew's father; his brother, Gee Moon Ben; and Ben's two sons, Gee Quong Sam and Gee Suey Gin. Having the file numbers is helpful for anyone who would like to do further research on the Gee Moon Jew family by obtaining copies of their files from the National Archives.

Quan Foy

Chinese Interpreter, Sumas

Quan Foy arrived in the United States at the Port of San Francisco at age seventeen and was admitted as the son of a merchant.[146] He registered during the Chinese registration period at Sacramento in January 1894 and received a certificate of residence. He started working as a Chinese interpreter in the immigration service in 1901.

On September 12, 1908, Quan Foy, a Chinese interpreter at the Sumas, Washington immigration center, received a letter granting him 30 days' annual leave of absence and 220 days' leave without pay so he could visit

Quan Foy in his USIS interpreter uniform, 1908. *CEA case files, Quan Foy, file 7032/1398, RG 85, National Archives at Seattle.*

his former home in China. It also promised that after his return, he would resume his duties as Chinese interpreter. He left Sumas on October 27, 1908. Attached to the letter is a photograph of Quan Foy wearing his U.S. Immigration Service interpreter uniform. Quan Foy's uniform cap says "U.S.I.S. Interpreter."

An earlier letter in the file stated that Quan Foy would be entitled to bring his wife into the United States when he returned from China at the expiration of the leave provided his status remained the same. Quan Foy and his wife, Leung She, returned at the Port of Sumas on June 19, 1909.

In August 1931, Quay Foy and his wife applied for immigration return permits. They had not been to China since 1909, and Quay Foy's employment record was above reproach. The immigration inspectors had a hard time deciding if he should be classified as a traveler or a laborer. Their permits were denied, but they were granted laborers' return certificates. The leave was for seven months without pay.

The next item in Quan Foy's file is a 1941 letter from R.P. Bonham, district director of the Seattle Office, to Mr. Thomas D. Shoemaker of the Immigration and Naturalization Service in Washington, D.C. Bonham wrote that in 1933, Quan Foy lost his job because of reductions in staff. Bonham didn't know why Quan was let go instead of someone else. He thought he "should have put up a battle royal to keep him in the service."

After Quan Foy was let go, he went back to China, leaving his family in the United States. His children were all born in this country. He came back to San Francisco in 1939 as a visitor and in 1941 asked for an extension for his visit. Bonham wrote to Shoemaker,

> *He came to the United States when he was sixteen or seventeen and has spent nearly all his life here. He is now aged 74. I earnestly hope that this very deserving gentleman may be from time to time granted an extension of his visit, so that he may spend his declining years with his sons and daughters. As you know, there are very few people in whose behalf I would*

> *write this kind of a letter, and I do it without any mental reservations whatsoever.*[147]

In September 1944, Bonham wrote a "personal" letter to Shoemaker,

> *I am writing you in behalf of an old friend of mine, named Quan Foy. I first came to know Quan Foy personally in 1914, when I was sent by the Department to Seattle to investigate the graft and rottenness then existing in the Chinese Division at this port. You may remember then I established the fact that Frank Tape had extorted in five years approximated fifty thousand dollars from the Chinese that passed through this port. Unquestionably others were involved in these dishonest practices. There were two murders over the case.*
>
> *In this investigation the record of Quan Foy stood out, to quote Robe Carl White, Assistant Secretary of Labor under three presidents, "like a new dollar in a mudhole." My investigation then was a thorough one. As a result of it, I acquired a high respect for Quan Foy. Never in all the time that he was in the Service was there even a whisper that would adversely involve his integrity.*

An August 1944 letter from Bonham further praised Quan Foy for his honesty. It also mentioned that Judge Clay Allen of the superior court held Quan Foy in high esteem. Bonham wrote to the San Francisco immigration office again in December 1945 saying he recommended extending Quan Foy's visit for another year. Quan Foy's final extension was granted to February 1947. He would be required to leave the United States if his next extension was not granted. The last document in his file is a letter stating Quan Foy died in Seattle on January 3, 1947.

> *Quan Foy was Chinese Interpreter at Seattle for very many years and was one of the most respected employees of this Service on this coast, of acknowledged and exceptional integrity.*[148]

Even though the people he worked with directly thought very highly of Quan Foy, he had been an interpreter for immigration services for thirty-two years, and the Chinese Exclusion Act was repealed in 1943, he had to apply for an extension every year to stay in the United States.

CHAPTER 8

THE 1909 ALASKA-YUKON-PACIFIC EXPOSITION

Seattle hosted the Alaska-Yukon-Pacific Exposition (A-Y-P Expo) from June to mid-October 1909 on grounds designed by Olmsted Brothers on the University of Washington campus. More than three million visitors attended during the fair's 138-day run. The founders of the expo wanted to promote Alaska, Seattle, and the Pacific Northwest and thought the expo was a good way show off the area's resources.[149]

The Chinese population in Washington had been decimated by the 1882 Chinese Exclusion Act and the 1885–86 expulsion of the Chinese from Seattle, Tacoma, and other areas. The Chinese were slowly returning. There were about four hundred Chinese people living in Seattle in 1900, and that number had doubled by 1910. The leading Chinese merchants in Seattle thought the A-Y-P Expo was an opportunity to gain acceptance

Opposite: Yip Sang (*center*) and family, 1909, Canadian Certification of Identity 10. *CEA case files, Yip Sang, file RS 2396, RG 85, National Archives at Seattle.*

Left: Kee Sing's Canadian naturalization photo, 1909. *CEA case files, Kee Sing, file RS 2319, RG 85, National Archives at Seattle.*

in the community and could lead to the federal government easing immigration laws.

Because anti-Chinese feelings ran high in the United States in the early 1900s, the Chinese government did not sponsor an exhibit at the expo. Well-known and respected Seattle Chinese community leaders—Goon Dip, Ah King, and several others—were instrumental in organizing China Day and its parade, the Chinese Village, entertainment, and many of the Chinese activities for the exposition. They raised money for the exhibits and the Chinese pavilion. Chinese visitors came from Vancouver, Victoria, Tacoma, Portland, Everett, Bellingham, and other cities for the expo.[150]

Visiting from Vancouver, British Columbia, was Yip Sang (Yip Chun Tien), head of the Chinese Nationalist League. He brought his family to the A-Y-P. He originally entered the United States at San Francisco in 1864 and worked for seventeen years as a dishwasher, cook, and cigar maker before settling in Vancouver's Chinatown and becoming a leading businessman.[151]

Kee Sing, a silk merchant from Vancouver, British Columbia, also visited the A-Y-P Expo in Seattle.[152]

Goon Dip does not have a Chinese Exclusion Act file because he arrived in the United States and established his business interests well before the act went into effect.

Ah King, 1909. *CEA case files, Ah King, file RS 2164, RG 85, National Archives at Seattle.*

Ah King, although an early settler of Seattle, does have a file.[153] When he traveled to China in 1908 to bring concession workers, actors, and acrobats, about twenty workers in total, to Seattle to work at the expo, he had to go through the same process and interrogations as any other Chinese person departing the United States with plans to return. He paid the passage of the laborers, put up the money guarantees, obtained the necessary bonds, and paid each of the workers a monthly salary. They earned about fifty dollars a month in Chinese currency. There were no written contracts, only oral agreements. The workers were required to return to China within thirty days after the closing of the fair.

The Chinese Village was located near the busiest area of the fair. It included a bazaar and three buildings: a Chinese temple brought intact from China, a restaurant, and a tearoom. The Chinese exhibits and curios were displayed on the village grounds behind the main building.[154]

The stars of the Chinese Village were theater performers, who caused a sensation with their juggling, magic, and feats of great strength. The featured performances of the Tin Yung Qui Troupe changed daily. One of the magicians was a woman, which was not unusual for a Chinese troupe in 1909 but would have been very unusual for an American troupe. The Tin Yung Qui Troupe was popular with fairgoers throughout the exposition. It was one of the few imported attractions to achieve widespread fame.[155]

Chee Yu San, one of the most prominent performers of the Tin Yung Qui Troupe, was held over in Vancouver because he had trachoma, a serious bacterial infection of the eye. His wife elected to stay with him. Because he was one of the stars of the troupe, this was a crisis. Chee Yu San and his wife were finally admitted on June 24, more than three weeks after the other Chinese workers had been admitted into the country. According to Henry A. Monroe, Chinese inspector in Seattle, Chee Yu San was allowed into the country:

under bond conditioned upon your remaining in the Chinese Village and remaining apart from the public or from other Chinese, and that you must comply with certain requirements laid down by our physician here as to sleeping in apartments to be used exclusively by yourself and wife, disinfection of all table linen, etc., weekly change of all linen, bathing hands and face with sublimate solution, and at the conclusion of your engagement at the exposition all effects to be thoroughly disinfected by steam or formaldehyde.[156]

J.E. Chilberg, president of the A-Y-P, wired the authorities in Washington, D.C., asking for immediate action in releasing Chee Yu San. This negotiation highlighted the problems Chinese people sometimes had trying to get into the United States. Chilberg obtained affidavits of physicians in Vancouver, British Columbia, saying there was nothing wrong with Chee Yu San physically or mentally and suggested that Chee was the victim of overzealous inspectors. Ah King made a special trip to Vancouver, British Columbia, to resolve the issue. After ten long days, Chee Yu San (Shin Yu) finally arrived at the fairgrounds on June 20.[157]

52314-1 Box 136

No. 1

Department of Commerce and Labor
IMMIGRATION SERVICE

DUPLICATE

CHINESE EMPLOYEE'S RECORD OF ADMISSION
ALASKA-YUKON-PACIFIC EXPOSITION, 1909

This is to Certify, That Lim Sing *a native of* China, *who is duly accredited as an Employee of* Ah King Company *of* Seattle, Wash., *an Exhibitor (or concessionaire) at the*

ALASKA-YUKON-PACIFIC EXPOSITION,

has been permitted to enter the United States as such employee in pursuance of an Act of Congress approved April 29, 1902.

(NAME.) John H. Sargent

(TITLE.) Inspector in Charge.

PORT OF Seattle, Wash.

DATE May 21st, 1909.

[SEAL.]

(Affix photograph on reverse side.)

11—2012 (DUPLICATE TO BE FORWARDED TO COMMISSIONER-GENERAL OF IMMIGRATION.)

Lim Sing, Chinese Employee's Record of Admission, 1909. *Correspondence file Chinese at the Alaska-Pacific Yukon Exposition, folder 52,314-1, RG 94, National Archives at Washington, D.C.*

Although the Chinese did not make a profit at A-Y-P Expo, they gained status and respect in the community. A relatively small community of Chinese pulled off an amazing feat during the expo; the Chinese Village was popular, and the Tin Yung Qui Troupe was an enormous hit. The Chinese parade and dragon were loved by huge crowds of people. Many Chinese dignitaries from far and wide visited the fair. Curious people tried their food and examined their curios. It would be another thirty-five years before the Chinese Exclusion Act would finally be overturned, but the white community was now more aware of the unfairness of immigration restrictions on the Chinese. The Chinese were respected by white community leaders like J.E. Chilberg, A-Y-P president. The success of the Chinese at the expo was an enriching experience, something to be proud of and a legacy to pass on to future generations.[158]

CHAPTER 9
OTHERS

World War II Veterans

Wong F. Pershing

Seaman on the USS Explorer

In 1917, Wong F. Pershing's father, Wong Chun Wah, applied to immigration for pre-investigation as a merchant intending to visit China. The examining inspector believed that the place Wong was working, W.J. London Company, was involved in gambling. The inspector did not believe Wong qualified as a merchant according to the exclusion law. Wong abandoned his connection with this employer and became a merchant for the Quan Yuen Chong Company, a legitimate and bona fide mercantile concern. His status as a merchant was reinstated.

Wong Chun Wah again applied to take his wife and three sons, Raymond Wong, Pershing Wong, and Chester Wong, to China with him in 1921. Wong showed immigration inspector B.A. Hunter the Seattle birth certificates of his children. They were issued return certificates but did not use them. The family did not travel to China, and several more children were born in Seattle.

Pershing F. Wong applied to visit Vancouver, British Columbia, by bus via Blaine, Washington, in October 1941.[159] He had three days of leave from the Merchant Marine. He was a seaman on the USS *Explorer*, a Coast and Geodetic Survey ship. He gave the following information in his interview:

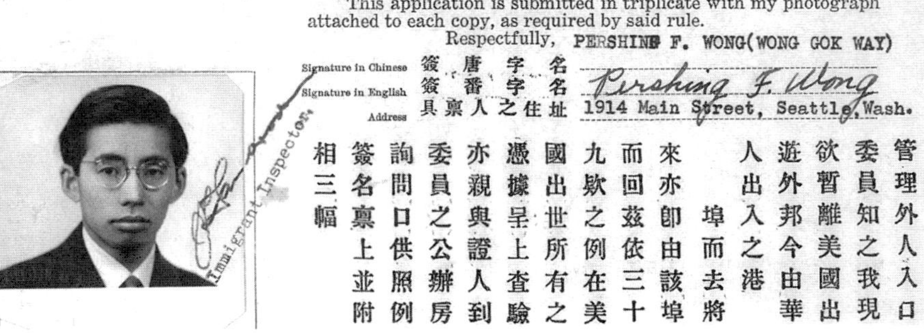
This application is submitted in triplicate with my photograph attached to each copy, as required by said rule.

Respectfully, PERSHING F. WONG(WONG GOK WAY)

Signature in Chinese 簽唐字名

Signature in English 簽番字名 Pershing F. Wong

Address 具稟人之住址 1914 Main Street, Seattle, Wash.

管理外人入口委員知之我現欲暫離美國出遊外邦今由華人出入之港埠而去將來亦即由該埠而回茲依三十九款之例在美國出世所有之憑據呈上查驗亦親與證人到委員之公辦房詢問口供照例簽名稟上並附相三幅

Wong F. Pershing's Form 430 photo, 1942. *CEA case files, Wong F. Pershing, file 7030/13628, RG 85, National Archives at Seattle.*

His Chinese name was Wong Gok Way. He was born on October 27, 1919, in Seattle, the son of Wong Chun Wah (Wah Fat) and Ann Quan Gee. His mother died in Virginia Mason Hospital in Seattle in 1930. Pershing had five brothers and one sister. He had attended Garfield High School before joining the marines. Ensign John Guthrie of the *Explorer* verified that Pershing F. Wong was the correct name for W.F. Pershing Wah, the name he used on his original application.

The reference sheet in Pershing Wong's file lists the file numbers for his father, mother, two brothers, and sister.

A newspaper article from the February 6, 1945 edition of the *Seattle Daily Times* states that Pershing Wong was the only Chinese deck officer sailing out of Seattle in the American Merchant Marine; he was a member of the Masters, Mates and Pilots' Association; and he joined the Merchant Marine in 1941. Wong had just spent 110 days in the Pacific combat arena. It was a turbulent time; besides the heavy World War II bombing, three navy craft were sunk by a typhoon.[160]

According to Pershing F. "Perky" Wong's obituary in the July 14, 1999 *Oregonian* newspaper, he retired as a captain in 1985.[161]

Harry Chinn

World War II Veteran and Prisoner of War in Germany

Harry Chinn, a World War II veteran, died in 1951 from complications of frostbite of both feet and pulmonary tuberculosis, which he developed when he was a prisoner of war in Germany.[162]

Harry Chinn (Chin King Ging), son of Shaw Chinn and Moy Shee, was born in Seattle on August 25, 1922.[163] He attended Bailey Gatzert School and Broadway High School in Seattle. Harry, his parents, and his four brothers and sister visited China in August 1937 and returned in November 1938. While in China, in January 1938, Harry married Lee Til Wui (Lee Tie Win) according to the old Chinese custom in May Hong Tune, How San province. Harry Chinn obtained his certificate of identity in 1942, a few days after he enlisted in the U.S. Army.

After the Chinese Exclusion Act was repealed in 1943, the quota for Chinese immigrants was 105. The War Bride Act of 1945 was passed to enable the admission of alien spouses and dependent alien children of U.S. citizens serving in the armed forces if they were admissible as non-quota immigrants. In 1946, the act was amended to admit Chinese wives of U.S. citizens on a non-quota basis.[164] About five thousand Chinese "war brides" came to the United States from 1945 to 1950.[165] One of them was Harry's wife.

Mrs. Harry Chinn arrived at the Port of San Francisco on March 6, 1947, as the wife of a U.S. citizen and a war veteran. She was admitted twenty-two days later. Harry Chinn was a patient in the U.S. Marine Hospital in Seattle when she arrived, so his father and brother went to San Francisco to meet her. They asked immigration services to expedite their investigation of Mrs. Chinn. They had been waiting three weeks for her release, and it was very expensive for them to stay in San Francisco. Paul D. Mossman, medical director of the U.S. Public Health Service in Seattle, verified that Harry Chinn, a patient in the hospital since January 2, 1947, was bedridden and unable to leave the hospital. His prognosis was guarded, and it was expected

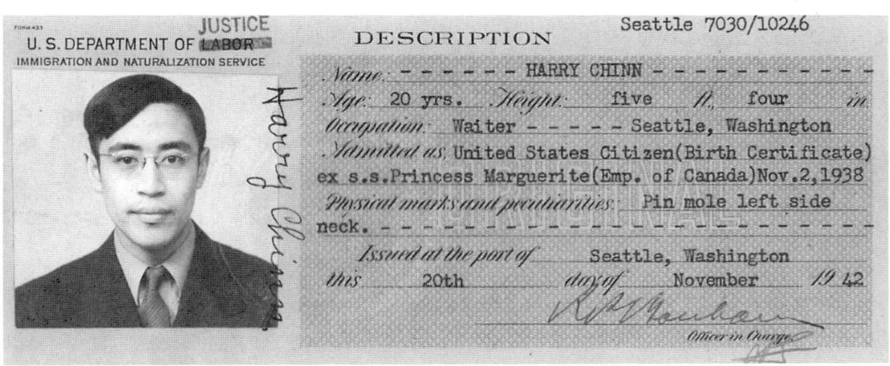
U. S. DEPARTMENT OF JUSTICE
IMMIGRATION AND NATURALIZATION SERVICE

Seattle 7030/10246

DESCRIPTION

Name: HARRY CHINN
Age: 20 yrs. Height: five ft. four in.
Occupation: Waiter - Seattle, Washington
Admitted as: United States Citizen(Birth Certificate) ex s.s.Princess Marguerite(Emp. of Canada)Nov.2,1938
Physical marks and peculiarities: Pin mole left side neck.
Issued at the port of Seattle, Washington
this 20th day of November 1942
Officer in Charge

Harry Chinn, Certificate of Identity No. 84891, 1942. *CEA case files, Harry Chinn, file 7030/10246, RG 85, National Archives at Seattle.*

that he would be in the hospital for some time. The reference sheet in the file contains the names and file number for Harry Chinn's grandfather, parents, four brothers, one sister, and his wife.

There is no information in the file about Harry Chinn's length of time in the hospital, but he died in July 1951. According to his obituary, Harry Chinn died in Vancouver, Washington, and was buried under the direction of the Cathay Post No. 186 in Washelli Cemetery in Seattle. He was survived by his wife, Lee Til Wui; his parents, Mr. and Mrs. Shew Hum Chinn; six brothers, Howard, Haley, Hopkin, Hansing, Horace, and Henning Chinn; and two sisters, Hannah Chinn, in Seattle, and Toy Su Chinn, in China. Two of his brothers were serving in the U.S. Army: Horace Chinn at Fort Lewis in Washington and Henning Chinn at Fort Hood in Texas.[166]

Paper Sons and Daughters

Immigration laws were very restrictive for the Chinese, and they tried to find ways around them. The more rigid the immigration officials became, the more enterprising the Chinese became. When a Chinese person who was exempt from exclusion, such as a merchant or someone born in the United States, returned from a trip to China, they often reported the birth of a child or a pregnancy. This created a "slot" for a child to come to the United States at a future date. Someone might purchase this slot for their child. When the child came to the United States, he came with the identity of the family who bought the slot. He would need to know his new family's history and have a thorough understanding of the extended family and their village. If he made it through the interrogation process, he would have to spend the rest of his life with this new identity. This was extremely stressful for these people and their adopted families.[167]

After the Chinese Confession Program and the Immigration Act of 1965, families who had so-called paper sons usually did not want to admit to it. They did not trust the government's forgiveness program.

Because of privacy issues, no Chinese Exclusion Act case files for paper sons are included.

NOTES

Introduction

1. Nicola, "Chinese Exclusion Act Records," 25–27.
2. Washington State University, "Chinese Americans."
3. Office of the Historian, "Chinese Immigration."
4. Chang, *Ghosts of Gold Mountain*, 146.
5. NARA, *Teaching with Documents*, 82–84.
6. U.S. Census Bureau, "Table VI."
7. *Compendium of the Tenth Census*.
8. Chin and Chin, *Chinese in Washington State*, 127, 128.
9. Chin and Chin, *Chinese in Washington State*, 127, 129.
10. Page Act (Sect. 141, 18 Stat. 477, March 3, 1875).
11. Peffer, "Forbidden Families," 32–38.
12. Klingle, "Timeline: Asian."
13. Chin and Chin, *Chinese in Washington State*, 128, 129.
14. Densho Encyclopedia, "Alien Land Laws."
15. Crowley, "Anti-Chinese Activism—Seattle."
16. Tacoma Chinese Reconciliation Park, "Expulsion: The Tacoma Method."
17. Chin and Chin, *Chinese in Washington State*, 46.
18. Chin and Chin, *Chinese in Washington State*, 45.
19. Chin and Chin, *Chinese in Washington State*, 48.
20. Chin and Chin, *Chinese in Washington State*, 49.

Chapter 1

21. "Act to Execute Certain Treaty Stipulations Relating to Chinese."
22. Lowell, reference information paper 99, 1.
23. Scott Act of 1888.
24. Geary Act; McCreary Amendment.
25. Immigration History, "Immigration Act of 1924."
26. Magnuson Act.
27. War Brides Act.
28. War Brides Act Amendment.
29. Immigration History, "Chinese Confession Program."
30. "*An Act to Amend the Immigration and Nationality Act, and for Other Purposes,*" *Public Law 89–236*, 89th Cong., 1st sess. (October 3, 1965).

Chapter 2

31. Woo Back (Bak) Sue(y), file 7030/10966, RG 85, National Archives at Seattle, CEA case files.
32. Quan Robert, file 7030/11495, RG 85, National Archives at Seattle, CEA case files.
33. Low Yow Edwin, file 7030/11920, RG 85, National Archives at Seattle, CEA case files.
34. U.S. Supreme Court, *Rassmussen v. United States*.
35. Emery, "Willard Jue"; Frederick Case, "Herbal Healers, Now."
36. Rose Leong, file 7030/13652, RG 85, National Archives at Seattle, CEA case files.
37. "Approval of Application for Rose Leong," CEA case files, file 7030/13652, RG 85, National Archives at Seattle, CEA case files.
38. Lee Share Yung, file 1010/18-8, RG 85, National Archives at Seattle, CEA case files.
39. "Lee Share Yung Affidavit," 1900, file 1010/16-8, RG 85, National Archives at Seattle, CEA case files.
40. Lee Gok Suey, CEA case file, file 7030/10684, RG 85, National Archives at Seattle, CEA case files.
41. "Lee Gok Suey and Lee Ling Hung Interviews," 1937, file 7030/10684, RG 85, National Archives at Seattle, CEA case files.
42. Beekman, "San Francisco Mayor Ed Lee."
43. "Photo Included on Woo Yen Tong's Affidavit," 1939, Woo Quin Lock case file, file 7030/12841, RG 85, National Archives at Seattle, CEA case files.

44. Wikipedia converted the 1939 Hong Kong dollars to pounds sterling; Measuringworth.com converted the pounds sterling to U.S. dollars.

Chapter 3

45. Ah Soon, "Affidavit," 1899, Ah Soon CEA case files, file RS 30384 RG 85, National Archives at Seattle, CEA case files.
46. FamilySearch.org, "Asian-to-Gregorian Calendar Converter"; Wikipedia, "Guangxu Emperor."
47. Ah Soon, "Mining Investment," CEA case files, file RS 30384, RG 85, National Archives at Seattle, CEA case files.
48. Ah Soon, "Stewart Note,"1913, file RS 30384, RG 85, National Archives at Seattle, CEA case files.
49. Ah Soon, "Overtime Certificate 25/1915," 1915, file RS 30384 RG 85, National Archives at Seattle, CEA case files.

Chapter 4

50. "Immigration, Exclusion of Chinese," 5189, 5190.
51. Leong Yip, file 34847/5-3, RG 85, National Archives at Seattle, CEA case files.
52. "Leong Yip Obituary," *Seattle Times*, June 30, 1943, included in file, file 34847/5-3, RG 85, National Archives at Seattle, CEA case files.
53. Chin Hing Yee, file 2355/21-16, RG 85, National Archives at Seattle, CEA case files.
54. Gin Mon Louie, file 7032/3549, RG 85, National Archives at Seattle, CEA case files.
55. Lew King, file 7032/521, RG 85, National Archives at Seattle, CEA case files.
56. Chan, "Chinese Head Tax."
57. U.S. Congress, *U.S. Statutes at Large*, vol. 25.
58. Hackworth, *Digest of International Law*, vol. 3, 792.
59. Leung Man Hoi (Yum Gong), file RS 29097, RG 85, National Archives at Seattle, CEA case files.
60. "San Francisco Immigration Office to Seattle Immigration Office, correspondence," May 28, 1920, Leung Man Hoi, file RS 29097, RG 85, National Archives at Seattle, CEA case files.
61. Ng Back Ging, file 7031/120, RG 85, National Archives at Seattle, CEA case files.
62. Green, "1924 Immigration Act."

63. University of Illinois, "Population of Chinese."
64. "H.E. Hull Correspondence #55476/519," November 20, 1929, "The First Supplement to Chinese General Order No. 13"; Ng Back Ging, file 7031/120, *RG 85, National Archives at Seattle, CEA case files.*
65. Dorothy S. Luke Lee (Mrs. Kaye Hong), file 7030/11435, RG 85, National Archives at Seattle, CEA case files.
66. Mallory, "Hollywood Heights—Keye Luke."
67. Wikipedia, "Edwin Luke."
68. Ah Yen, file RS 2168, RG 85, National Archives at Seattle, CEA case files.
69. Lee Wing Hing (Mrs. Mar Hing), CEA case file, file 7032/3680, RG 85, National Archives at Seattle, CEA case files.
70. "Lee Wong Hing Family photo," 1917, CEA case file, Lee Wing Hing (Mrs. Mar Hing), file 7032/3680, RG 85, National Archives at Seattle, CEA case files.
71. FamilySearch, "Washington Deaths and Burials, 1810–1960."
72. Look See (Mrs. Chin Quong), file 35205/1-4, RG 85, National Archives at Seattle, CEA case files.

Chapter 5

73. Chan, "Chinese American Identification Papers."
74. Mah Sun Inng, file 35100/4978, RG 85, National Archives at Seattle, CEA case files.
75. Fok Cheu (Fook Chew), file RS 2063, RG 85, National Archives at Seattle, CEA case files.
76. "Stephen B.L. Penrose Letter to Immigration, Seattle, Washington," 1922, Ng Shue Tong (Eng/Ng Se Tong), file 39540/3-1, RG 85, National Archives at Seattle, CEA case files.
77. "The Success of Whitman College" brochure, 1922, Ng Shue Tong (Eng/Ng Se Tong), file 39540/3–1, RG 85, National Archives at Seattle, CEA case files.
78. Mai Euon Lam, file 7032/2234, RG 85, National Archives at Seattle, CEA case files.
79. Nicola, "Going to Fly," 542.
80. Ng Fung Yuen, file 7032/469, RG 85, National Archives at Seattle, CEA case files.
81. "Ng Fung Yuen Photos—Exhibit G-1 & G-2," n.d., Ng Fung Yuen, file 7032/469, RG 85, National Archives at Seattle, CEA case files.
82. Long Tack Sam Company, file 38772/1-6, RG 85, National Archives at Seattle, CEA case files.
83. "Long Tack Sam Troupe," 1923, Long Tack Sam Company, files 10770/1-1 to 12 and files 38772/1-1 to 1-9, RG 85, National Archives at Seattle, CEA case files.

84. "Long Mi-Na & Long Nee-Sa correspondence photos," 1929, files 7022/18-3 and 7022/18-4, RG 85, National Archives at Seattle, CEA case files.
85. Soong May Ling, file RS 1483, RG 85, National Archives at Seattle, CEA case files.
86. "Correspondence between Harrison and Bonham," 1943, Soong May Ling, file RS 1483, RG 85, National Archives at Seattle, CEA case files.
87. Wikipedia, "Soong Ching-ling."
88. Encyclopedia of World Biography, "Madame Chiang Kai-shek."
89. Shao Chang Lee, file 36392/1–1, RG 85, National Archies-Seattle, WA.
90. "Letter Burford-White Letter," 1919, Shao Chang Lee, file 36392/1-1, RG 85, National Archives at Seattle, CEA case files.
91. *Seattle Post Intelligencer*, "Paying Honor to Visiting Chinese."
92. "Luther Weedin, Letter," 1929, Chen Ping-Huang, file 10360/1-1, RG 85, National Archives at Seattle, CEA case files.
93. Chen Ping-Huang, file 10360/1-1, RG 85, National Archives at Seattle, CEA case files.
94. Ferguson, "Mexican Silver Dollar."
95. "Choa Domingo Rufino, Passport," 1929, Choa Domingo Rufino, file 10360/1-2, RG 85, National Archives at Seattle, CEA case files.
96. "Letter from Walter P. Harris, Immigrant Inspector, U.S. Department of Labor to Seattle Commissioner of Immigration," May 24, 1929, Choa Domingo Rufino (Itsan Choa), file 10360/2-2, RG 85, National Archives at Seattle, CEA case files.
97. Lim Chu Cong (C.C. Lim), file 10360/1-2, RG 85, National Archives at Seattle, CEA case files.
98. A. Chua Clong, file 10360/2-1, RG 85, National Archives at Seattle, CEA case files.
99. Co Yong, file 10360/2-3, RG 85, National Archives at Seattle, CEA case files.
100. Wee C.G. (Wee Guan Chuan), file 10360/2-10, RG 85, National Archives at Seattle, CEA case files.
101. *Seattle Daily Times*, "Huskies May Play."
102. Immigration History, "Chinese Exclusion Act."
103. Sullivan T. Mar, file 7031/120, RG 85, National Archives at Seattle, CEA case files.
104. Britannica, "Second Sino-Japanese War."

Chapter 6

105. Immigration History, "Expatriation Act of 1907."
106. Immigration History, "Cable Act."
107. Seto More Fannie (alias Lew Tue Fannie), file 7030/12060, RG 85, National Archives at Seattle, CEA case files.
108. Rose Chin, file 30-3706, RG 85, National Archives at Seattle, CEA case files.
109. "Rose Chin, Birth Certificate," 1911, file 30-3706, RG 85, National Archives at Seattle, CEA case files.

Chapter 7

110. Chu Yong, file 41010/3/4, RG 85, National Archives at Seattle, CEA case files.
111. "Undertaker's Bill for Look Ah Pong," 1921, Look Gom Hong, file 7030/7291, RG 85, National Archives at Seattle, CEA case files.
112. Chin Hing (Chin Fook Hing), file 39666/1-1, RG 85, National Archives at Seattle, CEA case files.
113. *Seattle Times*, "Chin Fook Hing Funeral."
114. Chin Wing You, file 7030/13441, RG 85, National Archives at Seattle, CEA case files.
115. For more information about Chin Ching Hock, Chin Gee Hee, and Chin (Chun) Wa, see Riddle, "Chun Ching Hock," Dougherty, "King, Eng Ah," and Lange, "Chinese Funeral."
116. Lew Wa Hoo, file 35100/5245, RG 85, National Archives at Seattle, CEA case files.
117. Supreme Court of Washington, "*Lew You Ying v. Kay*."
118. Lock Ling (Lock Loon), file 7032/3676, RG 85, National Archives at Seattle, CEA case files.
119. Denfeld, "General Rossell O'Brien Promotes."
120. "Lock Ling (Lock Loon), file 7032/3676, RG 85, National Archives at Seattle, CEA case files.
121. Ng Ah Yun, file 7030/6363, RG 85, National Archives at Seattle, CEA case files.
122. Lowell, Reference Information paper 99, 1996, 1.
123. U.S. Selective Service System, "World War I."
124. Ng Ah Yun, 1919 Passport Application No. 4551.
125. This case study was originally published in the *Seattle Genealogical Society Bulletin*. See Nicola, "Chinese and the Northwest," 39–47.
126. Kershner, "Spokane Neighborhoods"; Chin and Chin, *Chinese in Washington State*, 39.

127. "Eng Gin Affidavit," 1907, Ah Kong, CEA files, file RS 29169, RG 85, National Archives at Seattle, CEA case files.
128. Ah Kong, file RS 29169, RG 85, National Archives at Seattle, CEA case files.
129. Yee Gim (Ah Tai), file RS 939, RG 85, National Archives at Seattle, CEA case files.
130. "Excerpt from Chinese Exclusion Act included in file," 1905, Yee Gim, file RS 939, RG 85, National Archives at Seattle, CEA case files.
131. Hui Hin, file 7031/636, RG 85, National Archives at Seattle, CEA case files.
132. Nelson Wah Chan King, file 7030/11344, RG 85, National Archives at Seattle, CEA case files.
133. Civilian Conservation Corps, "CCC Legacy."
134. Goon Fon, file 7032/3500, RG 85, National Archives at Seattle, CEA case files.
135. "F.W. Southworth Affidavit with photo of Ah Fook," 1907, (Wong) Ah One, file 7030/13432, RG 85, National Archives at Seattle, CEA case files.
136. Pfaelzer, *Driven Out*, 229.
137. Gim Bing, file 9347/9-3, RG 85, National Archives at Seattle, CEA case files.
138. Chin Yick Thlew, file 7030/13465, RG 85, National Archives at Seattle, CEA case files.
139. Chin Yick Thlew, file 7030/13465, RG 85, National Archives at Seattle, CEA case files.
140. Huie Taong, file 31-223, RG 85, National Archives at Seattle, CEA case files.
141. "Correspondence between Honorable Henry M. White and Mr. E. E. Wagen," 1920, Huie Taong, CEA, case files, file 31-223, RG 85, National Archives at Seattle, CEA case files.
142. "Photo Ah Gooey family and infant Fung Gall," 1903, See Jan, file RS 1392, RG 85, National Archives at Seattle, CEA case files.
143. Lock Yet, file RS 32260, RG 85, National Archives at Seattle, CEA case files.
144. Gee Moon Jew, file 7030/1001, RG 85, National Archives at Seattle, CEA case files.
145. Chan, "Chinese American Identification Papers."
146. Quan Foy, file 7032/1398, RG 85, National Archives at Seattle, CEA case files.
147. "Correspondence, re: Quan Foy," 1941, Quan Foy, file 7032/1398, RG 85, National Archives at Seattle, CEA case files.
148. "Correspondence, re: Quan Foy," 1944, 1945, 1947, Quan Foy, file 7032/1398, RG 85, National Archives at Seattle, CEA case files.

Chapter 8

149. Ott, "Alaska-Yukon-Pacific Exposition"; Ott, "Chealander, Godfrey"; Lange and Stein, "Alaska-Yukon-Pacific Exposition."
150. Chesley, "Goon Dip"; "Chinese Day Procession Unique."
151. Yip Sang, RS 2396, RG 85, National Archives at Seattle, CEA case files.
152. Kee Sing, file RS 2319, RG 85, National Archives at Seattle, CEA case files.
153. Ah King, file RS 2164, RG 85, National Archives at Seattle; Dougherty, "Alaska-Yukon-Pacific Exposition."
154. "Ah King," *Seattle Daily Times*.
155. Dougherty, "Alaska-Yukon-Pacific Exposition."
156. "Order Admitting Applications," 1909, Chee Yu San (Chee Sang) and Chee Chun She, files RS 2225, RS 2226; RG 85, National Archives at Seattle, CEA case files.
157. *Seattle Daily Times*, "Chinese Performer Kept Out"; *Seattle Daily Times*, "Chinese Magician Comes Across Line."
158. Nicola, "Day of the Dragon," 14–17.

Chapter 9

159. Wong F. Pershing, file 7030/13628, RG 85, National Archives at Seattle, CEA case files.
160. *Seattle Daily Times*, "American Ship Has Chinese."
161. *Oregonian*, "Pershing F. 'Perky' Wong."
162. *Seattle Daily Times*, "Harry Chinn."
163. Harry Chinn, file 7030/10246, RG 85, National Archives at Seattle, CEA case files.
164. War Brides Act.
165. *Tampa Bay Times*, "WW II Brides."
166. *Seattle Daily Times*, "Harry Chinn."
167. Nicola, "Paper Sons: How It Worked."

BIBLIOGRAPHY

"An Act to Amend the Immigration and Nationality Act, and for Other Purposes." Public Law 89–236. In *The Statutes at Large of the United States of America*[…], vol. 79, 89th Congress, 1st session (1965): 911–922.

"An Act to Execute Certain Treaty Stipulations Relating to Chinese." May 6, 1882. In *Enrolled Acts and Resolutions of Congress, 1789–1996.* General Records of the United States Government, Record Group 11. National Archives and Records Administration.

A. Chua Clong. File 10360/2-1. National Archives at Seattle, Record Group 85, Records of the Immigration and Naturalization Service, Chinese Exclusion Act case files.

Ah King. File RS 2164. National Archives at Seattle, Record Group 85, Records of the Immigration and Naturalization Service, Chinese Exclusion Act case files.

Ah Kong. File RS 29169. National Archives at Seattle, Record Group 85, Records of the Immigration and Naturalization Service, Chinese Exclusion Act case files.

(Wong) Ah One. File 7030/13432. National Archives at Seattle, Record Group 85, Records of the Immigration and Naturalization Service, Chinese Exclusion Act case files.

Ah Soon. File RS 30384. National Archives at Seattle, Record Group 85, Records of the Immigration and Naturalization Service, Chinese Exclusion Act case files.

Ah Yen. File RS 2168. National Archives at Seattle, Record Group 85, Records of the Immigration and Naturalization Service, Chinese Exclusion Act case files.

Beck, Katherine. "Luke, Keye (1904–1991)." HistoryLink.org, Essay 21023, May 4, 2020.

Beckman, Daniel. "San Francisco Mayor Ed Lee, Who Grew Up in Seattle, Dies at 65." *Seattle Times*, December 15, 2017.

Britannica. "Second Sino-Japanese War, 1937–1945." https://www.britannica.com.

Center for the Study of the Pacific Northwest. "Timeline: Asian Americans in Washington State History." https://www.washington.edu.

Chan, Arlene. "Chinese Head Tax in Canada." Canadian Encyclopedia, Historica Canada. https://www.thecanadianencyclopedia.ca.

Chan, Ruth. "Chinese American Identification Papers, 1882–1955 (Introduction)." History Hub, May 30, 2024. https://historyhub.history.gov.

Chang, Gordon H. *Ghosts of Gold Mountain*. Houghton Mifflin Harcourt, 2019.

Chee Chun She. File RS 2226. National Archives at Seattle, Record Group 85, Records of the Immigration and Naturalization Service, Chinese Exclusion Act case files.

Chee Yu San (Chee Sang) RS 2225. National Archives at Seattle, Record Group 85, Records of the Immigration and Naturalization Service, Chinese Exclusion Act case files.

Chen Ping-Huang. File 10360/1-1. National Archives at Seattle, Record Group 85, Records of the Immigration and Naturalization Service, Chinese Exclusion Act case files.

Chesley, Frank. "Goon Dip (ca. 1862–1933)." HistoryLink.org, Essay 9026, May 26, 2009.

Chinese Exclusion Act case files. National Archives at Seattle, Seattle, Washington.

Chinese Exclusion Act of 1882. Forty-Seventh Congress, Session 1, Chap. 126, May 6, 1882.

Chinese Reconciliation Project Foundation. https://crpftacoma.org.

Chin Hing (Chin Fook Hing). File 39666/1-1. National Archives at Seattle, Record Group 85, Records of the Immigration and Naturalization Service, Chinese Exclusion Act case files.

Chin Hing Yee. File 2355/21-16. National Archives at Seattle, Record Group 85, Records of the Immigration and Naturalization Service, Chinese Exclusion Act case files.

Chin Wing You. File 7030/13441. National Archives at Seattle, Record Group 85, Records of the Immigration and Naturalization Service, Chinese Exclusion Act case files.

Chin Yick Thlew. File 7030/13465. National Archives at Seattle, Record Group 85, Records of the Immigration and Naturalization Service, Chinese Exclusion Act case files.

Chin, Art, and Doug Chin. *Chinese in Washington State*. OCA Greater Seattle, 2013.

Choa Domingo Rufino (Itsan Choa). File 10360/1-2. National Archives at Seattle, Record Group 85, Records of the Immigration and Naturalization Service, Chinese Exclusion Act case files.

Choa Domingo Rufino. File 10360/2-2. National Archives at Seattle, Record Group 85, Records of the Immigration and Naturalization Service, Chinese Exclusion Act case files.

Chu Yong. File 41010/3/4. National Archives at Seattle, Record Group 85, Records of the Immigration and Naturalization Service, Chinese Exclusion Act case files.

Civilian Conservation Corps. "CCC Legacy." https://ccclegacy.org.

Compendium of the Tenth Census (June 1, 1880)[...]. Government Printing Office, 1885. https://www2.census.gov/library/publications/decennial/1880/1880-compendium/1880b_p1-01.pdf.

Co Yong. File 10360/2-3. National Archives at Seattle, Record Group 85, Records of the Immigration and Naturalization Service, Chinese Exclusion Act case files.

Crowley, Walt. "Anti-Chinese Activism—Seattle." HistoryLink.org, Essay 1057. May 2, 1999.

Denfeld, Duane Colt. "General Rossell O'Brien Promotes Practice of Standing for Playing of 'The Star-Spangled Banner' at a Meeting of Union Civil War Veterans on October 18, 1893." HistoryLink.org, Essay 11102, November 16, 2015.

Densho Encyclopedia. "Alien Land Laws." https://encyclopedia.densho.org/Alien_land_laws.

Dorothy S. Luke Lee (Mrs. Kaye Hong). File 7030/11435. National Archives at Seattle, Record Group 85, Records of the Immigration and Naturalization Service, Chinese Exclusion Act case files.

Dougherty, Phil. "Alaska-Yukon-Pacific Exposition (1909): Chinese Village." HistoryLink.org, Essay 8964, March 25, 2009.

———. "King, Eng Ah (1863–1915)." HistoryLink.org, Essay 10629, September 26, 2013.

Encyclopedia of World Biography. "Madame Chiang Kai-shek Biography." http://www.notablebiographies.com.

FamilySearch. "Asian-to-Gregorian Calendar Converter." https://www.familysearch.org.

———. "Washington Deaths and Burials, 1810–1960." Entry for Lee Shee Mar Hing and Lee Mar Hing, January 26, 1946. https://www.familysearch.org.

Ferguson, Jody. "Mexican Silver Dollar." March 21, 2021. https://www.jodyferguson.com.

Fleming, Ann Marie. *The Magical Life of Long Tack Sam: An Illustrated Memoir.* Riverhead Books, 2007.

Fok Cheu (Fook Chew). File RS 2063. National Archives at Seattle, Record Group 85, Records of the Immigration and Naturalization Service, Chinese Exclusion Act case files.

Geary Act. U.S. Statutes at Large, 27 Stat. 25, Sec. 7, 52nd Congress.

Gee Moon Jew. File 7030/1001. National Archives at Seattle, Record Group 85, Records of the Immigration and Naturalization Service, Chinese Exclusion Act case files.

Gim Bing. File 9347/9-3. National Archives at Seattle, Record Group 85, Records of the Immigration and Naturalization Service, Chinese Exclusion Act case files.

Gin Mon Louie. File 7032/3549. National Archives at Seattle, Record Group 85, Records of the Immigration and Naturalization Service, Chinese Exclusion Act case files.

Goon Fon. File 7032/3500. National Archives at Seattle, Record Group 85, Records of the Immigration and Naturalization Service, Chinese Exclusion Act case files.

Green, Jay D. "Passage of the 1924 Immigration Act." Teaching American History, April 23, 2024. https://teachingamericanhistory.org.

Hackworth, Green Haywood. "Chapter 11: Aliens." In *Digest of International Law* vol. 3: *Chapters 9–11*. Government Printing Office, 1942.

Harry Chinn. File 7030/10246. National Archives at Seattle, Record Group 85, Records of the Immigration and Naturalization Service, Chinese Exclusion Act case files.

Hui Hin. File 7031/636. National Archives at Seattle, Record Group 85, Records of the Immigration and Naturalization Service, Chinese Exclusion Act case files.

Immigration Act of 1965 (Hart-Celler Act). H.R. 2580; Pub.L. 89–236, 79 Stat. 911 United States Statutes at Large, Volume 79, 89th Congress, 1st Session.

Immigration History. "Cable Act of 1922." 67th USC 411, 42 Stat. 1021 (1922). https://immigrationhistory.org.

———. "Chinese Confession Program (1956–1965). https://immigrationhistory.org.

———. "Chinese Exclusion Act Aka 'An Act to Execute Certain Treaty Stipulations Relating to Chinese.'" https://immigrationhistory.org.

———. "Expatriation Act of 1907." 59th USC § 34 Stat. 1228. Sec. 3 (1907). https://immigrationhistory.org.

———. "Immigration Act of 1924 (Johnson-Reed Act)." https://immigrationhistory.org.

Kee Sing. File RS 2319. National Archives at Seattle, Record Group 85, Records of the Immigration and Naturalization Service, Chinese Exclusion Act case files.

Kershner, Jim. "Spokane Neighborhoods: Old Chinatown—Trent Alley—Thumbnail History." HistoryLink.org, Essay 8120, March 30, 2007.

Klingle, Matthew W. "Timeline: Asian Americans in Washington State History." Center for the Study of the Pacific Northwest. https://www.washington.edu.

Lange, Greg. "Chinese Funeral Is Held for Chun Wa in Seattle on July 21, 1873." HistoryLink.org, Essay 1617, August 9, 1999.

Lange, Greg, and Alan J. Stein. "Alaska-Yukon-Pacific Exposition Groundbreaking Ceremonies Take Place on June 1, 1907." HistoryLink.org, Essay 692, January 14, 1999.

Lee Gok Suey. File 7030/10684. National Archives at Seattle, Record Group 85, Records of the Immigration and Naturalization Service, Chinese Exclusion Act case files.

Lee Share Yung. File 1010/18-8. National Archives at Seattle, Record Group 85, Records of the Immigration and Naturalization Service, Chinese Exclusion Act case files.

Lee Wing Hing (Mrs. Mar Hing). File 7032/3680. National Archives at Seattle, Record Group 85, Records of the Immigration and Naturalization Service, Chinese Exclusion Act case files.

Leong Yip, file 34847/5-3. National Archives at Seattle, Record Group 85, Records of the Immigration and Naturalization Service, Chinese Exclusion Act case files.

Leung Man Hoi (Yum Gong). File RS 29097. National Archives at Seattle, Record Group 85, Records of the Immigration and Naturalization Service, Chinese Exclusion Act case files.

Lew King. File 7032/521. National Archives at Seattle, Record Group 85, Records of the Immigration and Naturalization Service, Chinese Exclusion Act case files.

Lew Wa Hoo. File 35100/5245. National Archives at Seattle, Record Group 85, Records of the Immigration and Naturalization Service, Chinese Exclusion Act case files.

"*Lew You Ying v. Kay*." Supreme Court of Washington, 174 Wn. 83 (Wash. 1933). https://case-law.vlex.com/vid/lew-you-ying-v-893715744.

Lim Chu Cong (C.C. Lim). File 10360/1-2. National Archives at Seattle, Record Group 85, Records of the Immigration and Naturalization Service, Chinese Exclusion Act case files.

Lock Ling (Lock Loon). File 7032/3676. National Archives at Seattle, Record Group 85, Records of the Immigration and Naturalization Service, Chinese Exclusion Act case files.

Lock Yet. File RS 32260. National Archives at Seattle, Record Group 85, Records of the Immigration and Naturalization Service, Chinese Exclusion Act case files.

Long Mi-Na. File 7022/18-3. National Archives at Seattle, Record Group 85, Records of the Immigration and Naturalization Service, Chinese Exclusion Act case files.

Long Nee-Sa. File 7022/18-4. National Archives at Seattle, Record Group 85, Records of the Immigration and Naturalization Service, Chinese Exclusion Act case files.

Long Tack Sam Company. Files 10770/1-1 to 12. National Archives at Seattle, Record Group 85, Records of the Immigration and Naturalization Service, Chinese Exclusion Act case files.

———. Files 38772/1-1 to 1-9. National Archives at Seattle, Record Group 85, Records of the Immigration and Naturalization Service, Chinese Exclusion Act case files.

Look Gom Hong. File 7030/7291. National Archives at Seattle, Record Group 85, Records of the Immigration and Naturalization Service, Chinese Exclusion Act case files.

Look See (Mrs. Chin Quong). File 35205/1-4. National Archives at Seattle, Record Group 85, Records of the Immigration and Naturalization Service, Chinese Exclusion Act case files.

Lowell, Waverly B., comp. "Chinese Immigration and Chinese in the United States: Records in the Regional Archives of the National Archives and Records Administration (NARA)." Reference Information paper 99, 1996.

Low Yow Edwin. File 7030/11920. National Archives at Seattle, Record Group 85, Records of the Immigration and Naturalization Service, Chinese Exclusion Act case files.

Magnuson Act, or an Act to Repeal the Chinese Exclusion Acts. 1943. H.R. 3070; 57 Stat. 600.

Mah Sun Inng. File 35100/4978. National Archives at Seattle, Record Group 85, Records of the Immigration and Naturalization Service, Chinese Exclusion Act case files.

Mai Euon Lam. File 7032/2234. National Archives at Seattle, Record Group 85, Records of the Immigration and Naturalization Service, Chinese Exclusion Act case files.

Mallory, Mary. "Hollywood Heights—Keye Luke." *Daily Mirror*, June 20, 2022.

McCreary Amendment. U.S. Statues at Large, Vol. 28 (1893–1895), 53rd Congress.

MeasuringWorth.com, "Converting 1939 Pounds Sterling to U.S. Dollars."

National Archives and Records Administration. *Teaching with Documents: Using Primary Sources from the National Archives*. National Archives Trust Fund Board, 1989.

Nelson Wah Chan King. File 7030/11344. National Archives at Seattle, Record Group 85, Records of the Immigration and Naturalization Service, Chinese Exclusion Act case files.

Ng Ah Yun. File 7030/6363. National Archives at Seattle, Record Group 85, Records of the Immigration and Naturalization Service, Chinese Exclusion Act case files.

———. 1919. Passport Application #4551. National Archives and Records Administration (NARA), Washington, D.C. *Passport Applications for Travel to China, 1906–1925*. Collection Number: ARC Identifier 1244180 / MLR Number A1 540; Box 4448; Volume 35. Database online. Ancestry.com.

Ng Back Ging, RG 85. File 7031/120. National Archives at Seattle, Record Group 85, Records of the Immigration and Naturalization Service, Chinese Exclusion Act case files.

Ng Fung Yuen. File 7032/469. National Archives at Seattle, Record Group 85, Records of the Immigration and Naturalization Service, Chinese Exclusion Act case files.

Ng Shue Tong (Eng/Ng Se Tong). File 39540/3–1. National Archives at Seattle, Record Group 85, Records of the Immigration and Naturalization Service, Chinese Exclusion Act case files.

Nicola, Patricia Hackett. "Chinese Exclusion Act Records: A Neglected Genealogical Source." *Association of Professional Genealogists Quarterly* (March 2006): 25–30.

Nicola, Trish Hackett. "Chinese and the Northwest." *SGS Bulletin* 64, no. 1 (Winter 2014): 39–47.

———. *Chinese Exclusion Act Case Files* (blog). https://chineseexclusionfiles.com.

———. "Day of the Dragon." *Columbia: The Magazine of Northwest History* (Summer 2010): 14–17.

———. "I Think I Am Going to Fly: Chinese Pilots Trained in Portland During the 1930s." *Oregon Historical Quarterly* (Winter 2021): 532–45.

———. "Paper Sons: How It Worked." *Chinese Exclusion Act Files* (blog), 2020. Legacy PowerPoint presentation.

Office of the Historian. "Chinese Immigration and the Chinese Exclusion Acts." Milestones in the History of U.S. Foreign Relations." https://history.state.gov/milestones/1866-1898/chinese-immigration.

Oregonian (Portland, OR). "Pershing F. 'Perky' Wong." July 14, 1999.

Ott, Jennifer. "Alaska-Yukon-Pacific Exposition (1909): The Olmsted Legacy." HistoryLink.org, Essay 8873, December 23, 2008.

———. "Chealander, Godfrey (1868–1953)." HistoryLink.org, Essay 8847, January 29, 2008.

Page Act. Forty-Third Congress, Session 2, Sect. 141, Stat. 477, 1875.

Peffer, George Anthony. "Forbidden Families: Emigration Experiences of Chinese Women Under the Page Law, 1875–1882." *Journal of American Ethnic History* 6, no. 1 (Fall 1986): 28–46.

Pfaelzer, Jean. *Driven Out: The Forgotten War Against Chinese Americans*. Random House, 2007.

Quan Foy. File 7032/1398. National Archives at Seattle, Record Group 85, Records of the Immigration and Naturalization Service, Chinese Exclusion Act case files.

Quan Robert. File 7030/11495. National Archives at Seattle, Record Group 85, Records of the Immigration and Naturalization Service, Chinese Exclusion Act case files.

Reading (PA) Eagle. "'Shaving Feast' Given Babies." October 23, 1920.

Riddle, Margaret. "Chun Ching Hock Opens the Wa Chong Company in Seattle on December 15, 1868." HistoryLink.org, Essay 10800, June 13, 2014.

Rose Chin. File 30-3706. National Archives at Seattle, Record Group 85, Records of the Immigration and Naturalization Service, Chinese Exclusion Act case files.

Rose Leong. File 7030/13652. National Archives at Seattle, Record Group 85, Records of the Immigration and Naturalization Service, Chinese Exclusion Act case files.

Scott Act of 1888. Fiftieth Congress. Sess. 1. 25 Stat. 115, Chap. 1064.

Seattle Daily Times. "Ah King, Chinese Concessionaire." July 14, 1909.

———. "American Ship Has Chinese as Third Officer." February 6, 1945.

———. "Chinese Day Procession Unique." September 13, 1909.

———. "Chinese Magician Comes Across Line." June 20, 1909.

———. "Chinese Performer Kept Out." June 19, 1909.

———. "Harry Chinn." July 21, 1951.

———. "Herbal Healers, Now." February 2, 1984.

———. "Huskies May Play All-Star Chinese Five." January 3, 1929.

———. "Willard Jue, UW Herb-Gardener, Dies." June 25, 1984.

Seattle Post Intelligencer. "Paying Honor to Visiting Chinese." April 9, 1919.

Seattle Times. "Leong Yip Obituary." June 30, 1943, CEA, NARA. File 34847/5-3.

———. "Obituaries: Chin Fook Hing Funeral to Be Held Tomorrow." November 26, 1941.

———. "San Francisco Mayor Ed Lee, Who Grew Up in Seattle, Dies at 65." December 15, 2017.

See Jan. File RS 1392. National Archives at Seattle, Record Group 85, Records of the Immigration and Naturalization Service, Chinese Exclusion Act case files.

Seto More Fannie (Lew Tue Fannie). File 7030/12060. National Archives at Seattle, Record Group 85, Records of the Immigration and Naturalization Service, Chinese Exclusion Act case files.

Shao Chang Lee. File 36392/1–1. National Archives at Seattle, Record Group 85, Records of the Immigration and Naturalization Service, Chinese Exclusion Act case files.

Soong May Ling. File RS 1483. National Archives at Seattle, Record Group 85, Records of the Immigration and Naturalization Service, Chinese Exclusion Act case files.

Sullivan T. Mar. File 7031/120. National Archives at Seattle, Record Group 85, Records of the Immigration and Naturalization Service, Chinese Exclusion Act case files.

Tacoma Chinese Reconciliation Park. "Expulsion: The Tacoma Method." www.tacomachinesepark.org/tacoma-chinese-park/expulsion-the-tacoma-method.

Tampa Bay Times. "Parade Magazine—Report on WW II Brides." July 17, 1965, 14.

U.S. Census Bureau. "Compendium of the Tenth Census, June 1, 1880." https://www.census.gov/library/publications/1885/dec/1880-compendium.html.

———. "Table VI, Population of the United States, (by States and Territories,) Classified by Race and Place of Birth, Showing the Number of Persons Born in Each State and Territory and Specified Foreign Country." In *1870 Census: Vol. 1. Statistics of the Population of the United States.* Government Printing Office, 1872. https://www2.census.gov/library/publications/decennial/1870/population/1870a-32.pdf.

U.S. Congress. *The Statutes at Large of the United States of America*[…]. Vol. 25, 50th Congress, 1888–89. Government Printing Office, 1889. https://www.loc.gov/item/llsl-v25.

U.S. Selective Service System. *World War I Selective Service System Draft Registration Cards, 1917–1918.* Database online. National Archives and Records Administration. M1509. Accessed August 26, 2014. Ancestry.com. Wah Young, Hartford, Conn., No. 1597; citing FHL, Roll 1561897; Draft Board 2.

U.S. Supreme Court. *Rassmussen v. United States*. 197 U.S. 516 (1905). https://chanrobles.com/usa/us_supremecourt/197/516/case.php.

United States Compiled Statutes, Annotated, 1916. Vol. 5. West Publishing, 1916.

University of Illinois. "Population of Chinese in the United States, 1860–1940." *The Chinese Experience in 19th Century America.* http://teachingresources.atlas.illinois.edu/chinese_exp.

War Brides Act Amendment. Public Law 713, 1946.

War Brides Act. 59 Stat. 659, Act of Dec. 28, 1945.

Washington State University. "Chinese Americans in the Columbia River Basin—Historical Overview." https://content.libraries.wsu.edu/digital/collection/cchm/custom/ca-overview.

Wee C.G. (Wee Guan Chuan). File 10360/2-10. National Archives at Seattle, Record Group 85, Records of the Immigration and Naturalization Service, Chinese Exclusion Act case files.

Wikipedia. "Converting 1939 Hong Kong Dollars to Pounds Sterling." https://en.wikipedia.org.

———. "Edwin Luke." https://en.wikipedia.org.

———. "Guangxu Emperor." https://en.wikipedia.org.

———. "Soong Ching-ling." https://en.wikipedia.org.

Wong F. Pershing. File 7030/13628. National Archives at Seattle, Record Group 85, Records of the Immigration and Naturalization Service, Chinese Exclusion Act case files.

Woo Back (Bak) Sue(y). File 7030/10966. National Archives at Seattle, Record Group 85, Records of the Immigration and Naturalization Service, Chinese Exclusion Act case files.

Woo Quin Lock. File 7030/12841. National Archives at Seattle, Record Group 85, Records of the Immigration and Naturalization Service, Chinese Exclusion Act case files.

Yee Gim (Ah Tai). File RS 939. National Archives at Seattle, Record Group 85, Records of the Immigration and Naturalization Service, Chinese Exclusion Act case files.

Yip Sang. File RS 2396. National Archives at Seattle, Record Group 85, Records of the Immigration and Naturalization Service, Chinese Exclusion Act case files.

INDEX

A

Abbott, Charles W. 74
Aberdeen 145
Adcox School of Aviation 74
Admiral Oriental Line 98
Ah Chung 39
Ah Don Ng 113
Ah Fook 130
Ah Foon 38
Ah Gee 63
Ah Gong Yen. *See* See Jan
Ah Gooey 142
Ah Gow 77
Ah Him 133
Ah June 120
Ah King 37, 38, 42, 64, 153, 155
Ah King Company 37, 38, 42, 64
Ah Kong 120
Ah Lan 68
Ah Len 143
Ah Loy 143
Ah Lun 143
Ah Lung 131
Ah One 130
Ah Quan 67. *See also* Look See
Ah Que 38, 42
Ah Quong. *See* Ah Kong
Ah Soon 37, 38, 42, 43, 44
Ah Wah 105, 130
Ah Wing 68
Ah Yen 62, 142
Ah Yun 115, 116, 117
Alaska 25, 37, 46, 66, 128, 133, 152
Alaskan Eskimo 26
Alaska-Yukon-Pacific Exposition 40, 152
Alien Registration Act of 1940 66
alien registration number 10
Allen, Arn 72
Allen, Clay Judge 151
all-male Chinese population 13
Amoy, Fukien, China 86
Angel Island 36, 55
anti-Chinese 11, 12, 14, 130, 131, 153
anti-Chinese riots 131
anti-immigration laws 12
appeal 30, 35, 53, 77, 93, 124, 130
Astoria, Oregon 45, 46
Astoria Savings Bank 47
A-Y-P Expo. *See* Alaska-Yukon-Pacific Exposition

B

baby names 42, 140
Bailey Gatzert School 159

Bak Sar village 69
Barber, George H. 134
Bartlett, C.C. 114
Bartlett, Frank A. 116
Bates, U.C. 66
Beaven, Joseph H. 40
Bellingham 16, 136, 153
Bellman, W.W. 144
Bill Huie. *See* Hui Hin
Billings, William 15
Bing Quong 115
Black Diamond 14
Blackman, Henry 139
Blaine, Washington 61, 78, 89, 93
Blue Funnel Line 98
Boeing 28
Boise, Idaho 120
Bok Fook 57
Bok Teung 119
Bok Wong 118
Bonham, Raphael P. 82, 137, 150
Bo San Wo Company 54
Boston 100
bound or natural feet 117
Bow On Drug Company 48
Boxer Rebellion 11
Brattstom, A. 57
Bremmeyr, Peter 47
British citizenship 95
British Columbia, Canada 85
Broadway High School 159
Brotchi, Charles 47
Brunton, E.L. 134
Burford, S.J. 85
burial ceremony 35
Burke, Thomas 85
Butte, Montana 68

C

Cable Act of 1922 97
Calgary 78
California 11, 12, 13, 29, 36, 38, 55, 61, 74, 84, 95, 126, 147
California Restaurant 140
Callahan, W.P. 100
Camp Sheridan, Illinois 28
Canada 50, 52, 56, 58, 61, 69, 83, 89, 93, 126
Canadian border 10, 16
Canadian certificates of identity 93
Canadian Chinese exclusion file 52
Canadian Chinese Immigration Act of 1923 53
Canadian head tax 53, 58
Canadian Pacific head tax guarantee 71
Canadian Pacific Railroad 85
Canadian Pacific Railway 92, 98
cannery contractor 26
Canoe Pass Packing Company 46
Canton, China 38, 63, 72, 103
Canton Province Mining Company 40
Canton University 110
Carleton, C.E. 121
Carlton, F.T. 50
Cathay Post No. 186 160
Caucasian 12, 22, 37, 47, 70, 88, 93, 134, 143
Caucasian workers 13
CCC Camp 127
cemetery 112
Central Public School 74
certificate of identity 19, 30, 33, 35, 46, 54, 58, 100, 102, 117, 122, 130, 148, 159
certificate of residence 10, 19, 40, 43, 46, 89, 112, 122, 130, 134, 144, 149
lost 145
Cha Chung village 62
chak chi 122
Chan, Charlie 61
Chang Chang Ching 78
Changehow 86
Chang, Hao-Jan 113
Chan Go 50
Chan, Lee 61
Chan Man Yai. *See* Gin Mon Louie
Chan Yee 50
Chee Yu San 154
Chen Ping-Huang 86
Chen Shee 34
Chew See 22
Chicago 72, 89, 100
Chicago Hotel 35
Chilberg, J.E. 155
China Club of Seattle 85
China Day 153
Chin Ah Wing 105, 106
Chin, Annie M. 68
China's Great Recession 11
Chin Bing village 48

Chin Ching Hock 68, 105, 106, 121
Chin Dan 68
Chinese Air Force 74
Chinese Basketball Team 85
Chinese Confession Program 20, 160
Chinese consulate in Seattle 93
Chinese Exclusion Act 7, 9, 13, 19, 22, 37, 45, 53, 69, 78, 83, 109, 113, 123, 128, 139, 144, 151, 152, 156, 159, 160, 192
Chinese Exclusion Act of 1882 9, 17
Chinese Exclusion Act of 1888 54
Chinese Historical Society of the Pacific Northwest 26
Chinese interpreters 64, 93, 149
Chinese laborers 17, 19, 54, 69
Chinese logging camps 38
Chinese magicians 78
Chinese marriage customs 112
Chinese Masonic Lodge 47
Chinese names 11
Chinese Nationalist League 153
Chinese overtime certificate 43, 44, 50, 100
Chinese riots in 1886 93
Chinese Village 153, 154, 155, 156
Chin Fook Hing 103
Chin Gee Hee 44, 67, 105, 121
Chin Gem (Jim) Wah 104
Chin Hing. *See* Chin Hing Yee; Chin Fook Hing
Chin Hing, Henry 103
Chin Hing Yee 47, 48, 50
Chin Hui Quock. *See* Chin Ah Wing
Chin Jim Wah 105
Chin, Josephine 103
Chin Kee 67, 95
Chin Kee, Tom 95
Chin King Ging. *See* Chinn, Harry
Chin Lai 48
Chin Lee, Pansy 33
Chin, Loretta 78
Chin May Goon 68
Chin May Young 68
Chinn, Haley 160
Chinn, Hannah 160
Chinn, Hansing 160
Chinn, Harry 158, 160
Chinn, Harry, Mrs.. *See* Lee Til Wui
Chinn, Henning 160
Chinn, Hopkin 160
Chinn, Horace 160
Chinn, Howard 160
Chinn, Shaw 159
Chinn, Shew Hum, Mr. and Mrs. 160
Chinn, Toy Su 160
Chin Quok Jon 68
Chin Quong 66, 68
Chin, Rose 95, 97
Chin Sang 48
Chin See. *See* Leong Yip
Chin She 54, 133. *See also* Leung Man Hoi
Chin Shee 28
Chin Suey 103
Chin Suie Heung (Helen) 26
Chin Tan 55
Chin Tong 137
Chin Wing 68, 104, 106
Chin Wing Mow 68
Chin Wing Moy 105
Chin Wing Yon 68
Chin Wing You 104, 105, 106
Chin W. Kee 85
Chin Yen Gee 68
Chin Yick 103
Chin Yick Goon 137
Chin Yick Thlew 136
Chin Yock Can 137
Choa, Domingo Rufino 86, 87
Chong Hing and Company 103
Chong Hing Knitting Company 104
Chow Shee 35
Chua Ciong 88
Chung Chi village 131
Chung-Lee Company 108
Chun Wong. *See* Ah One
Chu Yong 98, 100
Civil War Union veteran 108
Cleveland, Grover 14
Coast and Geodetic Survey ship 157
Coaster Tea Company 47, 48, 110
Colfax, Washington 62
Collins Brothers Undertaking Company 102
Colman Building 38
Colman School 61

Colorado 12
Commercial Dock 131
Connell, J.J., Mrs. 85
Coombs, Samuel F. 68
Co Yong 88
Crawford, Samuel L. 105
Crawford, S.L. 93
credible witnesses 45, 70, 116

D

Dallas, Texas 24
Dan, Charley 42
Davis, Clark 110
DeBruler, Ellis 40, 145
Deep Sea Salmon Cannery Company 133
detention 19, 22, 23, 29, 32, 68, 112, 137
diplomatic passport 89
discharged from custody 29
discharge papers 22, 29, 117
discrepancies 30, 32, 34, 39, 75, 135
distraught parents 138
Dobbs, Milton 63
domiciled broker 40
Dong Shee 137
Doon Hen. *See* Lew King
Dow Dung village 63
Down Cook 60
draft registration card 118
Dr. Woo. *See* M. Hee Woo
Dune, Jim 135
Dunton, John F. 75
Duwamish Junction 38

E

Ellensburg, Washington 139, 140
Ellis, Parker 145
Eng Ah Quan 24
Eng Fang 71
Eng Fong Hock 120
Eng Gay 63
Eng Gin 120
Eng Hong (See Fat) 70
Eng, Lily 142
Eng Se Tong. *See* Ng Shue Tong
(Eng) Yee Quay 120
Eng Yee Tung 115
Evansville, Indiana 88
Everett 153
Expatriation Act of 1907 92
extension of visit request 150
extortion 151

F

Fang Ching Hai 78
Farrar, Rhonda 27
Farrell, J.E. 140
Fee Lon 137
fire 48, 93, 121, 131
Fisher, Thomas M. 23, 47, 108
Fisher, T.M. 71
Fleming, Ann Marie 82
Flyer Dock 133
Flynn, M.E. 140
Fok Cheu 70, 71
Fong Ngow hill 35
Foochow, China 89
Fook Yen Tong 35
Fook Yung 71
Foo Lee Laundry 145
Forester, John J. 95
Fort Hood, Texas 160
Fort Lewis, Washington 160
French Charlie's 39
Frye, Mr. 77
Fulton, A.S. 41, 131
Fung Gall 143
Fung King 143
Fung, Paul 85
Fung Sing 143

G

gardeners 71, 119, 134
Garfield High School 24, 28, 158
Geary Act 19, 116, 139, 148
Gee, Ann Quan 158
Gee Fee Yee 147, 149
Gee Hee, Chin, Mrs. 66
Gee Moon Ben 147, 149
Gee Moon Jew 147
Gee Moon Taw 147
Gee Quong Sam 149
Gee Suey Gin 149
generation book 103
Germany 158
Gerson, Max 62
Get Kee Company 63
Get Tuck 70
Gill, Hiram 133
Gim Bing 134
Gim Sing Wing. *See* Gim Bing
Gim Wing 64
Gin Mon Louie 50, 52
Godfrey, J.E. 51
Gok Suey Lee 32, 33
gold mines 11, 13, 103
Gong Sen 42. *See also* Ah Soon
Gong Shee 107
Gong Yen. *See* See Jan

Goon Dip 46, 54, 128, 153, 154
Goon Fon 128
Goon Sam 128
governor general of Manila 86
Gowan, Herbert H. 91
great fire of Seattle, 1889 93
Great Northern Railway 79
Greene, Mrs. 67
Guangdong, China 55
Guangdong Province 11
Guptill, Elthea S. (Mrs. Charles Guptill) 143
Guthman, Otto 103
Guthrie, John 158

H

habeas corpus 9, 19, 22, 29, 56
Hai Ping Fong 102
Hallinger, H. 143
Hall, Purely G. 60
Hambeck, Mrs. 66
Hanford, C.H. 22, 143
Hansen, P.J. 35
Harker, Aloysuis 121
Harman, George 105
Harmon, Mr. 131
Harold Ng. *See* Ng Back Ging
Har Pang Village 39
Harrison, Earl G. 82
Harry Quong Eng 24
Hart-Celler Act 21
Hartford, Connecticut 117
Harvey, Fred R. 48
Hatch Mill 15
Hatch sawmill 131
Hawthorne School 124
Hedberg, Axel 51
Helena, Montana 37, 38, 43
Henman, O. 140
herb doctor 51
Her Ping village 120
He Wo. *See* M. Hee Woo
Hill, Mr. 135
Hing Lung Lay village 104
Hip Sing Company 102
Hock Fong. *See* Ah Soon
Hock Geng 122
Hock, Hen 115
Hock Hung 39
Hock, Jet 115
Hoe Sing 135
Hofius, W.D., Mrs. 112
Hok Fong. *See* Ah Soon
Hong Chong Company 110, 112
Hong Chong Wo Company 70, 71
Hong, Kaye Mrs. *See* Dorothy S. Luke Lee
Hong Kong 33, 44, 50, 53, 55, 63, 112, 118, 131, 142
Hong Po. *See* Louie Kay
Hong Sing 48
Hong Won Kee Kaye 61
Hong Yee Chung Company 93
hookworm 73, 142
hop business 141
Hop Lee 140
Hop Yick Company 46
Hop Yick Shing Kee Company 46
Hoquiam 144
Horr, James C. 108
Hoy Loy 134
Hubbell, J.C. 140
Huestis, F.D. 47
Hui Cheung 123, 125, 130
Huie, Bill 124
Huie Doo Taong. *See* Huie Taong
Huie Foy 140
Huie Hong Jack 141, 142
Huie Tai Ball. *See* Huie Taong
Huie Taong 139
Hui Hin 123
Hui Yut Seng 125
Hunter, B.A. 157

I

Immigration Act of 1924 20, 58
Immigration Act of 1965 21, 160
Immigration and Naturalization Service 20, 25, 150
Ing Gar Hong village 53
interpreter 57, 95, 103, 150, 151
Irondale, Jefferson County, Washington 143
Issaquah 15
Itsan Choa. *See* Choa Domingo Rufino

J

James, Martha 26
Jam Mon 71
Japan 126
  Twenty-One Demands (1915) 91
Japanese 20, 119
Japanese Imperial Army 90
Jenn, Alice Martha 148
Jenn, Eugene 148

Jenn, George W. *See* Gee Moon Jew
Jenn, George Walton 148
Jenn, Helen Elizabeth 148
Jenn, Mary Frances 148
Jenn, William Lawrence 148
Jew (Jue), Willard. *See* Jue, Willard
Jin Hing Lok 52
Jin Lip Moon. *See* Gin Mon Louie
Jin Mon Yuey. *See* Gin Mon Louie
Jin Ok Jung 52
Jobson, Frank 64
Johnson-Reed Act 20
Jones, Philip B. 36
Jong King Company 93
Jow Wah 28, 47
Jue, Willard 26
Jung Lun. *See* Lock Yet

K

Kai Gock village 54
Kalama 14
Keagy, C.E. 51, 52
Kee, Rose Chin. *See* Chin, Rose
Kee Sing 153
Kee Toy 143
Ken Chung Lung Store 40
Kent, Washington 78
Killisnoo, Alaska 26
King Chong Lung Company 54
King, Cora Smith (Eaton) 60
King, Harry N. 126
King, Lily S. 127
King, Paul Ming 126
King Tai Company 122
Kin Ham village 93
Kitsap County 105
Kuhn, Judge 142, 143
Kung Yick Company 146
Kwang Hu University 86
Kwong Chung Sing Company 135
Kwong Fat Lung Company 133
Kwong Nom Low Restaurant 126
Kwong Sin. *See* Gong Sen
Kwong Tung, China 33
Kwong Wa Chong Company 103

L

laborer's return certificate 44, 53, 74, 130
Lamb, Dr. 51
Lam Mai 74
Lam Yuk Tsun 74
Landon, Daniel 64
Larned, Kansas 149
Lavinthal, Louie 75
League of Nations 91
Learned, A.F. 128
leave of absence 149
Lee Chung 135
Lee, Dorothy S. Luke 60
Lee, Edwin Mah 33
Lee, Edwin S. Luke 60
Lee, Eugene Luke 60
Lee Gim 29, 32
Lee Gok Foo 29
Lee Gok Gong 29
Lee Gok Suey 30, 32
Lee Gok Sui 29
Lee Hong Gue 64
Lee Ling Hung 29, 30, 32
Lee Poo (Gee Woon) 71
Lee See 110
Lee Share Yung 29, 32
Lee Shee 35, 36, 71, 93, 112
Lee Shung 135
Lee Tie Win. *See* Lee Til Wui
Lee Til Wui 159, 160
Lee Wong (Wing) Hing 64, 66
Lee Yun Nam 136
Lehn, Fritz 71
Lem Shee 130
Leong, Gene 28
Leong Gim Lin 28
Leong Git Too 28
Leong, Jimmie 28
Leong, Robert 28
Leong, Rose 28
Leong Yip 28, 45, 46, 47
letters 23, 32, 35, 40, 42, 47, 55, 72, 73, 78, 82, 85, 86, 91, 95, 98, 137, 145, 149, 151
Leung Man Hoi 54
Leung She 150
Leung Yum Gong. *See* Leung Man Hoi
Lew Café 147
Lew Fong 140
Lew Geate Kay 93, 95
Lewis and Clark High School 124
Lew Jung Hen. *See* Lew Wa Hoo
Lew King 52, 53, 93, 108
Lew Tue. *See* More, Fannie Seto

Lew Wa Hoo 106
Lew York Lon 93
Lew York Lue. *See* More, Fannie Seto
Li Chee Gardens Restaurant 102
Li Koy Dohien 78
Lim, C.C. *See* Lim Chu Cong
Lim, C.C. (publisher) 87
Lim Chu Cong 87
Lim Shee 50
Lincoln High School 74
Lind, Judge 93
Lin She 117
Lin Shing Jewelry Store 59
Liw Ting 146
Locke, Gary 113
Lock Goey 112
Lock How 144
Lock Kim 110, 112
Lock Lad 145
Lock Ling 108, 110
Lock Loon. *See* Lock Ling
Lock Loui 110
Lock Loy 110
Lock Lung. *See* Lock Ling
Lock Mee 112
Lock Mee Oye 112
Lock Sang 146
Lock Sing 144
Lock Wing 144
Lock Yen. *See* Lock Ying
Lock Yet 144, 146
Lock Ying 110, 146
Lock You 147
Loey King. *See* Lew King
Long Lieu (Lan Ludovika) 78
Long Mi-Na 79
Long Nee-Sa 79
Long Tack Sam 78
Long Tack Sam Troupe 79
Look Ah Pong 100, 102
Look Gim Yook (York) 100
Look Gom Hong 100, 102
Look Kim Fun 102
Look See 66
Los Angeles 74, 89, 103, 126
Louie Hay 48
Louie Kay 93
Louie Kee 40
Louie See 121
Louie Shee 38, 42
Louis Gar On 53
Lou Shee 42
Low, Daisy and Rose 26
Low Yow 26
Low Yow, Amy 26
Low Yow, Edwin 25
Loy Lee Laundry 140
Luey Shee 30
Luke, Edwin 61
Luke, Kaye 61
Luke Lee 60
Luke Thick Kaye 60
Lum Shee 133
Lu Woo 121
Lynch, Charles I. 38, 39

M

Madame Chiang Kai-shek. *See* Soong May Ling
Magical Life of Long Tack Sam, The 82
Magnuson Act of 1943 20
Mah Fook Hing 44
Mah Lee, Edwin 33
Mah Sin Dung 69
Mah Sun Inng 69
Mai Euon Lam. *See* Lam Mai
Main Street School 61
Manchuria 74, 90
Mangels, G.H. 97, 146
Man Sing Lung Company 52, 53
manufacturing category 123
Mar, Gum Shu James 64
Mar Hing 40, 64
Mark Ten Suie Company 110
Mar, Lun Clarence 64
Mar, May. *See* May Fun Kim
marriage names 42
Mar, Saung Gew Myra 64
Mar, Shew Howard 64
Mar, Sullivan T. 89, 90, 91
Mar, Teh-Chien. *See* Mar, Sullivan T.
Mar, Wing Harry 64
Masters, Mates and Pilots' Association 158
Matterson, Roy C. 52
Maus, Edward 47, 48
May Fun Kim 28
McCool's Garden 136
McCreary Amendment of 1893 19, 148
McGoldrick, H.E. 70
McGougan, James 123
medical exam 54
Men Dan. *See* Dan, Charley
Merchant Marine 157
Merges, Edward E. 36
Me Wing Wah 104
Mexican currency 86, 120

M. Hee Woo 50
military draft 117
Mills, George G. 147
Milwaukee Railway 60
mining 10, 11, 13, 37
mining stockbroker 40
Minneapolis, Minnesota 78
Mires, Austin 140
Mitten, Frank L. 64
Mon Fong Restaurant 128
Monroe, Henry A. 48, 54, 115, 137, 154
Moose Club 24
More, Fannie Seto 92
Mossman, Paul D. 159
Mount Pleasant Cemetery 100
Moy Kee 135
Moy Shee 159
Moy Yuen District 54
Mr. Whitlock 66
Mullin, E.C. 75
Mun Low village 56, 59
murders 151
Murphy, S.J. 131
Mutual Paper Corporation 57

N

Nanking Noodle House 146
National Archives at Seattle 7, 9, 10, 27, 192
National Bank of Commerce 38, 47, 107
National Dollar Stores 126
National Surety Company 79
Native Americans 103
native-born citizens 22, 42
naturalized citizens 9
Nelson Wah Chan King 126
Neterer, Judge 56
Newcastle 14
New Haven, Connecticut 60
New York 100
New York Café 141, 142
New York CEA file 86
New York City 100, 118, 126, 128
New York Laundry 42
Ng Ah Don 113
Ng Ah Yun 113. *See also* Ah Yun
Ng Back Ging 56, 58, 60
Ng Bok Chung (Teung), 118
Ng Bok Sen 118
Ng Buck Look 56, 57, 58, 60
Ng Dok Baw 57
Ng Dok Foon 57, 58
Ng Fung Yuen 75, 77
Ng Joon Sam 72
Ng Kun 44
Ng See Tong. *See* Ah Yun
Ng Shue Tong 72
Ng Soon Aim 77
Ng Yee Loon 77
Nice, Herbert 124
noodles 75, 77
Noodles Café 130
Norse, Willard A. 50
Northern Pacific Railroad 14
North Pacific College 74
Northwest Chinese Basketball Tournament 61
North Yakima 135

O

Oakland, California 95
Ober, George F. 40
obituary 47, 104, 158, 160
O'Brien, P.J. 144
O'Brien, Rossell G. 108
Oklahoma 24, 57
Okmulgee, Oklahoma 24
O'Leary, Tom 146
Olsen, Ralph E. 60
Olympia, Washington 15, 92, 107, 144
Omaha, Nebraska 24
Opium Wars 11
Oppenheiser, Mose 122
Oregon 10, 12, 13, 30, 45, 66, 119
Oriental Café 121
Osaka Shosen Kaisha 98

P

Pacific College 59
Pacific National Bank 133
Pacific Northwest pioneers 47
Page Act of 1875 13
Pang, Archie 68
Pang Chung Cheong 68
Pang, Victor Ernest 68
Pantages Theatre Company 78
paper family 21

paper sons or daughters 160
paternity 125
Pauly, Fred M. 71
Payne, Mary Virginia. *See* Wee C.G.
Pearl River Delta 11
Peking Café 42
Peking Restaurant 41
Penrose, Stephen B.L. 72
Pershing, Wong F. 157
Philadelphia, Pennsylvania 82, 86
Phoenix Hotel 105
Pong Mon 97
Pon Shee 135
Poole, Louis 143
Portal, North Dakota 10
Port Discovery 119
Porter, Roy M. 29, 53, 149
Port Gamble 75
Portland, Oregon 10, 14, 29, 30, 70, 74, 89, 131, 140, 153
Port Ludlow 142
Port Townsend 10, 22, 37, 42, 48, 62, 66, 75, 82, 105, 110, 113, 120, 122, 128, 134, 135, 144
poultry farmer 147
prisoner of war 158
Proctor, Marie A. 54
professional witness 106
prostitution 13
Puget Mill Company 143
Puget Sound Mills & Lumber Company 106
pulmonary tuberculosis 158

Q

Quan Foy 97, 149
Quan, Robert 24. *See also* Quong, Robert
Quan Yuen Chong Company 157
queue 135
Quong, Charley 115, 116, 119
Quong Chaw village 60
Quong Chong Company 56, 60
Quong, Dorothy 24
Quong Eng, Harry. *See* Eng Ah Quan
Quong, Erma 24
Quong, Harry, Jr. 24
Quong, Jessie 24
Quong Ock 44
Quong, Robert 24
Quong Sang Wo Kee Company 29
Quong Tuck Company 32
Quong Yen Company 131
Quong Yuen Long Company 121
Quon On Company 70
quota 20, 21, 159

R

railroad industry 11
railroads 10, 11, 13, 91, 119
real estate 34, 37, 40, 105
red marriage paper 57, 68
Reed, B.F. 140
reference sheet 66, 102, 113, 158, 160
Renton, Washington 14
reparations 131
Richardson, A.F. 123, 140
Richmond Beach 133
Rieke, John E. 85
Riverfront Park 122
Roark, William Francis 60
Robb, J.D. 46
Robb, W.L. 46
Rock, Miss 61
Rogers, Charlotte Irene 148
Rondema, Theodore 71
Roosevelt, Eleanor 82
Roosevelt, Franklin D. 82
Rose Leong. *See* Leong, Rose
Ross, P.H.W. 140
Russell, Leo B. 98
Russia 75
Ryan, Frederick M. 95

S

Sacramento 149
Salt Lake City Tribune 127
Salt Lake City, Utah 126
Sam Choi 57
Sam Wah 141
Sam Yik Company 44
Sanborn, George O. 110
San Francisco 10, 14, 26, 29, 33, 35, 38, 48, 52, 55, 61, 70, 83, 95, 103, 107, 112, 125, 126, 130, 134, 147, 149, 151, 153, 159
San Francisco, mayor of 33
Sang Chi Hwa 78

sanipractor 51
San Pedro, California 74
Santa Cruz, California 36
Sapulpa, Oklahoma 24
Sargent, John H. 106
Sargent, William George 136
Schweigart, Julius 103
Scott Act of 1888 19, 53
Scott, R.B. 135
Seafair parades 78
Seattle Chinese Patriotic League 104
Seattle fire of 1889 121
Seattle Post Intelligencer 93
Seattle Times newsboys excursion 24
Seattle, Washington 13, 22, 36, 45, 48, 56, 61, 66, 75, 112, 159
Second Sino-Japanese War 91
See Jan 142
See Kin 70
See Yick 70
Senn, Earl H. 70
Seto, Maysien Geraldine 92
Seto More 92, 95. *See also* More, Fannie Seto
Seto, Wilfred Bientang 92
Shanghai Café 133
Shanghai, China 86
Shao Chang Lee 83, 85
shaving feast 115
Shea, James 47, 64
She Chew 75
Shee Chong village, Sunning District, China 46
She Get 62
Shem, Lily Dorothy Mowlan 126
ship manifests 130
Shoemaker, Thomas D. 150
Si Chuck 118
Sih Qua Ling 78
Sik Chee 54
Sik Yuen 54
silk merchant 153
Sing, Charley 38
Sing Fork and Company 60
Sing Kuan 70
Sing (Sun) Wo Company 107
Sing Wa 107
Sin Lim 63
Smith, Harold N. 106, 110
Smith, Miss Sadie E. 61
Smith, P.K. 110
Snaith, Thomas W. 40
Snowden, E.H. 140
Song Cheong, village 116
Soon En 72
Soong Ching Ling 82
Soong Mai-ling. *See* Soong May Ling
Soong May Ling 82
Southworth, F.W. 131
Souvenirs China & Japan Tour, Chinese Basket Ball Team 87
Spokane, Washington 35, 40, 62, 119, 121, 122, 123, 130
Squak Valley 15
status change from laborer to merchant 141, 146
Steilacoom, Washington 110
Steiner, Joseph 116
Stevenson, Anna C. 127
Stewart, J.V. 41, 75
St. John's University 86
Stockand, James W. 62
Stone, C.P. 110
Storey, James W. 118
Suey Gin 140
Suie Yen 143
Sumas, Washington 10, 60, 149
support jobs 10, 11, 119
Swatow 54
Swatow Section 6 merchant 55
Swedish Tribune 51

T

Tacoma expulsion 131
Tacoma method 14
Tacoma, Washington 14, 37, 41, 42, 74, 78, 98, 130, 133, 152, 153
Tah Soo Len 103
Talcott, Grant 146
Tang (Tseng) Chin-Yun 86
Tape, Frank 151
Thomas, L.R. 140
Thomas, Mrs. 66
Thompson, John 47
Thompson, John A. 57
Thorp, L.L. 40
Thurston County 93
Tibbals, H.L. 128
time of birth 103
Tin Yung Qui Troupe 154, 156
Tom Gubbins Company 127
Toy Sam 48

Toy Shee 29
trachoma 154
Troy, New York 130
Tseng, C.L. 89
Tsue Chong Company 75, 78

U

Union Pacific Railroad 12
University of California, Los Angeles 126
University of Louisville, Kentucky 88
University of Pennsylvania 86
University of Southern California 127
University of Washington 26, 61, 86, 89, 91, 152
unsatisfactory testimony 137
Upper, G.W. 38
Upper, G. Wyatt 108
U.S. Army 28, 159
U.S. census, 1870 13
U.S. census, 1890 20
USIS interpreter uniform 150
U.S. Marine Hospital in Seattle 159
U.S. Supreme Court 19
Utah birth certificate 126
UW Chinese Student Club 89
UW Huskies 89

V

Vancouver, British Columbia 28, 39, 52, 53, 58, 59, 66, 69, 70, 78, 83, 89, 92, 112, 126, 148, 153, 155, 157
Vashon Island 147
Victoria, British Columbia 24, 53, 64, 153
Villa, Mrs. 135
Vincent, W.D. 122

W

Wa Chong Company 23, 66, 103, 105
Wagen, E.E. 141
Wah Chung Company 68
Wah Chung Tai Company 68
Wah Hing Company 93
Wa Hing Company 107, 108
Wah Young 117. *See* Ah Yun
Wah Young Company 55
Wah Yuen Company 38
Waitsburg, Washington 39
Walk, Maurice 50
Walla Walla, Washington 13, 70, 71, 72, 134
Wang Kuh Yong 78
Wan Jew village, Toy San district 33, 35
War Bride Acts of 1945 and 1946 20, 159
Ward, Charlotte Irene 149. *See* See Rogers, Charlotte Irene
Ward, James E. 136
Ward, W.A. 29
Washelli Cemetery 160
Washington, D.C. 36, 89, 95, 98, 124, 150, 155
Washington Grade School 24, 28
Washington Rice Mill Company 103
Washington School 124
Washington State 10, 91, 98, 112, 137
Washington territorial census, 1850 13
Washington Territory 10, 13, 22, 108
Wau Yune Lung Kee Company 29
Wa Young Company store 117
Wee C.G. 88
Weedin, Luther 86, 100
Wee, George Richard 89
Wee Guan Chuan. *See* Wee C.G.
Wee Guan Wee. *See* Wee, George Richard
Wee Jee. *See* Jenn, Eugene
Weeks, Harold 61
White, Henry M. 85, 141
white workers 12
Whitlock, John C. 68
Whitlock, Mr. 66
Wilhelm, Fred 108
Wilson's Business College 24
Wilson's Modern Business College 69
Wilson, Woodrow 91
Wing Long Company 112

Wing Luke Museum 26
Wing Sing Company 128
Wing Wo Chinese Medicine Company 124
Wing Yick Tong Company 140
Winnipeg 78
W.J. London Company 157
woman magician 154
Wong, Chester 157
Wong Chew 135, 136
Wong Chun Wah 157
Wong Gok Way. *See* Pershing, Wong F.
Wong, Kathleen 28
Wong On 100
Wong, Pershing F. "Perky" 158
Wong, Raymond 157
Wong Sai Chuck 115
Wong She 117
Wong Shee 56, 112
Wong Shin How 40
Wong Shu Tong 55
Wong Sui 70
Wong Wam Fong 52
Won Mee Menie 66
Woo Ah Moy 106
Woo Bak Sue 22, 23, 24
Woo Bing Gee 23
Woo Fong Tong 35
Woo Gap 34
Woo Gen 23, 103, 105
Woo Jen 68
Woo Koon Sang 33
Woo Quin Kwock 33
Woo Quin Lock 33, 34
Woo, Raymond. *See* Woo Yen Tong
Woo Shee 103
Woo Sze Hong 23
Woo Tai Gap 22
Woo Yen Tong 33, 34
World War II 47, 119
World War II veterans 158
Wu Ah Young. *See* Ah Yun
Wychoff, Tom L. 126
Wyckoff, William P. 128
Wyoming 12

Y

Yakima, Washington 142
Yee Fon 142
Yee Gim 122
Yee Hep 70
Yee Kong 113, 114, 116, 118
Yee Kong's laundry 116
Yee Onlai 40
Yee Shee 52
Yee Sing 70
Yee Sing Wook Kee Company 115
Yee Wah Laundry 113
Yee Yuen Company 62
Yee Yuen Hong Kee Company 122
Yen Ling Lock 113
Yen On village 60
Yet Yue. *See* Eng Gin
Yik Fong Company 44
Ying Shing Lung Co. 46
Yin Lim. *See* Louie Kay
Yin Ling. *See* Lock Ling
Yip Chun Tien. *See* Yip Sang
Yip Sang 153
YMCA, Chinese Branch of 83
Young, David 87
Yung Foo 135

Z

Zamberlin, Joseph 146, 147
Zee Tai Company 63, 120

ABOUT THE AUTHOR

Trish Hackett Nicola, certified genealogist emeritus, is a public historian and retired librarian. She has a bachelor's degree in accounting, is a retired certified public accountant, and has a master's in library and information science. She has worked with the Chinese Exclusion Act files at the National Archives at Seattle as a volunteer since 2001. Trish has published numerous articles and given many presentations on various aspects of the Chinese Exclusion Act case files. Her blog at https://chineseexclusionfiles.com contains over 330 entries on individual Chinese case files from the National Archives. Her goal is to make it easier for family historians and researchers to access these files and share examples of the variety of information and photos that can be found in the files. The files are a treasure trove of information.